IMAGES
of America

CASTLE ROCK

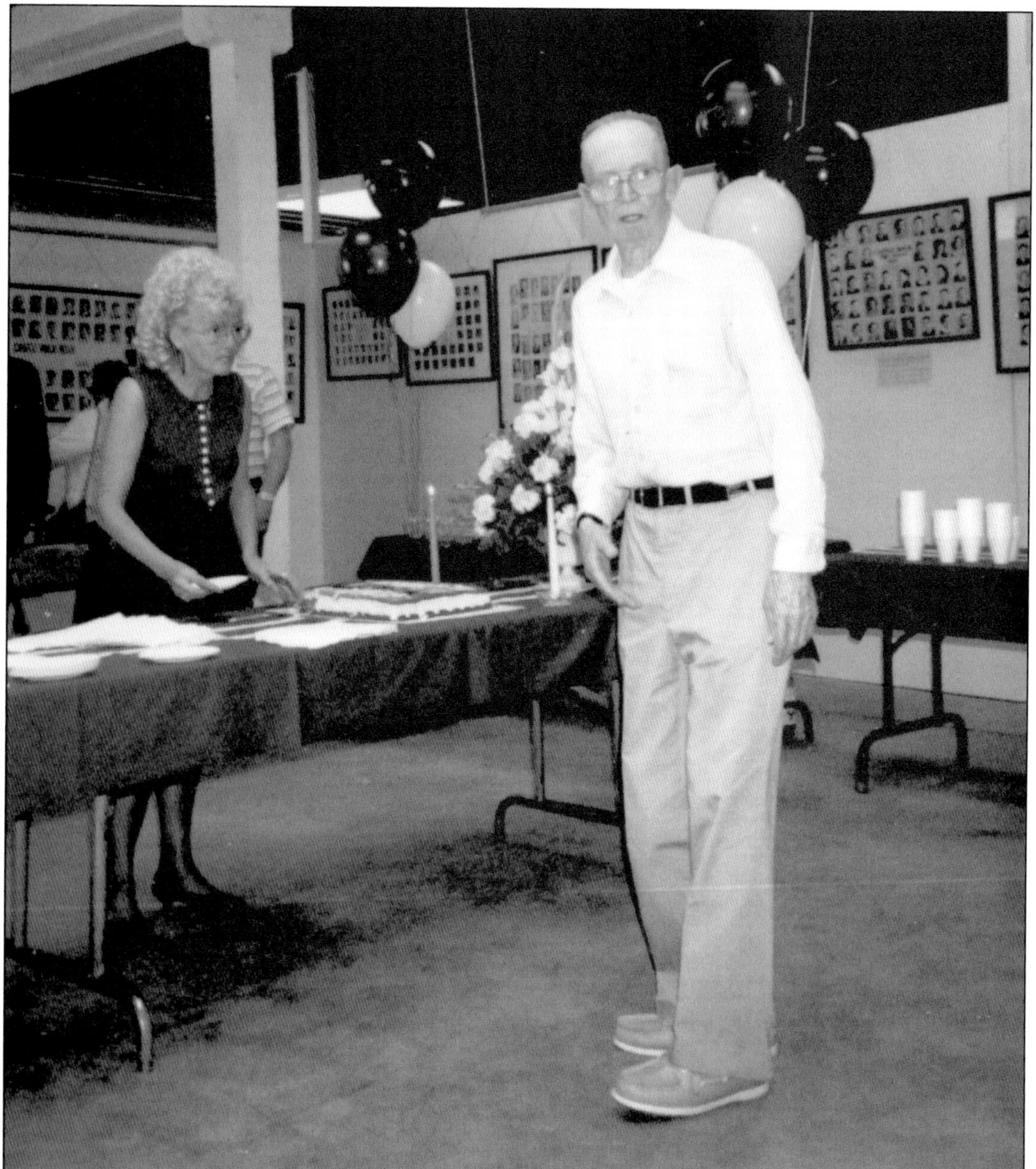

Arloween Rister and Leland Jackson are at the cutting of the town's birthday cake in 1990 during the 150th anniversary celebration of the settlement of Castle Rock. Jackson was the unofficial town historian whose work and extensive research has made up the bedrock on which any history of the Castle Rock area is bound to be found. (Courtesy Castle Rock Exhibit Hall Society.)

On the Cover: Young loggers Kenneth Dixon (right) and Frank Davis, are loading logs from a rollway in 1910. Young men often went to work "in the woods," as it is called locally, at age 16 or younger. (Courtesy Leland Jackson and the Castle Rock Exhibit Hall Society.)

IMAGES
of America

CASTLE ROCK

Vicki Selander

ARCADIA
PUBLISHING

ISBN 978-0-7385-7092-1

Published by Arcadia Publishing
Charleston, South Carolina

Printed in the United States of America

Library of Congress Control Number: 2009924714

For all general information contact Arcadia Publishing at:
Telephone 843-853-2070
Fax 843-853-0044
E-mail sales@arcadiapublishing.com
For customer service and orders:
Toll-Free 1-888-313-2665

Visit us on the Internet at www.arcadiapublishing.com

This book is dedicated to all my ancestors,
who helped create the town of Castle Rock:
the Pyles, the Merrills, the Hansons, the Fergusons,
and especially to my mother and father,
Dorothy Hanson Selander and Lloyd "Bud" Selander.

Contents

ACKNOWLEDGMENTS

Thank you to all the people of Castle Rock who offered information, guidance, and support for this book, especially Rita Baxter and Lanae Vestal at the Castle Rock Exhibit Hall. Thanks, also, to director David Freece and the staff and volunteers of the Cowlitz County Historical Museum (CCHM). All of the photographs and other images in this book are the property of the Castle Rock Exhibit Hall Society unless otherwise credited. Special thanks to my sister, Hope Selander, and my brothers, Nathan and Spencer Selander, for their patience during the creation of this book.

INTRODUCTION

It is difficult to imagine what this little town must have looked like when only the native peoples lived here. The forests were thick and lush. Food was plentiful, both on land and in the rivers and streams. This is what European and American immigrants saw, when they first arrived. The only visual records of these first arrivals are sketches and paintings made by early explorers.

Capts. Meriwether Lewis and William Clark had led the Corps of Discovery to the Pacific Ocean in 1805. Astoria had been founded in 1811. The United States, Britain, and Russia had all held conflicting claims to what was then the Oregon country. England's Hudson's Bay Company had established Fort Vancouver in 1825, Fort Nisqually in 1833, and Cowlitz Farms about 1837. Cowlitz Landing, a mile or so downstream from present-day Toledo, had been established about 1845 as an important transfer point between boat travel on the Cowlitz River and land travel to Puget Sound.

The beginning of the main route between the Columbia River and the Puget Sound region lay along the Cowlitz River. There was a footpath along the river where people who could walk would go with their livestock. Boats carrying their household goods would come on the river. As people traveled this route, some of them decided to stay.

The Cowlitz area was the scene of tremendous activity and growth following the settlement of the Canadian boundary dispute with England in 1846 and the designation of the Oregon Territory in 1848. Darby Huntington and his relatives founded the town of Monticello near the mouth of the Cowlitz River in 1849.

In the 1850s, the first land grants, where the town of Castle Rock now stands, were filed by William and Eliza Huntington and John Beek, north of them. (The latter was later purchased by Capt. George R. Pyle.) The two homesteads met at what is now Cowlitz Street. On the opposite side of the river, Henry Jackson, Elisha Jackson (father and son), William Whittle, and William Cagle filed their land grants. In the mid-1850s, William Cagle built a fort to provide shelter to the women and children of the pioneer families. Some of the local natives had tried to expel the settlers by force in other areas of the territory. People were killed on both sides, so it was felt prudent to be ready for such an occurrence here. No violence was offered by members of the Cowlitz tribe. In fact, Henry Cheholtz, son of a Cowlitz chief, filed his own land claim and became quite prosperous. Unused for war, the fort became the focal point of a small community for several years.

The name Castle Rock became formally attached to the area in 1853. At that time, William Huntington established a post office in his home, which was located just south of the rocky outcropping that had been christened by river boatmen. His was one of 10 post offices in existence when the Washington Territory was created in March 1853. A Christian church was approved for Castle Rock later in 1853, and meetings were held on a rotation in different homes. The first formal school was established in 1859. The classes were held in William Cagle's home on the west side of the river. The first teacher was William Marshall, a brother of Elizabeth Whittle. The schoolchildren from the east side of the river were brought to school by boat.

The Cowlitz River continued to be the lifeline for transportation and commerce in those early days. Canoes, bateaus, and rafts moved past Castle Rock almost constantly. The first successful steamer schedule was started in 1864, permitting travel from Portland to Cowlitz Landing in one day and back to Portland the next day. Also in 1864, the first horse-drawn stages travelled from Monticello to Olympia and back twice a week. A sawmill was built by Nathaniel Smith at Sandy Bend, a few miles downriver from Castle Rock.

The Civil War, from 1861 to 1865, was followed by the great immigration of settlers to the West. This brought growth and prosperity to the Castle Rock area. Alaska was purchased from Russia in 1867. The population of the Washington Territory at the end of the decade was 24,000. The county had 730 people, according to the census. By 1880, the territory had 75,116 inhabitants, and there were 2,062 people in Cowlitz County. Washington was made a state on November 11, 1889. In 1890, when Castle Rock was incorporated, 681 people lived in the town. By contrast, Kelso had only 354 residents.

After the Civil War, land was given to Union veterans who had survived the conflict. Capt. George Pyle brought his wife, Sarah, and daughters, Minnie, Laura, and Annie, and staked his first claim on the south shore of Silver Lake. No one knows why, but about 1872, the Pyle family bought the Beek homestead and moved next to the Huntingtons.

Captain Pyle platted most of his land into 1-acre lots. William Huntington soon followed his example. The town grew, and the lots were subdivided into smaller lots. Until 1883, there were only two houses in Castle Rock. Settlers were looking for farms and located in outlying areas.

Over the years of its existence, Castle Rock has endured many natural disasters. Two great floods struck in 1906 and 1933. An earthquake caused one fatality and much damage in 1949. In 1962, a Pacific hurricane, or typhoon, called the Columbus Day Storm (or Typhoon Freda) hit Oregon and Washington, with some of the worst damage done in the Castle Rock area. Most famously, Mount St. Helens, one of the Cascade Range volcanoes, erupted with a mighty blast in 1980, forever changing the Toutle and Cowlitz River Valleys. After these devastating occurrences, the people of Castle Rock cleaned up and rebuilt with the resilience of their pioneer ancestors.

During quiet times and good weather, the people of this area work hard to build and maintain their lives, often socializing and celebrating good times with music, festivals, and other forms of artistic expression and entertainment. They also follow in the steps of the early pioneers, harvesting the bounty of the forests and rivers by hunting and fishing. Often this is not only recreation, but also part of a family's food supply for a given year.

One

People Put Down Roots

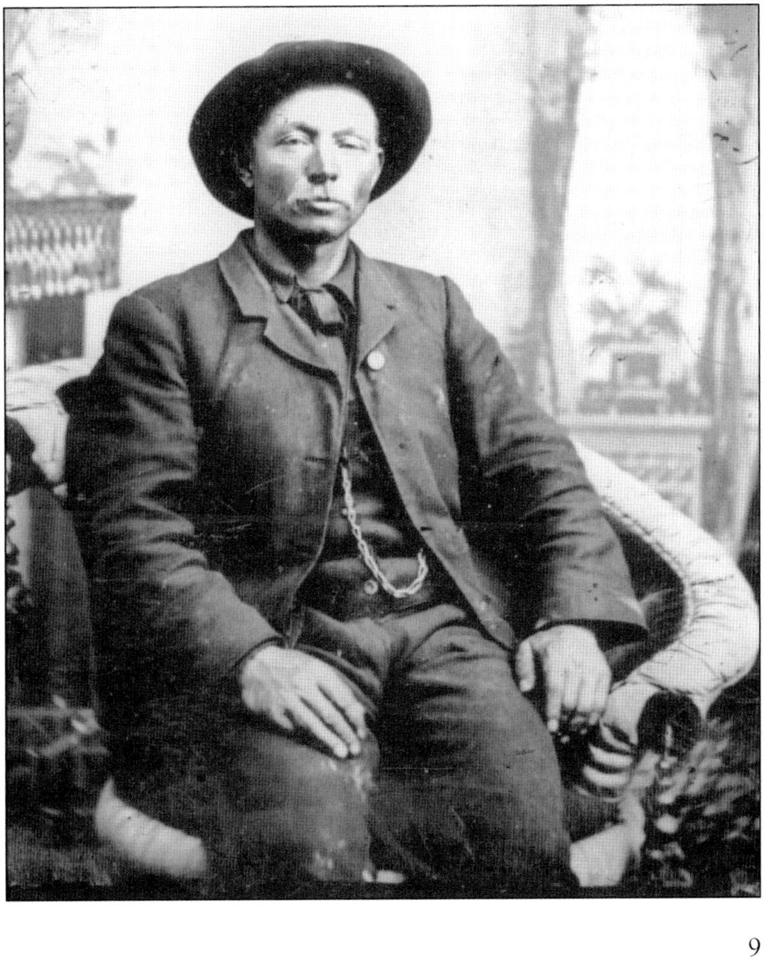

Henry Cheholtz was a Lower Cowlitz (who called themselves Taitinapum) Indian who received his own donation land claim from the U.S. government in 1890. He was born before 1840, was here before the white settlers came, and lived to be 116. He is buried in the Whittle Hubbard Cemetery.

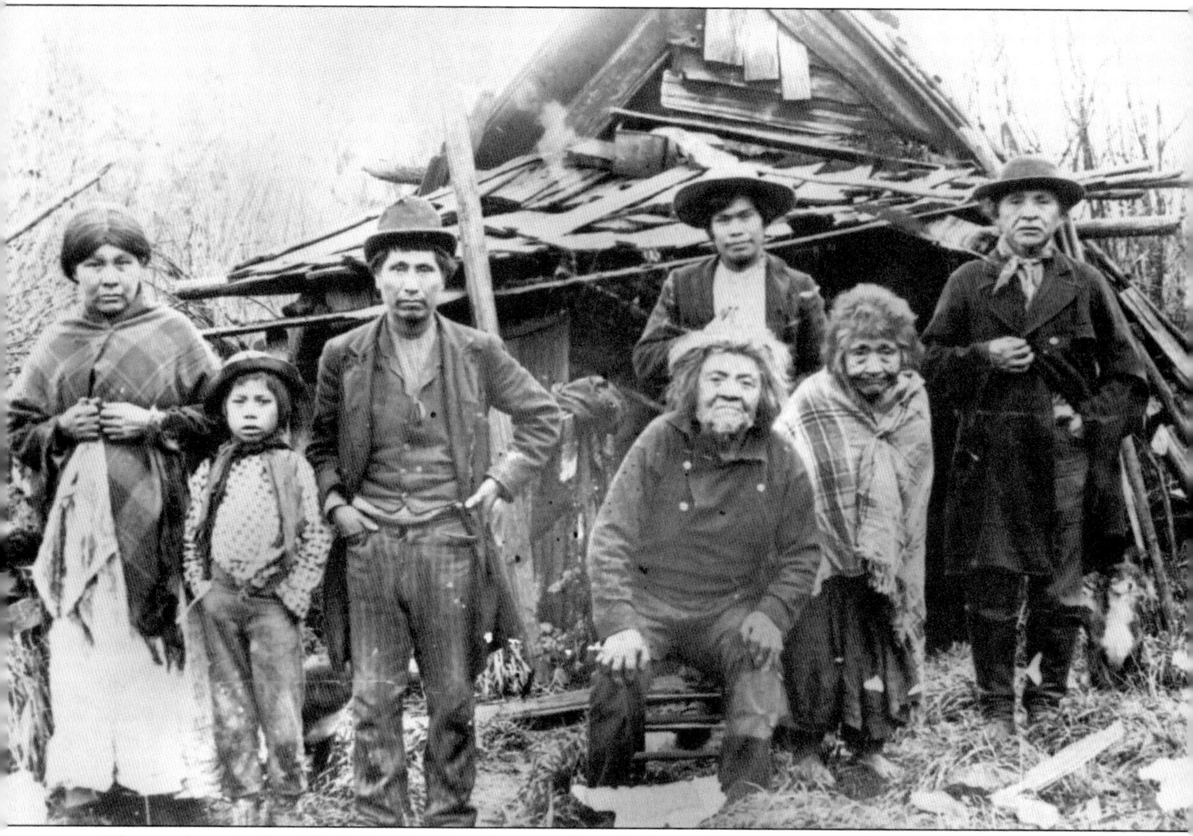

Shown here is the Cheholtz family, who are, from left to right, Kathleen Cheholtz, Elisha Cheholtz (who was named for Henry's great friend, Elisha Jackson and who was called Little Elisha), John Cheholtz, Capt. Peter Cheholtz, Lemmea Cheholtz, and Henry Cheholtz. The man standing in back is unidentified. Kathleen and Lemmea are identified as Henry's wives. Henry and his family lived on the banks of the Cowlitz River near the town and sold fresh salmon caught in the river. In a speech at a Fourth of July celebration in Castle Rock, he predicted the reduction in fish and wildlife, which he said would be due to the unrestrained fishing and hunting practices of the white immigrants. In 1911, he sold his homestead to Niles and Amanda Thurston, whose descendent Murray Hyde still owns and occupies 55 acres of the original 150-acre land grant. (Courtesy CCHM.)

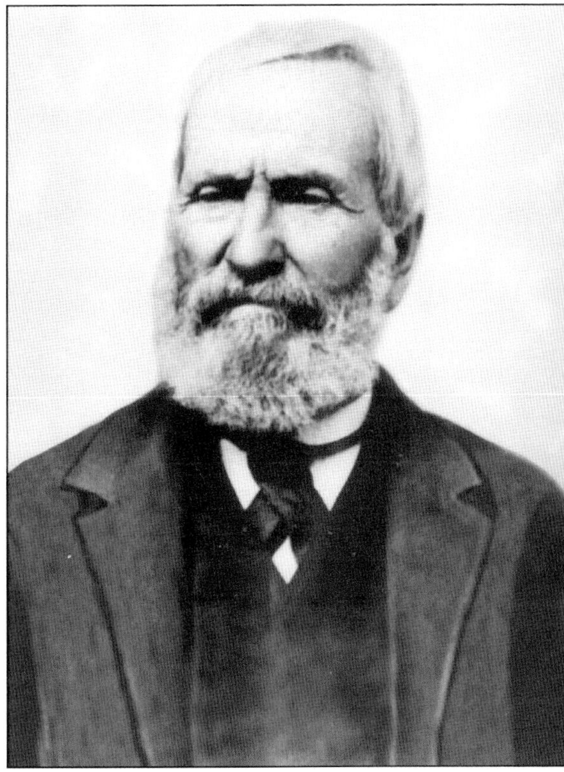

William Huntington, with his wife, Eliza, filed a donation land claim and built a log house near an 80-foot-high rock formation called Castle Rock. William, age 39, and Eliza had arrived in 1953 in wagons pulled by ox teams from St. Joseph, Missouri. They were accompanied by three children: Annette, Jacob, and Benjamin Franklyn. Four more were born later: Susan, Mary Emily, Charles Alvin, and George. William Huntington was the first postmaster of the town and the first minister, in addition to being a federal marshal and a member of the Washington Territorial Legislature.

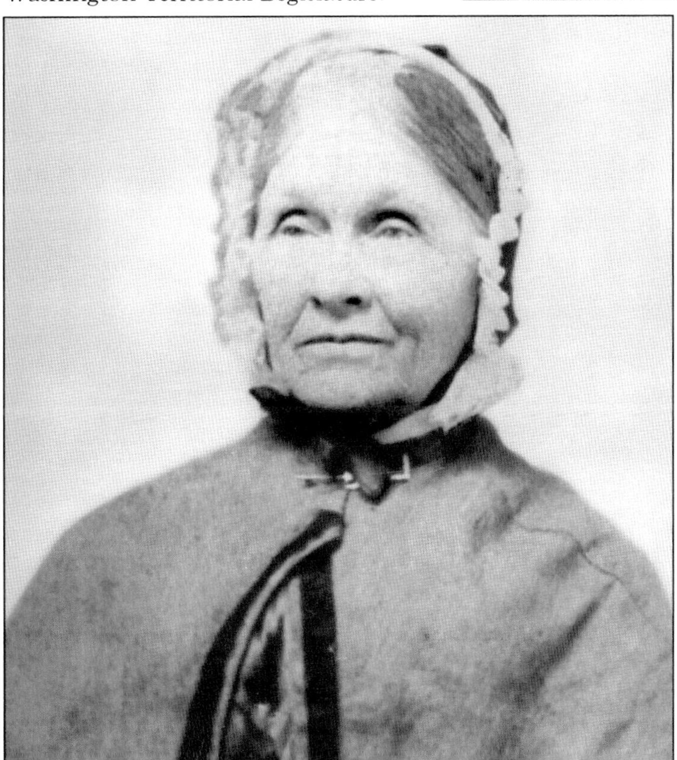

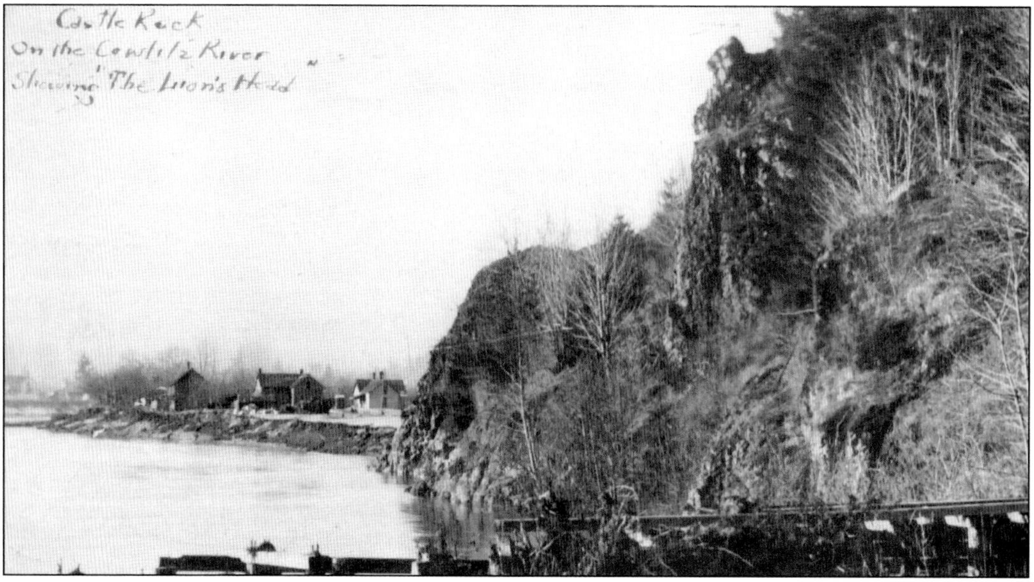

This is a view of Castle Rock. At first, it was the end of a ridge of rock that pointed out into the Cowlitz River. When the Northern Pacific Railroad brought tracks in, workers blasted through the ridge that made the rock into a separate formation from the rest of the ridge. There is a small road and path up to the top of Castle Rock, where a covered picnic table welcomes the person tenacious enough to get to the top.

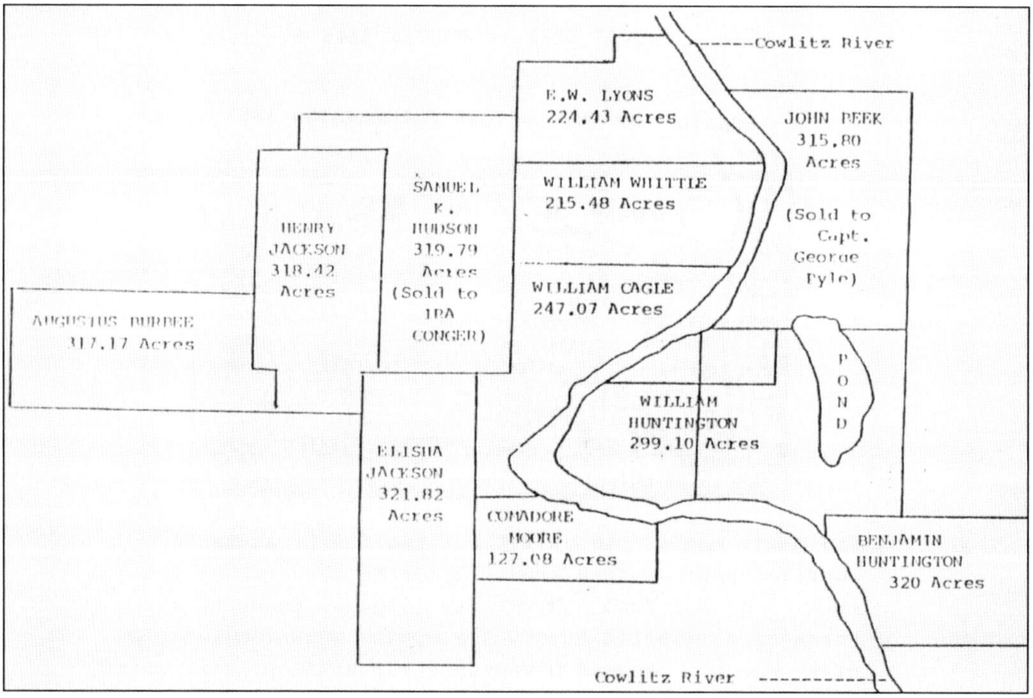

This map shows the unadjusted property lines of the original donation land claims of what are now Castle Rock and the Delemeter Valley (then called the Arkansas Valley). Federal government surveyors of 1859 altered many lines to correct mistakes and excess acreage. (Courtesy Castle Rock Public Library.)

Capt. George Robert Pyle served in the Union army during the Civil War. He received field promotions from sergeant to captain by the war's end. After filing his first land claim at Silver Lake, he was followed by his family. Later he bought the John Beek claim and built the first frame house in the town, the Pyle cottage. He also laid out part of his land in 1-acre lots.

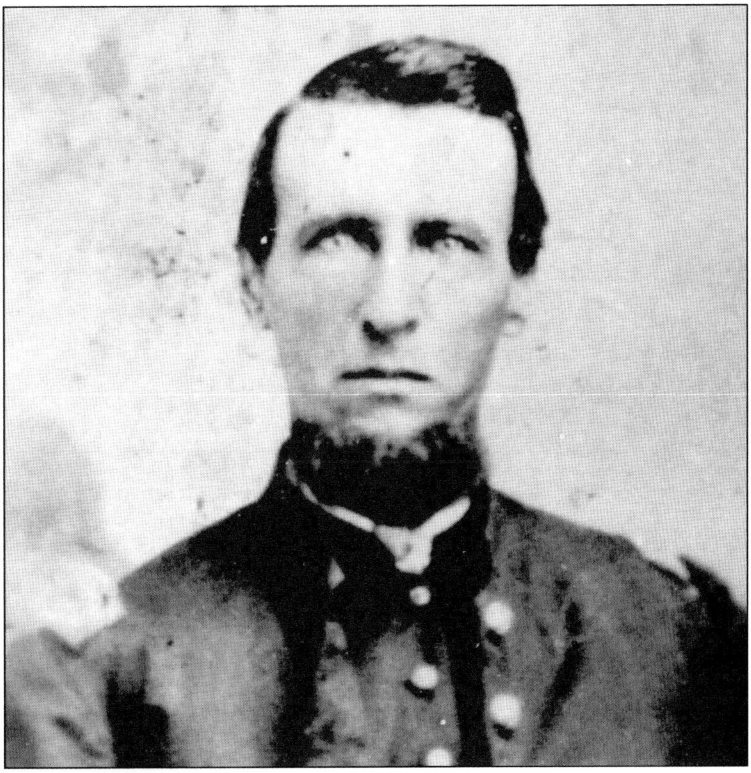

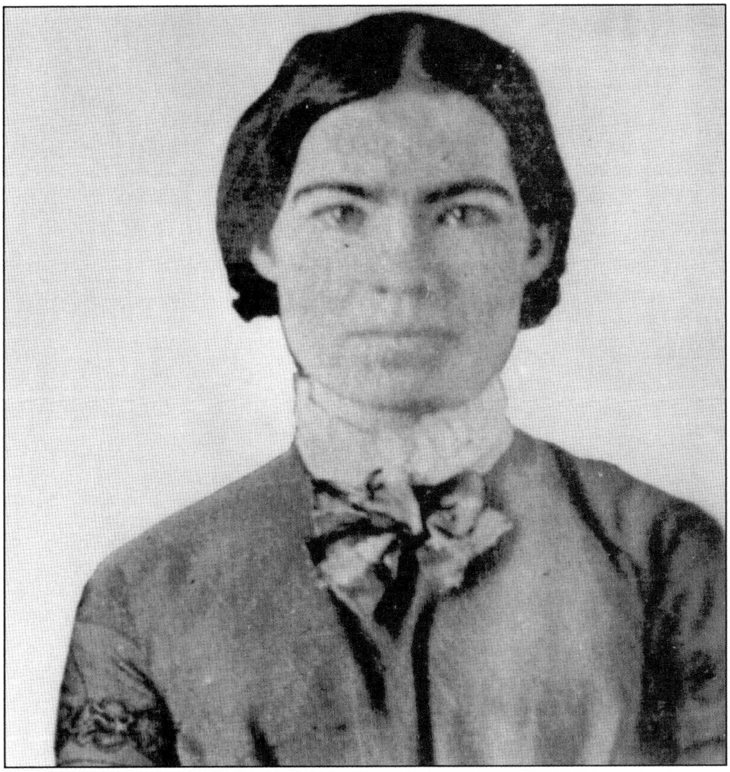

Sarah Hoar Pyle, wife of George Pyle, was the first schoolteacher at Silver Lake. She rowed a boat across the lake and back every day. After being widowed, she opened a shop in her house. She and her daughter, Laura, sold supplies to settlers as well as locals. They also served meals to working men in the area. This was the first store and restaurant in Castle Rock.

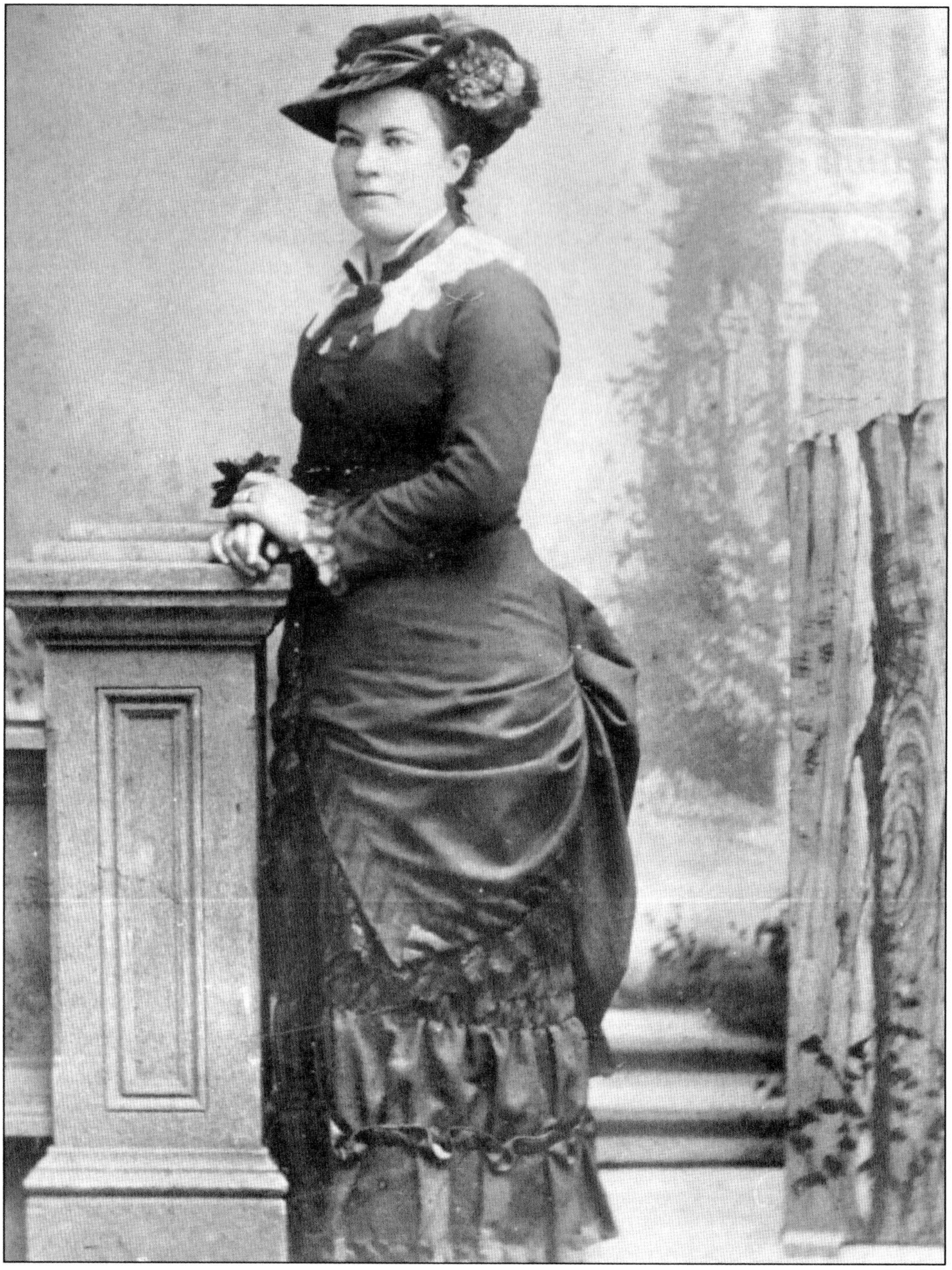

Laura Pyle Merrill was the daughter of Capt. George Pyle and his wife, Sarah. Laura married Roswell "Roddy" Merrill in 1883. This photograph may have been an engagement portrait. She helped her mother to establish and run the first store in the Pyle cottage, which was located at the corner of Huntington Avenue and Cowlitz Street East. The location is now a lumberyard behind Castle Rock Lumber. Later they built a store building in the developing business area near the Kellogg boat landing and the J. R. Robin and Sons shingle mill, about where a convenience store now stands. She was a literate woman and a dedicated letter writer. Some of her letters survive in the hands of one of her great-grandchildren and give an interesting picture of life in the town from 1910 to the 1920s.

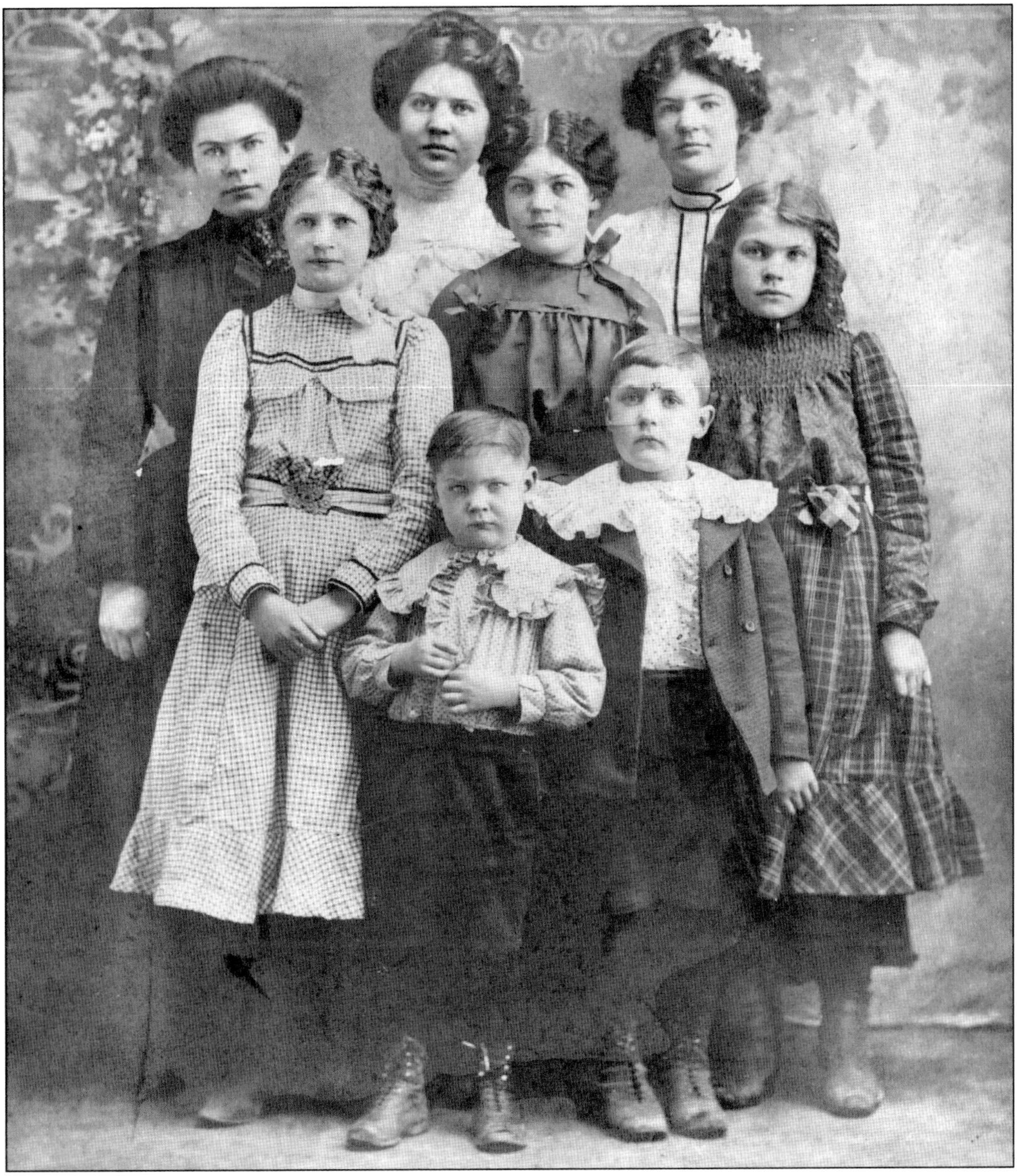

This portrait of the children of Roswell Merrill and Laura Pyle Merrill was taken in 1910. They are, from left to right, (first row) Albert Merrill and Harlan Merrill; (second row) Alice Merrill McCormick, Sara Merrill Murphey Selander, and Frances Merrill Underdahl; (third row) Mary Merrill Smith Fuller, Grace Merrill McKinley, and Annie Merrill Finley Buck. Elwood George Merrill was not born at the time this photograph was taken. Alice Merrill McCormick and her husband, William "Billie" McCormick, owned and operated a butcher shop in downtown Castle Rock. Sara Merrill Murphey Selander was a woman ahead of her time. As the mother of three young girls, she divorced her first husband because of his drinking problem and supported the family by becoming a housekeeper. She later married Victor Selander, and they had two more children together. (Courtesy Ellen Jacobson.)

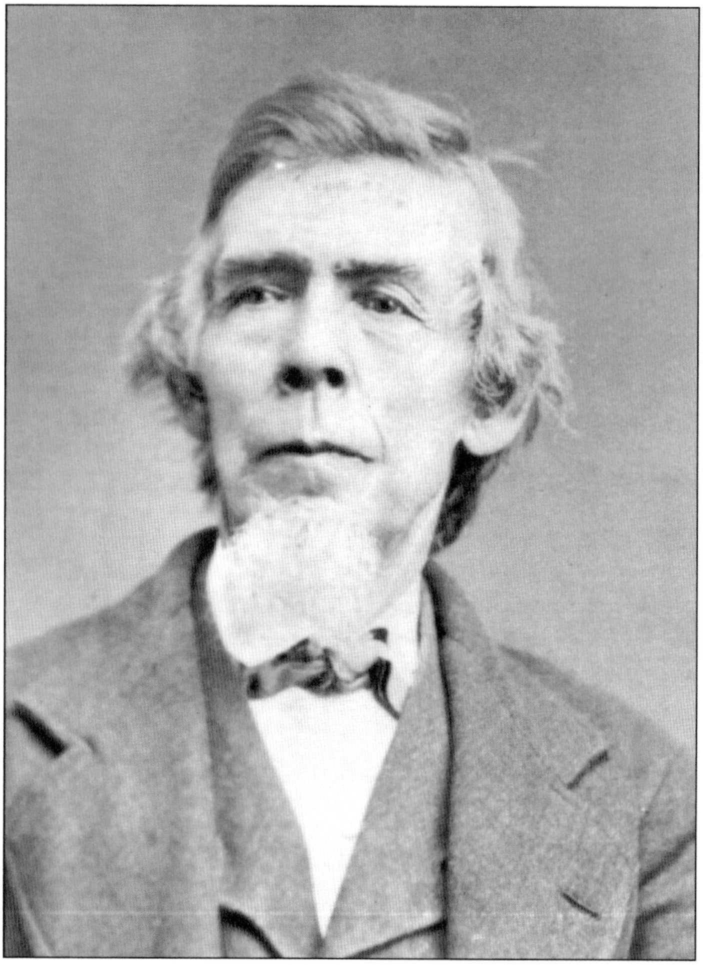

Henry Jackson was born 1810 in Kentucky and died in Castle Rock in 1889. He came to this area with his wife, Elizabeth, in 1853 by crossing the plains in a covered wagon. When he learned that the Military Road was to pass his house, he decided that travelers would need a hotel with good food, lodging, and other amenities. He built the Jackson Inn on the west side of the Cowlitz River from the William Huntington home, which became a stagecoach stop on the Military Road in the 1860s and 1870s. A ballroom on the second floor held dances, parties, and church services. Shortly after the inn was built and opened, Henry's wife, Elizabeth, died. He was grief stricken. He later married the widow of Jonathan Burbee and, as Cynthia Jackson, she became a fine farm wife and hostess for the inn.

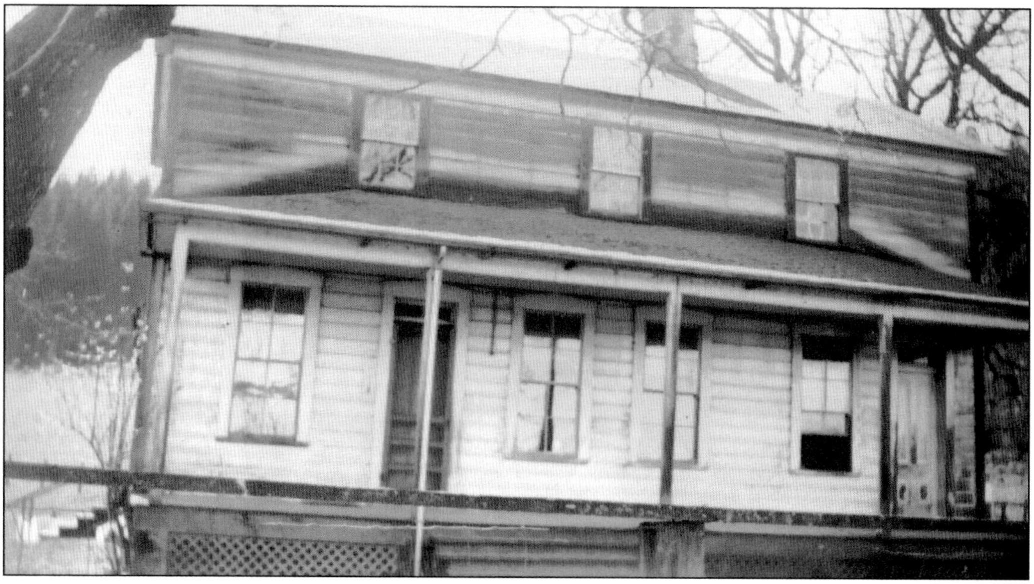

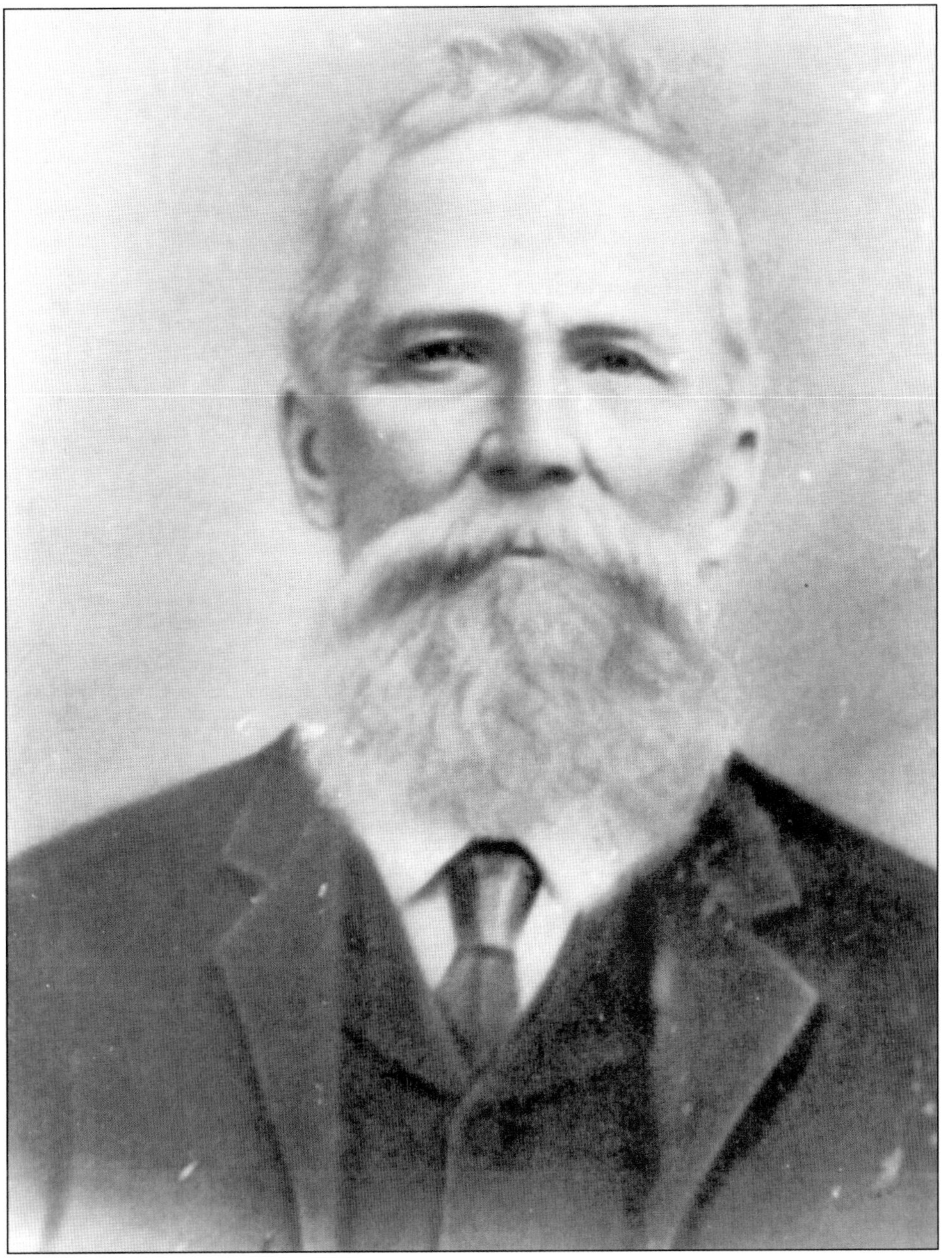

Elisha Jackson was born in 1828 in Indiana and died in Castle Rock in 1894. He came with his father in a wagon pulled by an ox team. He took out his own government donation land claim in the valley of the Arkansas Creek, now called Delemeter Valley, near his father. He was a good friend of Henry Cheholtz, a Cowlitz Indian, who lived not far away and who named one of his sons Elisha (called Little Elisha). In 1887, in his business journal, he stated that he paid Ira Conger $6.50 for two suits of red flannels and $1 for 7 yards of cotton flannel. Around 1880, he purchased a horse-powered hay baler at a high price. Baled hay was a valuable commodity, even at the cost of shipping it as far as California. The baler was not portable, so he bought loose hay, baled it, and sold it to farm suppliers, who shipped it out. His journal lists more than 64 different people with whom he did business during a five-year period.

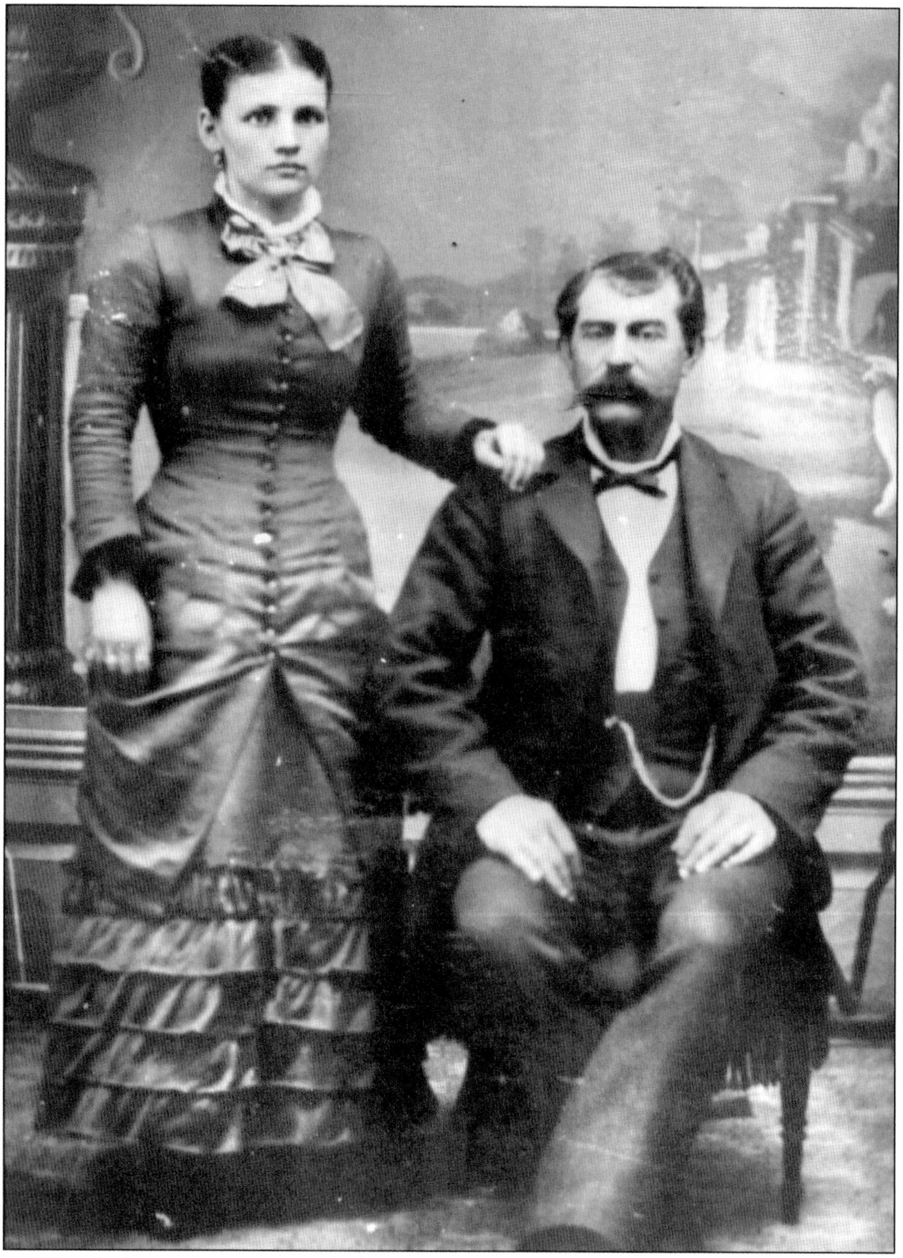

William Whittle filed a donation land claim north of William Huntington's and across the river, where the high school now stands. He is shown here in 1898, with his wife, Elizabeth Marshall Whittle. He built the first sawmill in northern Cowlitz County on the Arkansas Creek in 1859, where lumber was made into building materials. This made sawed lumber affordable, and people could then build houses instead of log cabins. He also established the first meat market in the town prosperous enough to employ a butcher. His other firsts included making it possible to get from one side of the Cowlitz River to the other by launching the first ferry, and he started the first store in Silver Lake in 1882. In addition to providing jobs, his efforts provided goods to be sold out of the area and brought in income. His employees needed houses, stores, and hotels for single men. All this fed the growth of the town.

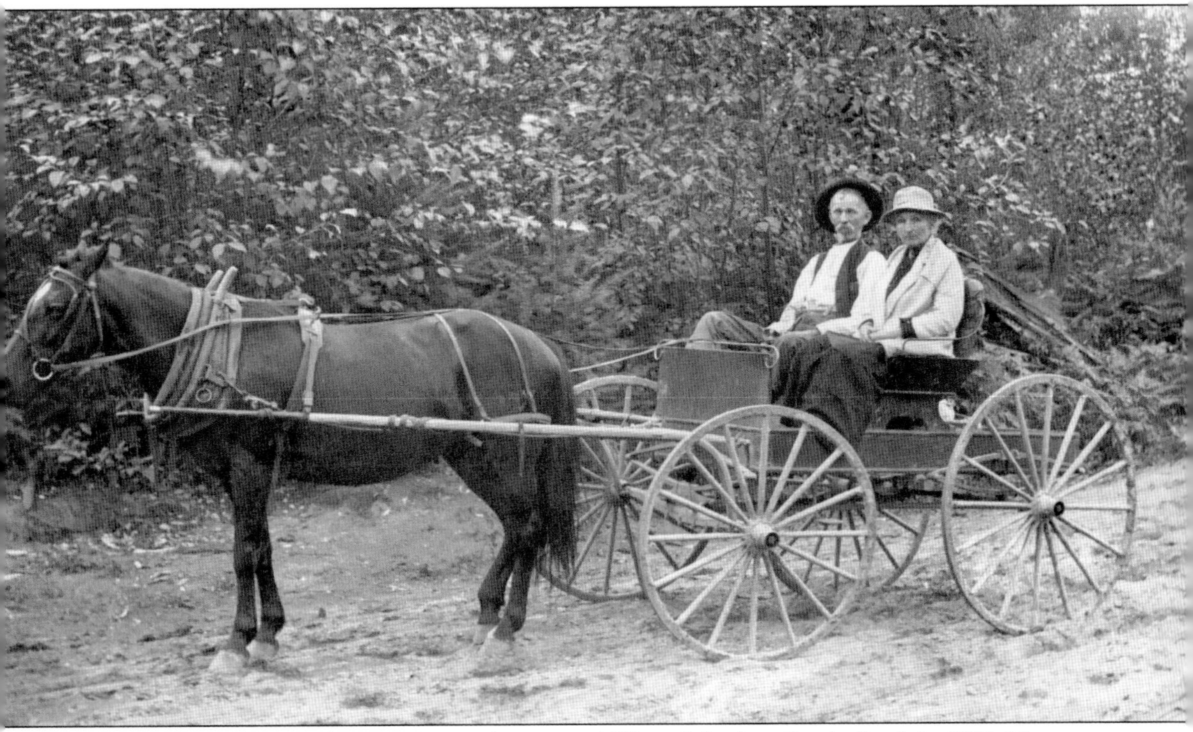

William Studebaker was born in Pennsylvania in 1851 and died in Castle Rock in 1921. He was a brother of James Studebaker, who was a partner with George Pyle in the purchase of the Beek claim. Both Studebakers had large families. Their children married the children of many other pioneer families, such as the Huntingtons, the Pyles, and the Merrills. William Studebaker and his wife are shown in 1890 on their way into town in a horse and buggy from what is now the North Pacific Highway. This was the common mode of transportation of people wealthy enough to own one. However, during the rainy season, wheeled vehicles were not always able to negotiate the muddy roads.

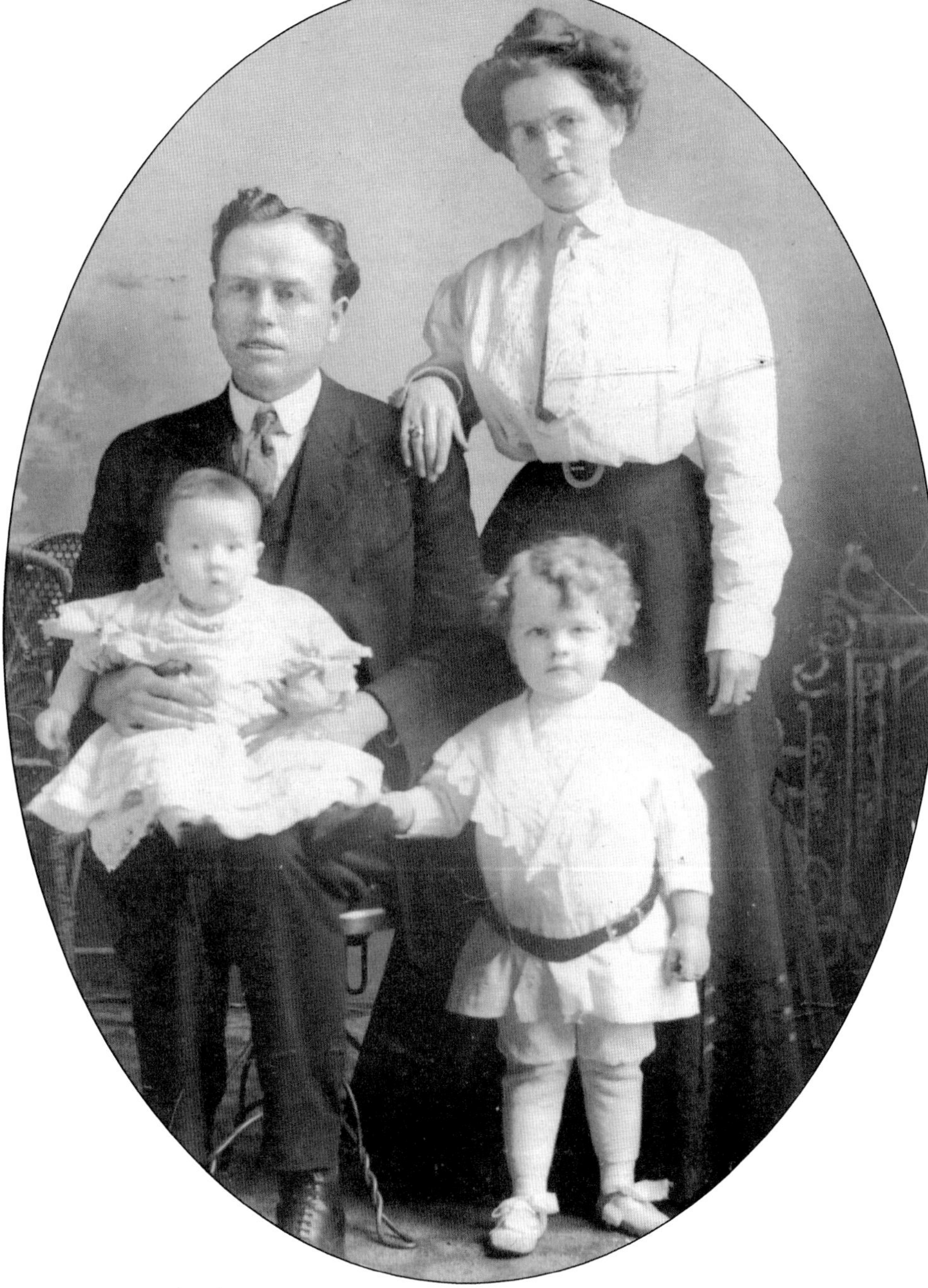

In 1890, Harvey Richardson and Myrtle Ott Richardson are pictured with their two young sons, Vernon Richardson and Calvin Richardson. The baby, Vernon, seated on his father's lap, is wearing a dress, as was customary at the time for infant boys. Richardson was a jeweler by trade. He built a store on Cowlitz Street to house his jewelry business and several other businesses. He was also an accomplished musician. He played in groups with other musicians in town and started a mandolin band. There were not yet radios or televisions and only the most rudimentary and expensive phonographs, so musical ability was a highly prized commodity in early Castle Rock.

Two

Building and Growing

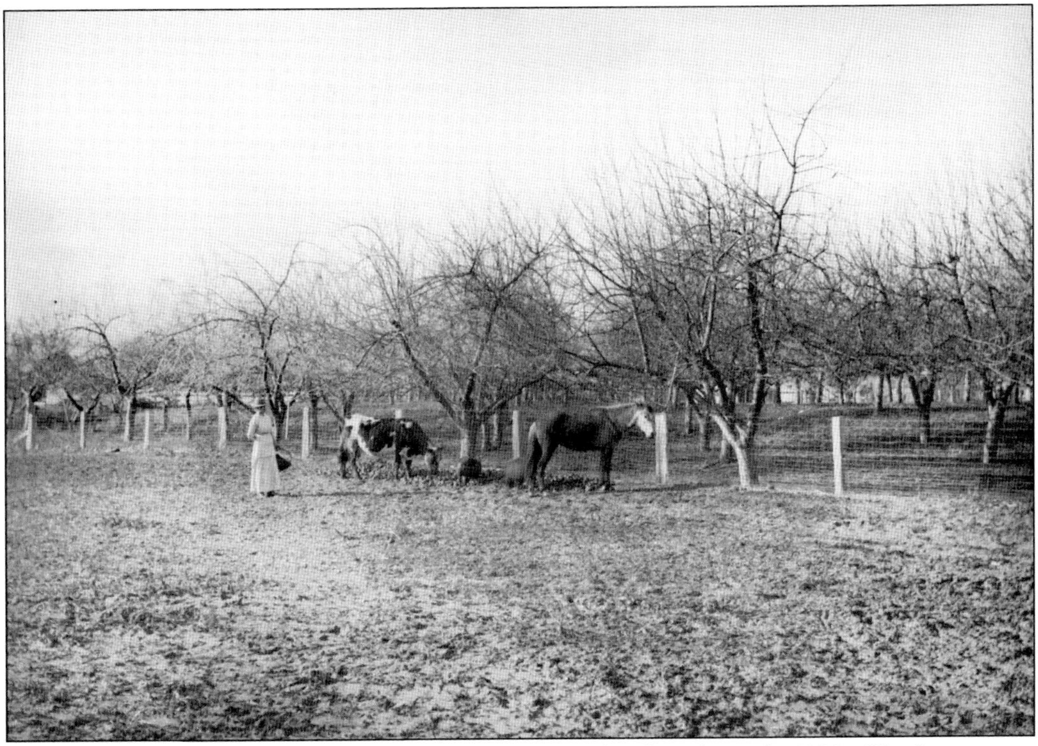

A Mrs. Laird is standing in her pasture next to her orchard in the early 1900s. The horse, cow, and two pigs are eating apples gathered from the trees behind the fence. The location of this farm is at what is now the southwest corner of Fourth Avenue and Warren Street SW in the heart of the residential area of Castle Rock.

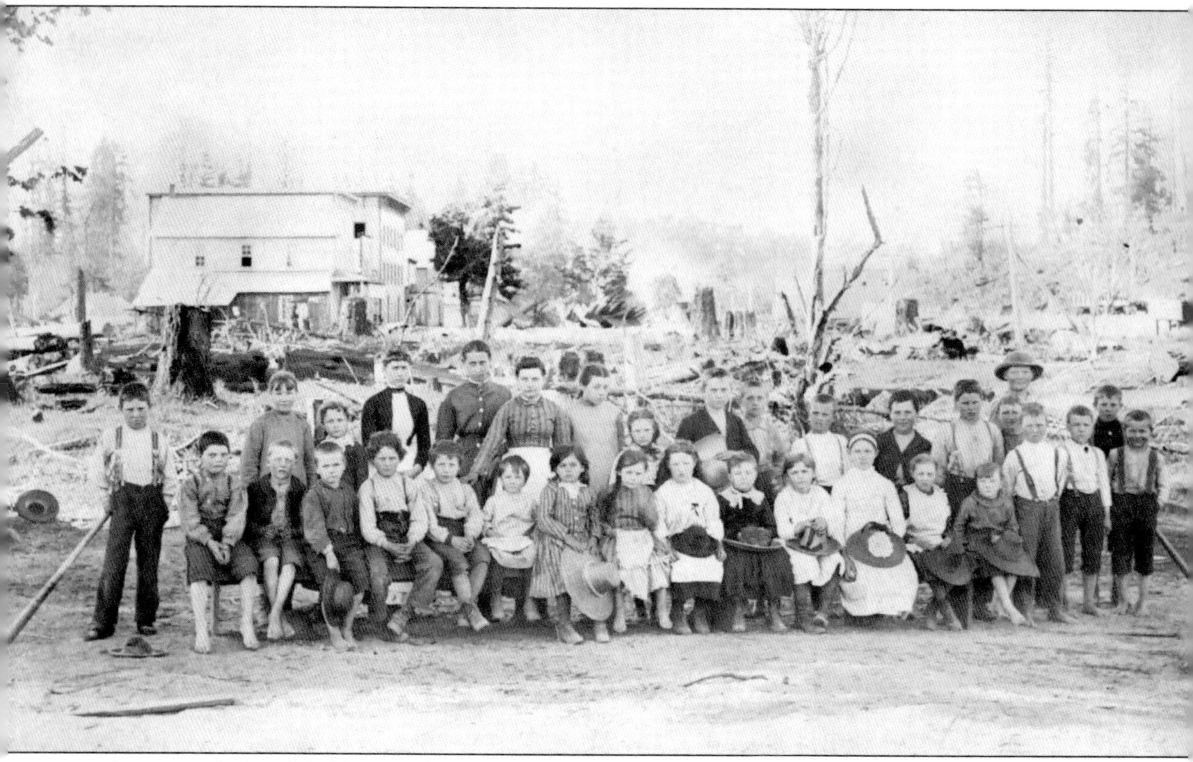

A group of schoolchildren and teachers poses on the street in 1887. None of them are identified. This view shows only a handful of buildings in what must be the business area behind them. The largest structure is the Spencer Hotel, built by James Spencer, which later became the Castle Rock Hotel. This three-story building occupied the corner where the Baptist church now stands. Many stumps are visible where trees have been cut to clear the area to make way for more streets and businesses. The building that can be seen in the upper-right corner of this photograph is the first actual railroad depot in the town. The Northern Pacific tracks were situated where Huntington Avenue is now. (Courtesy CCHM.)

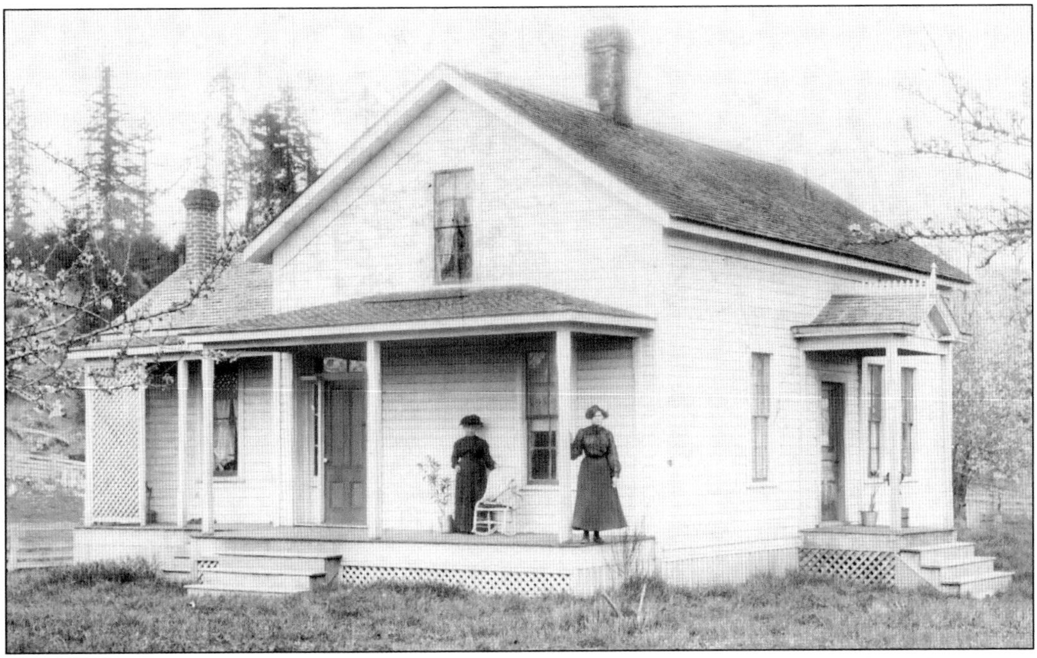

Sarah Hoar Pyle (left) and her daughter, Laura Pyle Merrill, pose on the porch of the Pyle cottage. Capt. George Pyle built this first milled-lumber house in Castle Rock. Roswell Merrill, Laura's husband, hand-hewed the timbers and the fireplace mantle for the living room. For many years this was the finest home in Castle Rock.

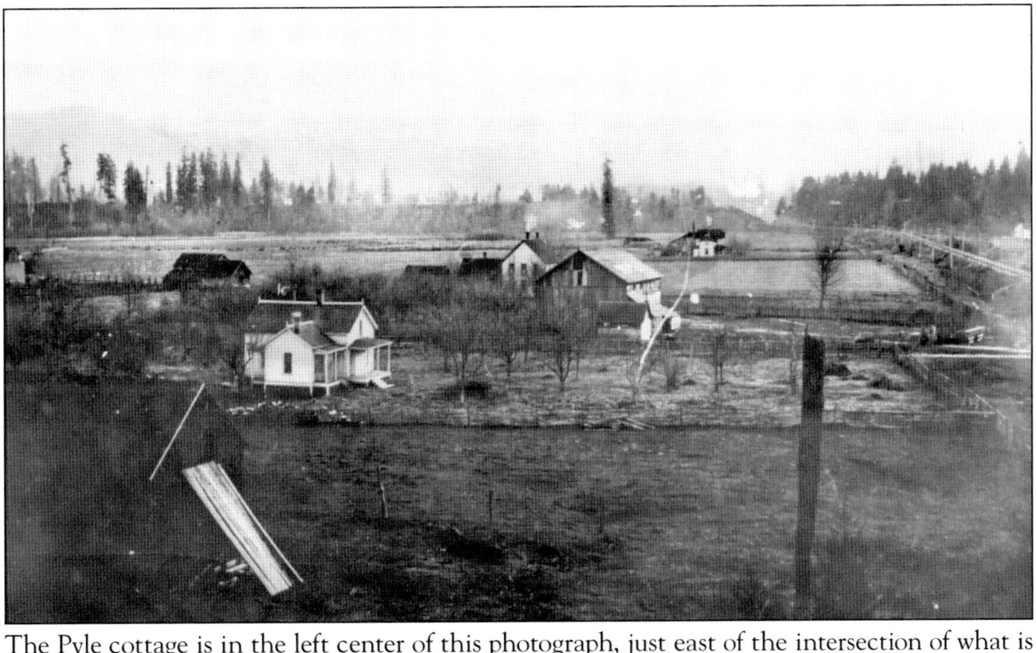

The Pyle cottage is in the left center of this photograph, just east of the intersection of what is now Huntington Avenue and Cowlitz Street East. It remained standing until the 1960s. The site is now the lumberyard behind Castle Rock Lumber. The building in the center of the picture is a large barn. The house behind and to the left is George Huntington's. In the center and farthest back is the Charley Huntington home.

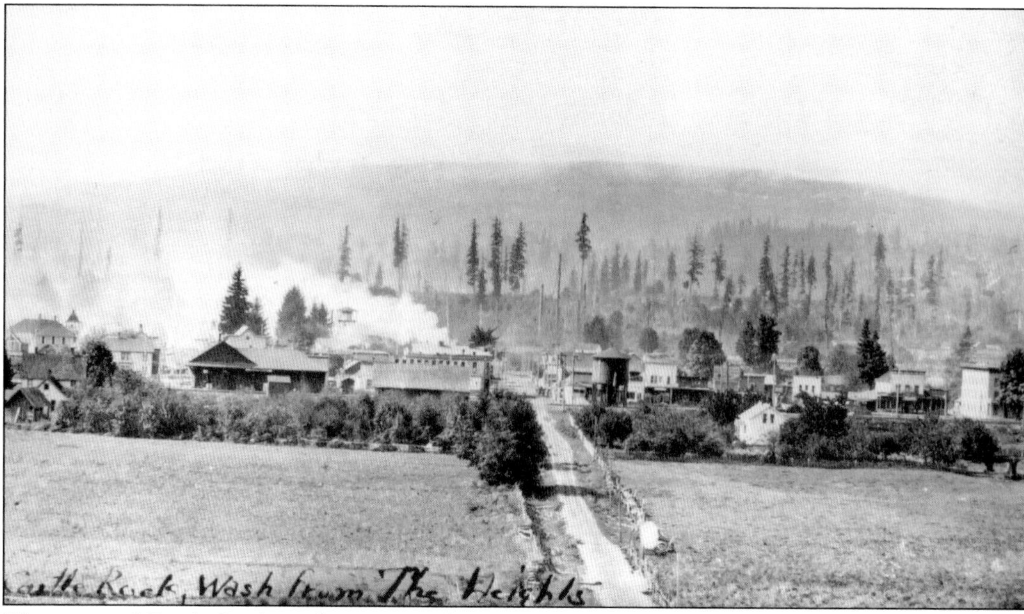

This view of Castle Rock in the 1880s is looking west from a hill east of town. The road in the middle is Cowlitz Street. The Northern Pacific train depot can be seen in the center left and a water tower in the center. Cowlitz Street was then a rutted wagon road. After Cowlitz Street crosses Front Avenue, poles can be seen that carry electric power provided by an early electrical generating plant, which was built near downtown.

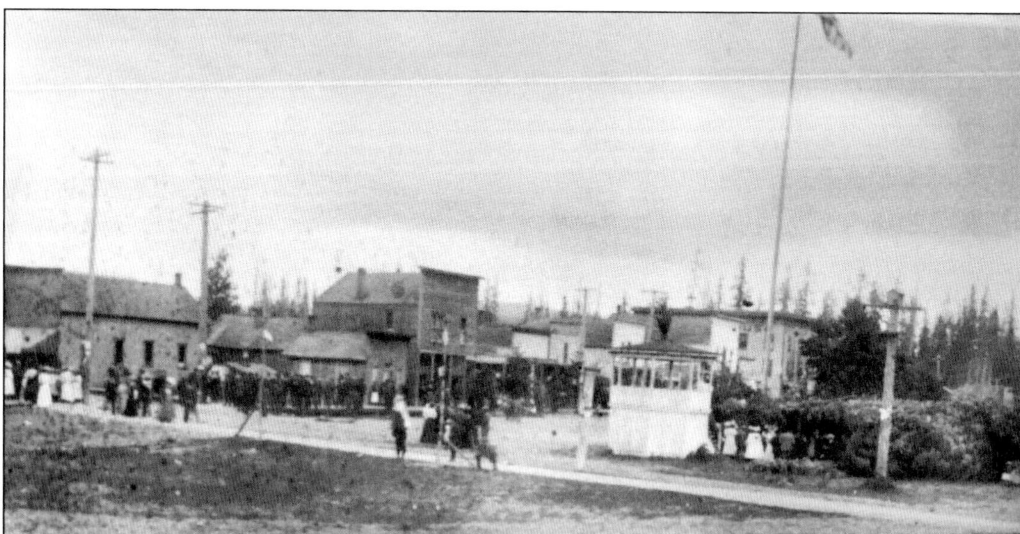

On July 4, 1887, downtown Castle Rock celebrates Independence Day. A flag is flying over the downtown next to the bandstand on the corner of Cowlitz Street and Front Avenue. People have lined up along Front Avenue to see the festivities. Washington had not become a state yet (that would happen on November 11, 1889), but people celebrated Independence Day with gusto anyway.

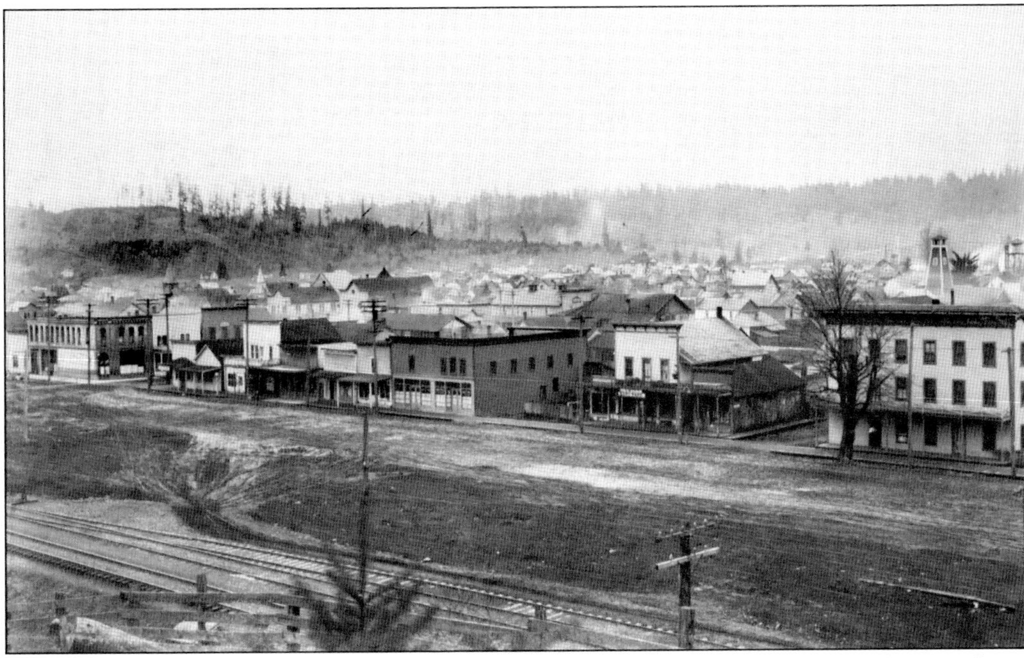

A view of the downtown area, looking southwest, shows the businesses on Front Avenue facing the railroad tracks. The building at the far left is on the south corner of Cowlitz Street and Front Avenue. There is a hardware store at the center right, then Jackson Street, and, finally, the Spencer Hotel on the far right.

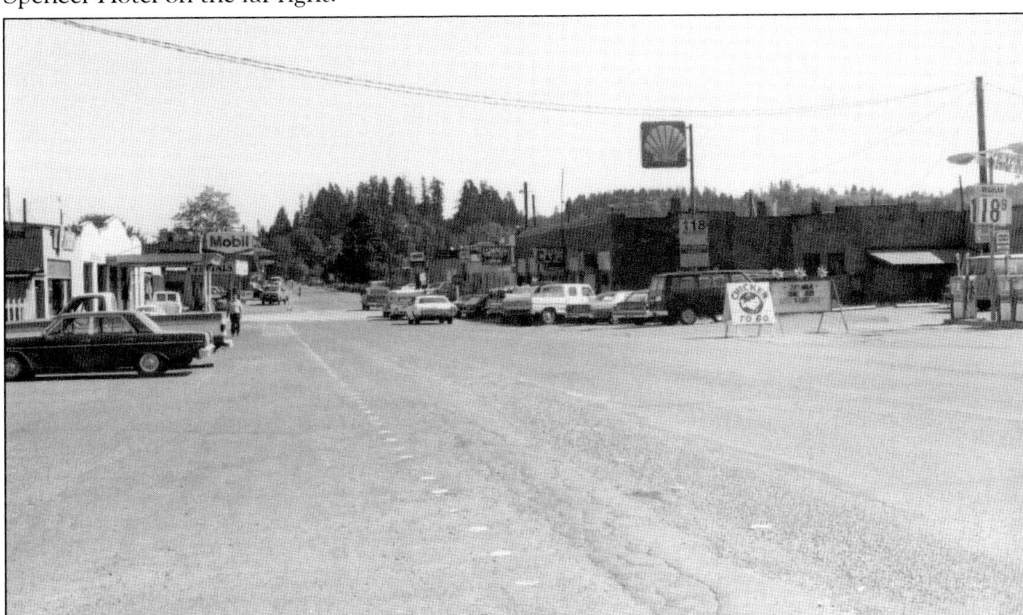

A view of Castle Rock in the 1960s shows the intersection of Huntington Avenue and Cowlitz Street looking south. The clump of trees in the background is the Castle Rock. Huntington Avenue has been paved, and there is a flashing signal light at the intersection of Huntington Avenue and A Street. The Mobile station on the left is where Hill Creek Outdoors is now. (Courtesy CCHM.)

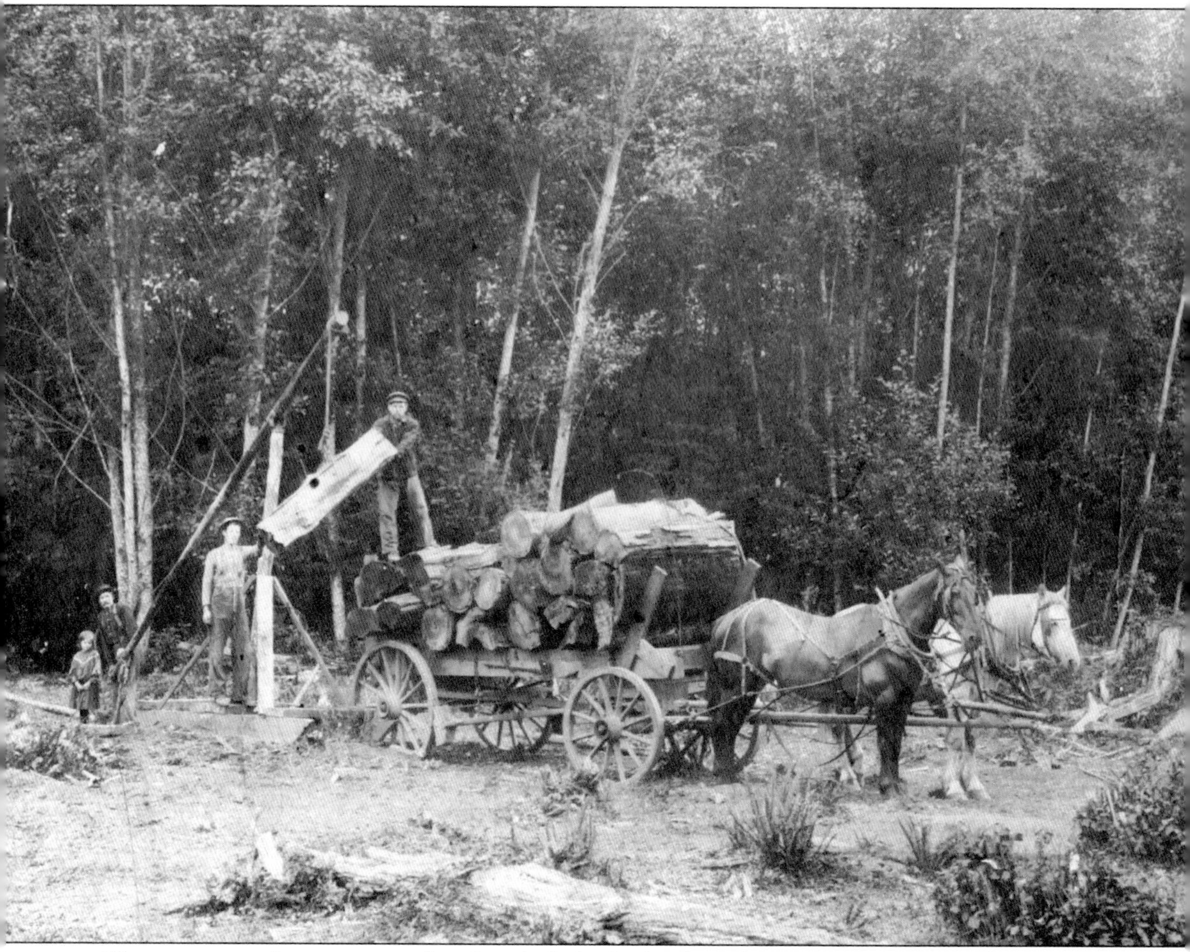

These men are harvesting cedar shingle bolts by loading them into a wagon pulled by a two-horse team in the 1890s. For ease of handling, most trees were cut into bolts. The bolts were 55 to 60 inches long and were split into a size that could easily be handled by two men. They were bought and sold by the cord, which was the equivalent of a stack measuring 4 feet by 8 feet. Over time, the size of bolts became standardized, and 18 were considered to be a cord. Farmers could often make money selling the wood as it was cleared from their farms. The bolts could be transported to the riverbank to float to a buyer or delivered directly to a nearby mill to be sawn into shingles.

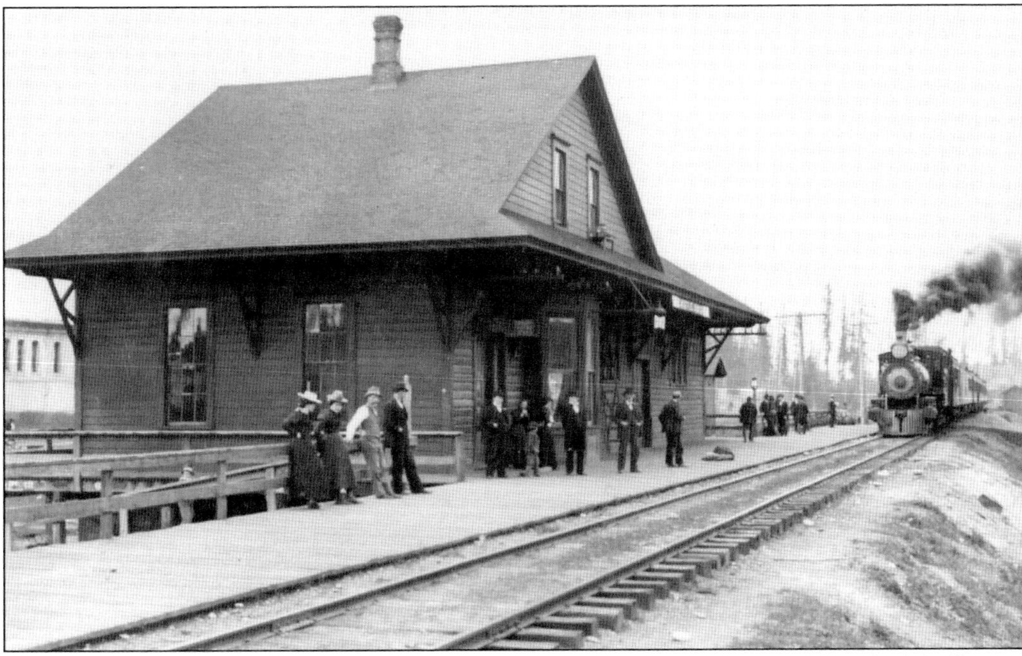

The first two stations in Castle Rock were platforms where passengers could stand while flagging the next train. Finally, in 1892, a depot building was constructed. It was located on the west side of the tracks at the end of A Street. This new structure had a ticket office, separate waiting rooms for men and women, restrooms, and a baggage and freight warehouse. The second story held the station agent's living quarters. The photograph below shows the fourth depot, which was built when the railroad tracks were moved about a quarter mile east out of downtown, and the old railroad bed became Huntington Avenue. It was made of red brick with a slate roof, glass windows, and a stone floor. Benches in the waiting room were oak, and the restrooms were finished in white tile. (Below, courtesy Judy Tinney.)

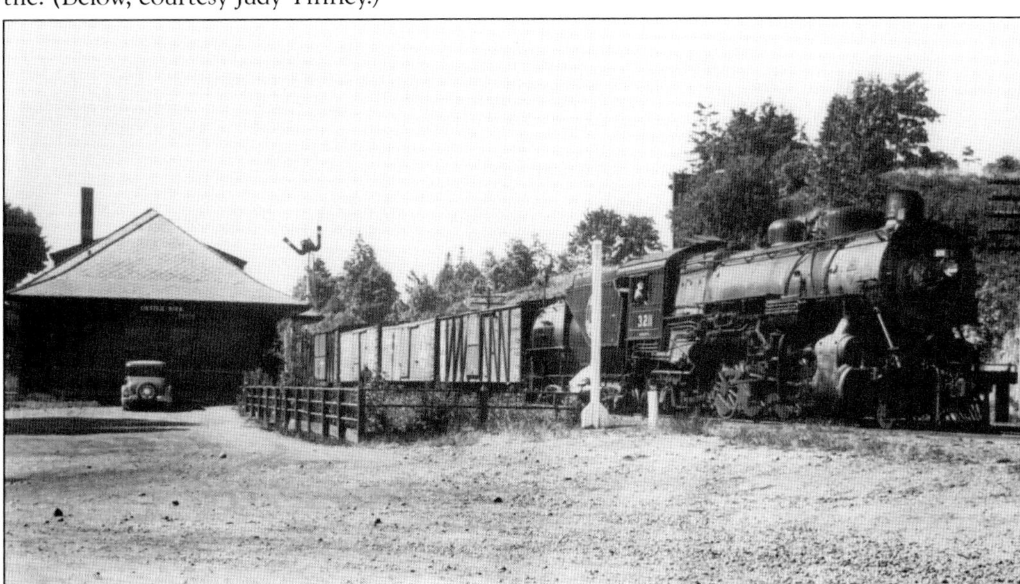

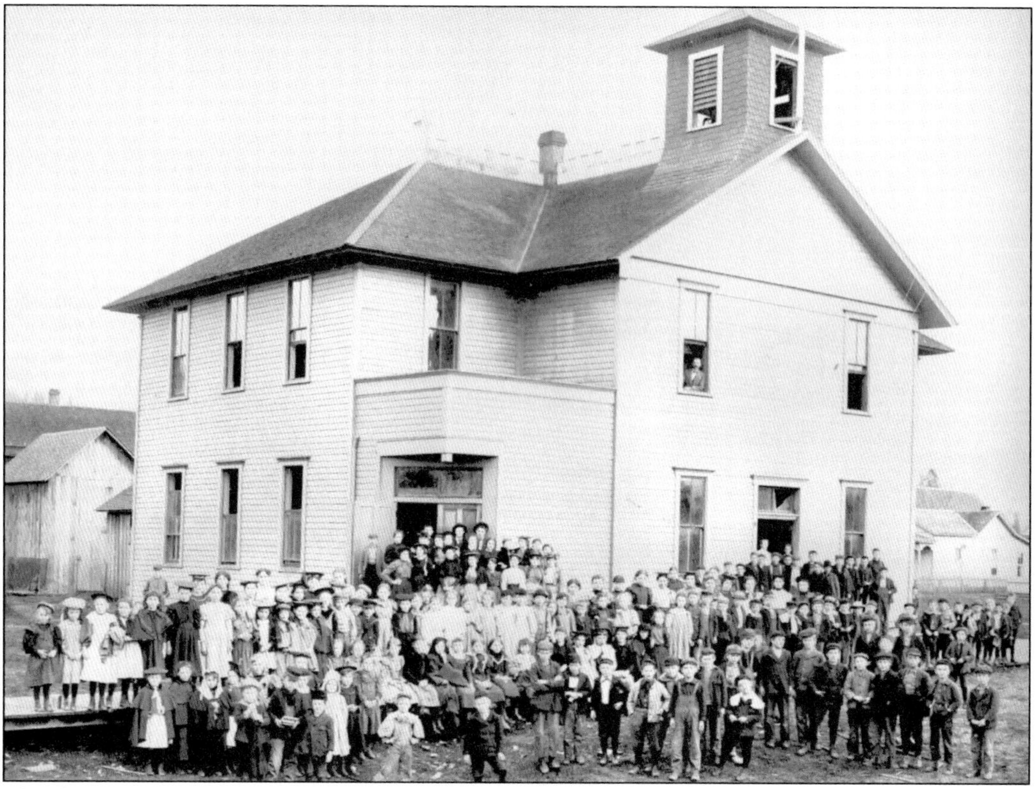

The first multiroom schoolhouse (pictured above) was in use in the 1890s. In 1899, two rooms were added, and the result was the building shown below. Castle Rock School District No. 18 was separated out of the Silver Lake district in 1876. The first board of directors was made up of Benjamin Huntington, James Spencer, and William Huntington. The board employed Antoinette Huntington to teach at $20 per month. There was no school building at that time, so classes were held in the front room of Huntington's home. There were eight pupils: the children of the teacher, Fred, Winnie, and Via Huntington; Erving and Hattie Merrill; Charley and George Huntington; and Belle Shear. Huntington taught all the classes until 1885.

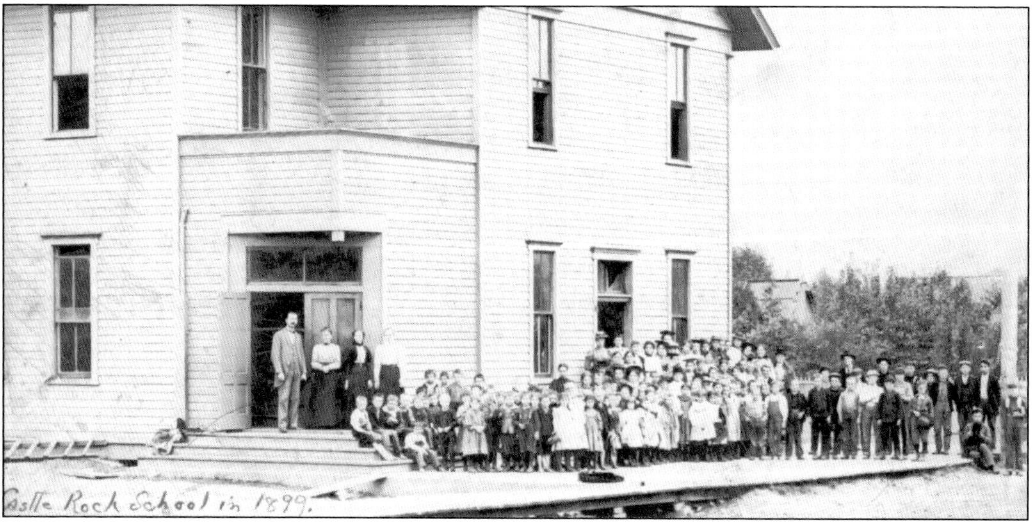

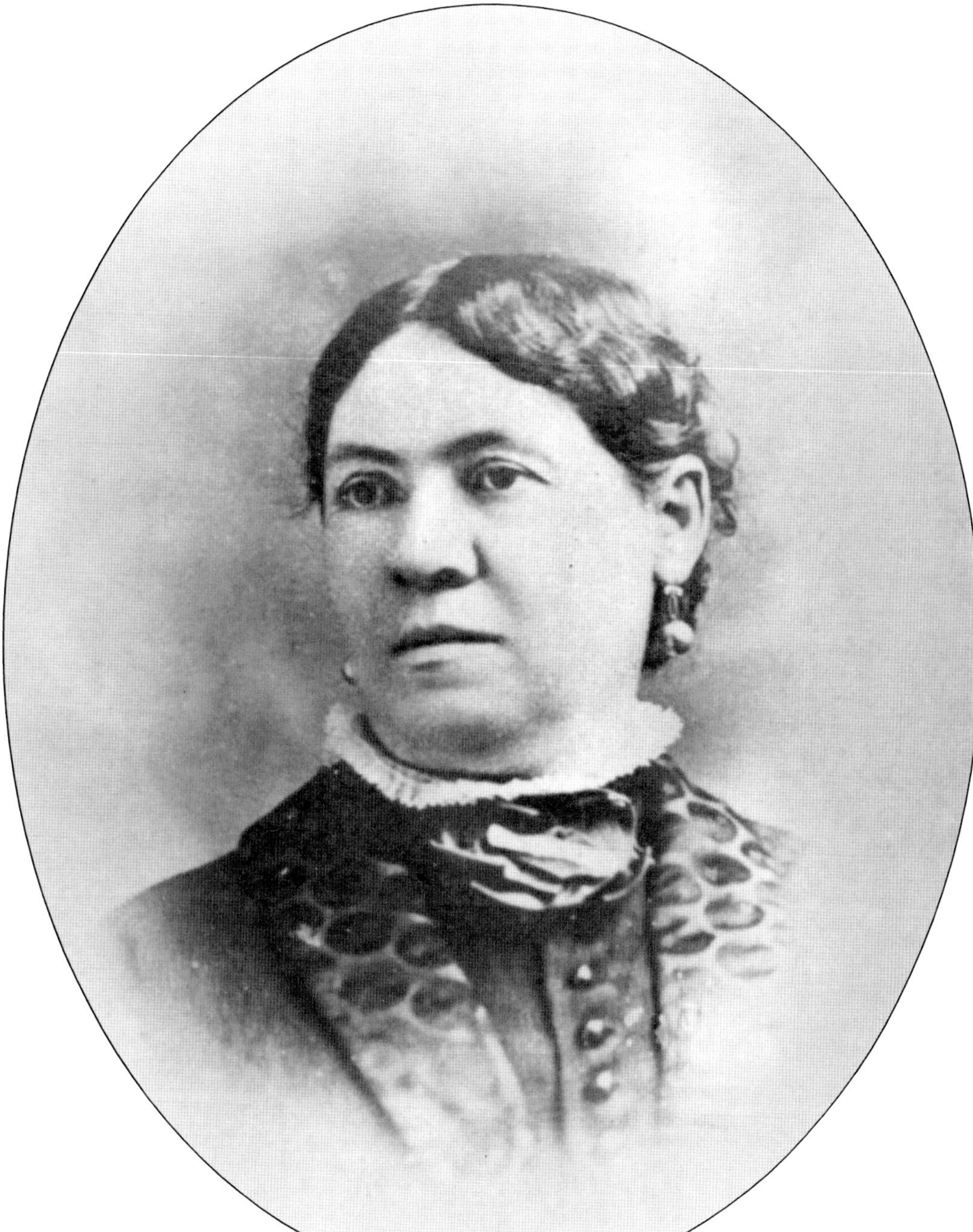

Antoinette Baker Huntington was one of the famous "Mercer Girls" brought to Seattle by Asa Mercer. She accepted a teaching position at Monticello. In 1865, she married Edwin Huntington, son of Darby. They moved to Castle Rock in 1876. She started the first school in Castle Rock in her own home. Eventually, she became the superintendent of public schools for the entire county.

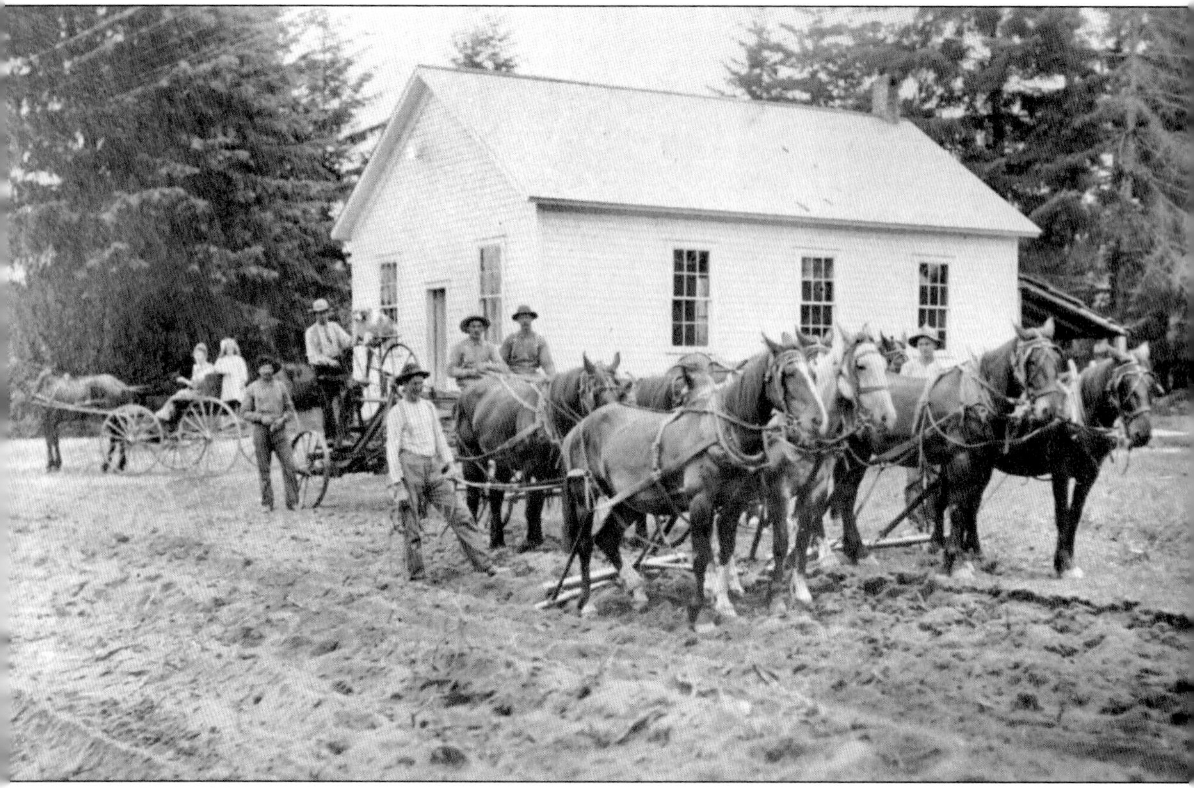

In front of the Sandy Bend schoolhouse, about 5 miles south of Castle Rock, a team of unidentified men with horse-drawn graders are seen grading the school yard. This is how grounds were prepared and landscaped before the invention of tractors using the internal combustion engine. Everything was by horsepower or manpower, such as push lawn mowers.

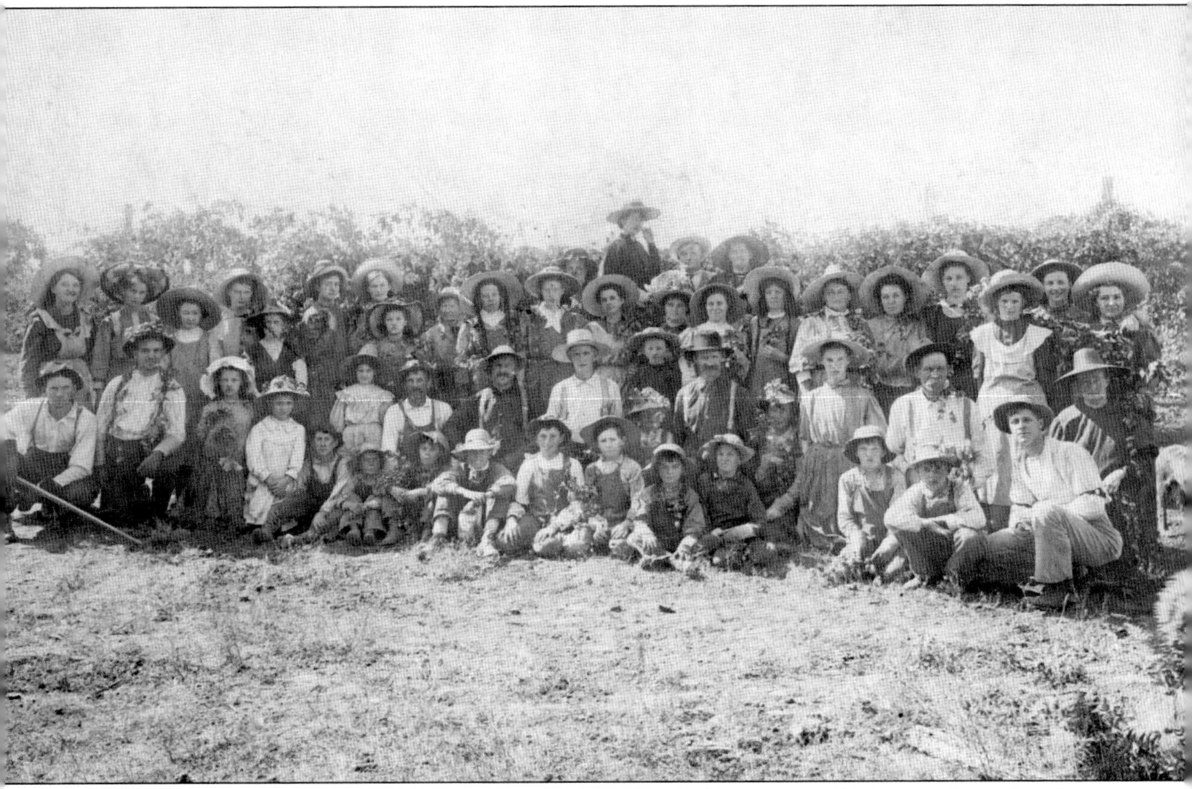

In 1880, there were several hop farms around Castle Rock. The town of Olequa, about 7 miles north on the Military Road, was a booming hop-producing area. This photograph was taken at the farm owned by Royal Smith at Pleasant Hill, about 3 miles south of Castle Rock. In the summer, families, including children, made extra money by participating in the hop harvest. At the end of the harvest, there was usually a party for all the workers. Hops are used in the production of beer. The first brewery in Washington was established in 1854 at Steilacoom, near Tacoma. Hops were a major crop in Cowlitz County in the latter half of the 19th century. An advertisement in the local newspaper for hop pickers in September 1897 called for 600 to 800 pickers. However, in 1891, there was an infestation of hop lice, which destroyed the crop and devastated the hop industry. It never recovered. Farmers turned to other crops, and hops are no longer grown in this area.

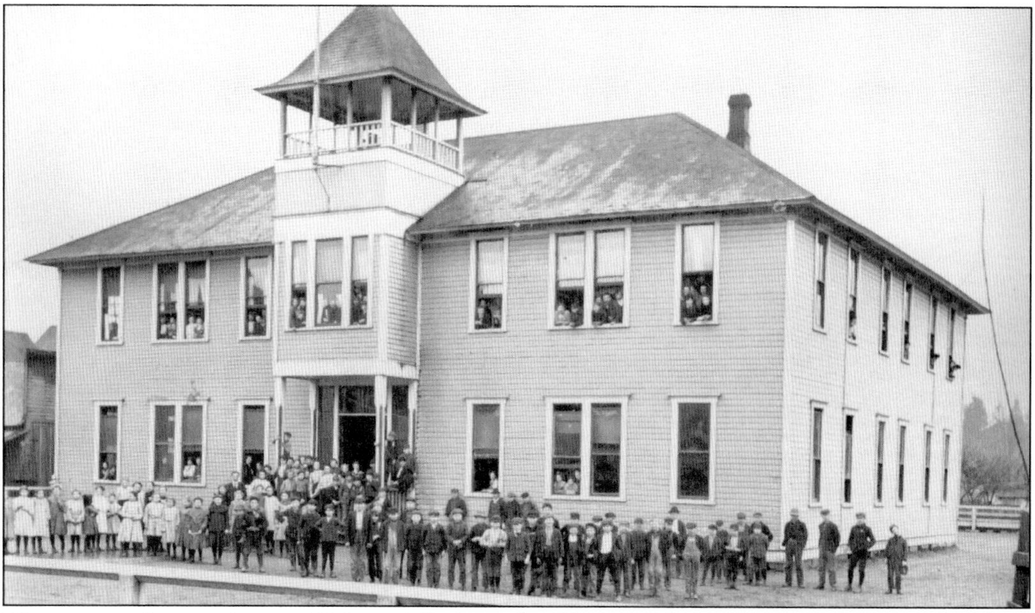

The picture above, taken in 1899, is of the last schoolhouse to hold all its classes in one building. This structure was located where city hall now stands on A Street. The picture below is of the first separate grammar school for lower grades to be built in Castle Rock, on Warren Street in 1903. When this building was constructed, the former school became the high school. Other schools that were consolidated into Castle Rock were the Leonard School, the Pleasant Hill School, the Keatley School, the Olequa schools, the Tower School, the Tucker School, and the Sandy Bend School.

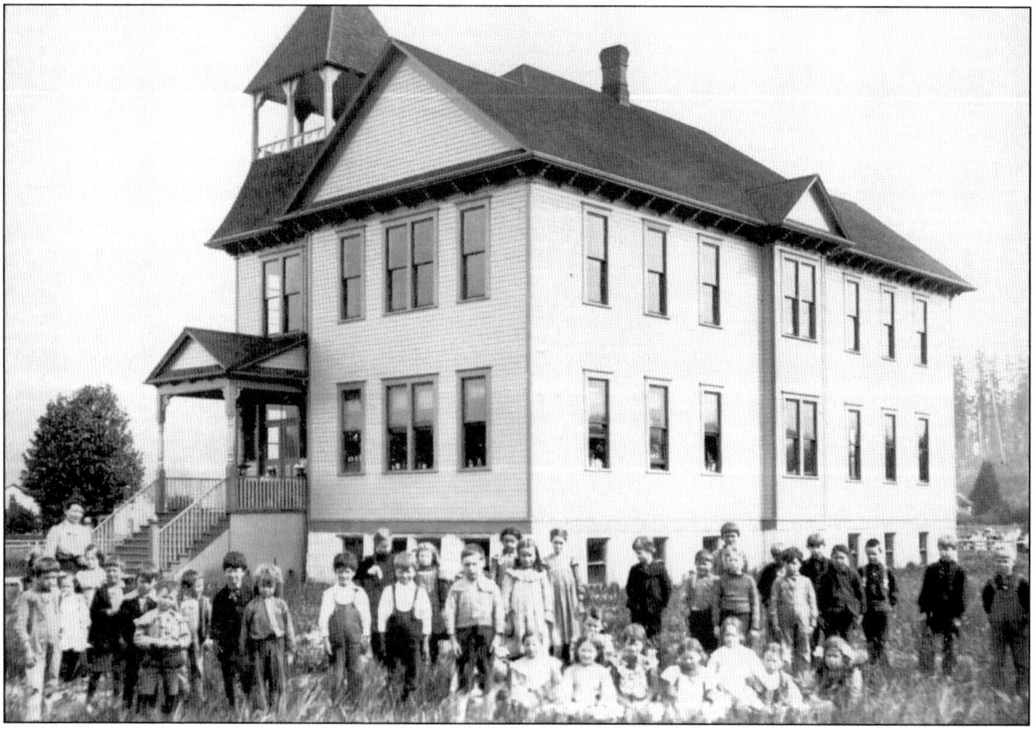

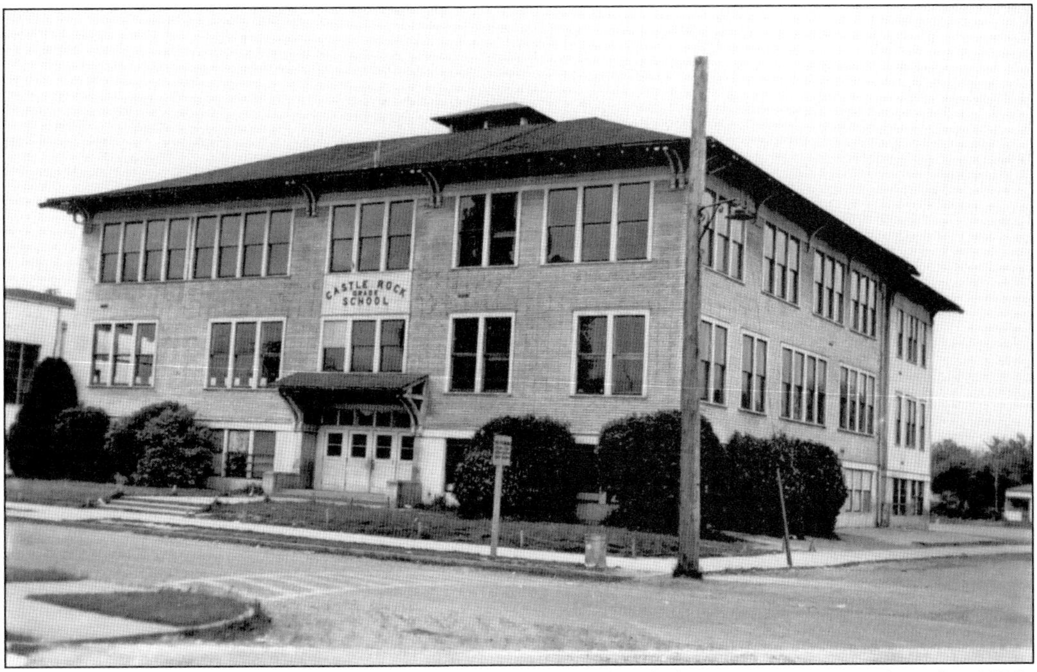

The photograph above is of the elementary or grade school that was constructed in the 1930s at the corner of Front Avenue and Warren Street. It was destroyed in the 1949 earthquake. The photograph below is of the middle school in 1981. It was built between the sites of the old wooden elementary school building and the old brick high school, both of which were torn down in the 1970s. The middle school was also expanded and remodeled in the 1980s when the voters refused to pass a bond to build a new building. (Below, courtesy CCHM.)

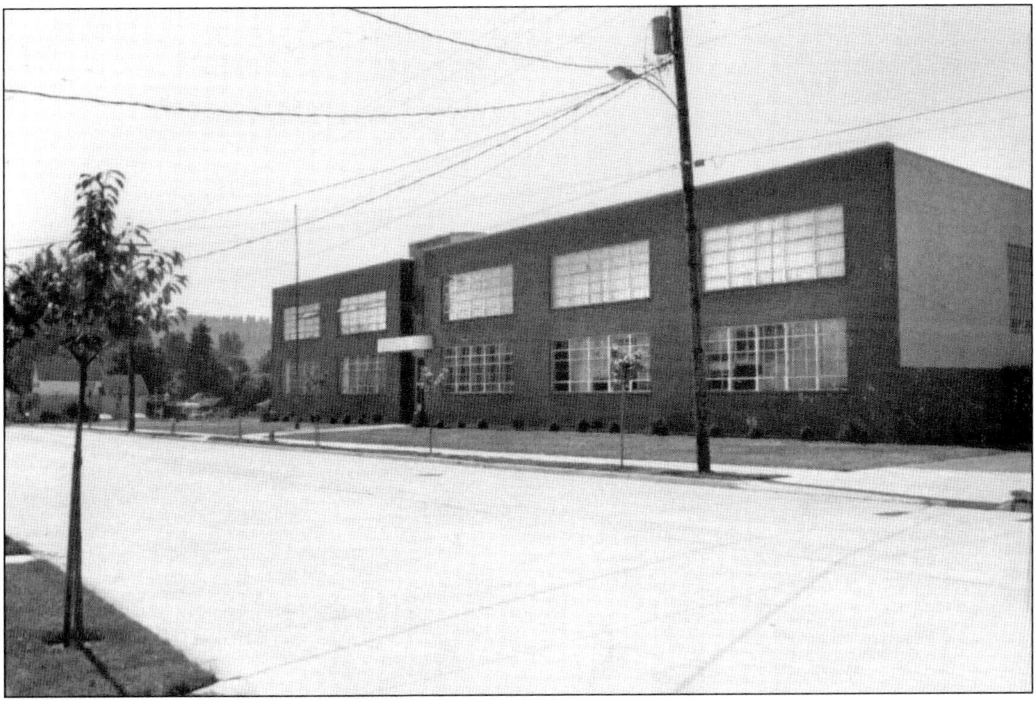

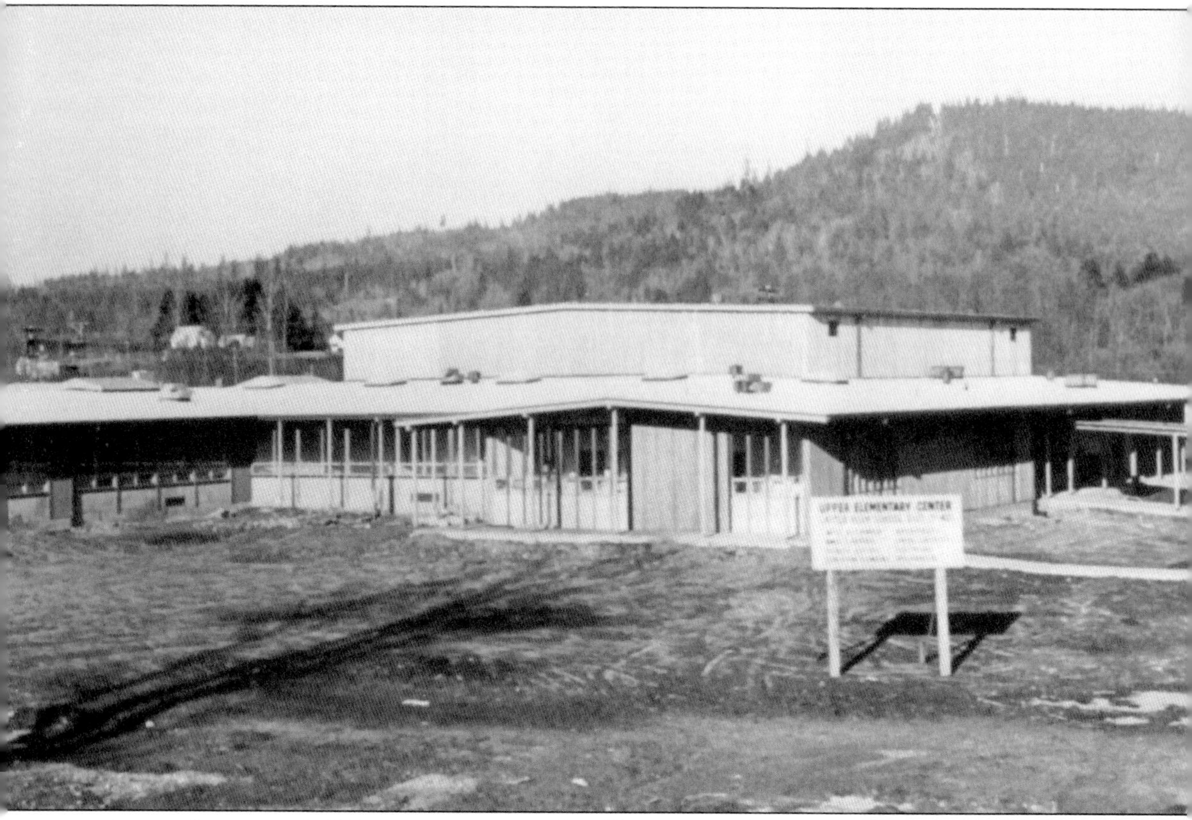

A new elementary building was constructed on Huntington Avenue in 1950 to accommodate the growing baby boomer population. It has been expanded and remodeled twice since then. By 1959, it had already been outgrown, so a new upper elementary building was constructed to expand the facilities. This building housed the sixth, seventh, and eighth grades and included a music room, a gymnasium, locker rooms with showers, and offices for the school district's administration. In a 1990s remodeling effort, this building was incorporated into the elementary school.

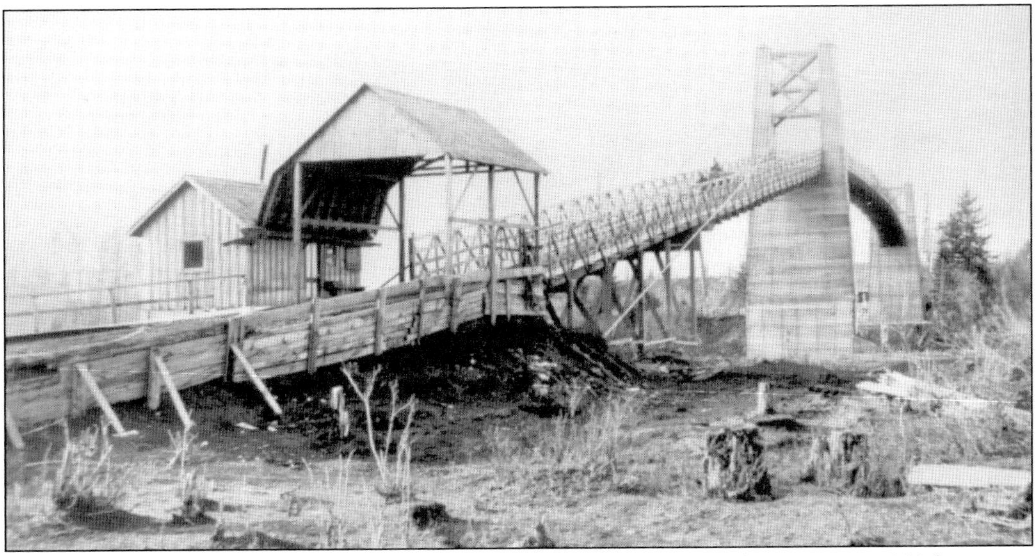

The wooden suspension toll bridge was constructed across the Cowlitz River in 1903 by a man named Eddy. This was the first vehicular bridge spanning the river in Cowlitz County. Its east end was on a long peninsula just southwest of town, and the west end was anchored to a prominence next to the present West Side Highway, or State Route 411. The east end had a long ramp to bring vehicles up to the level of the bridge. Warren Street was then extended to connect to the new bridge. A toll was charged to cross the bridge, and the owner hoped to make a profit on his investment. A ferry was also operating in this area, so the traffic fees were not highly profitable to either business. In 1906, a fire erupted on both piers of the bridge, and it fell into the river. Arson was suspected, but no one was ever prosecuted for the fire.

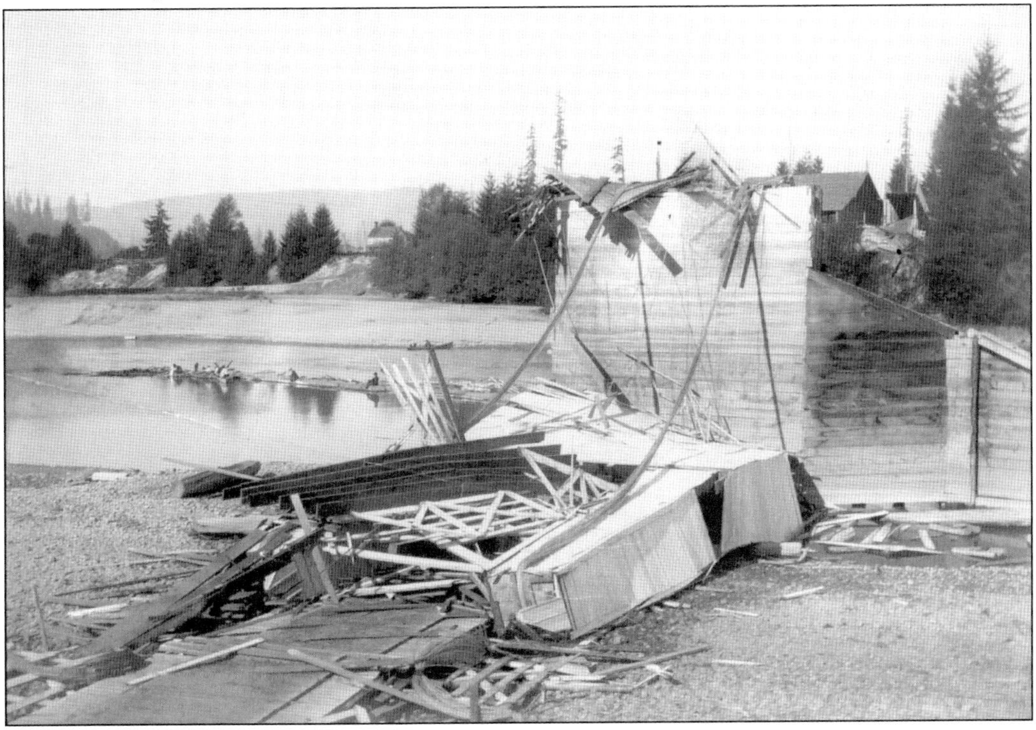

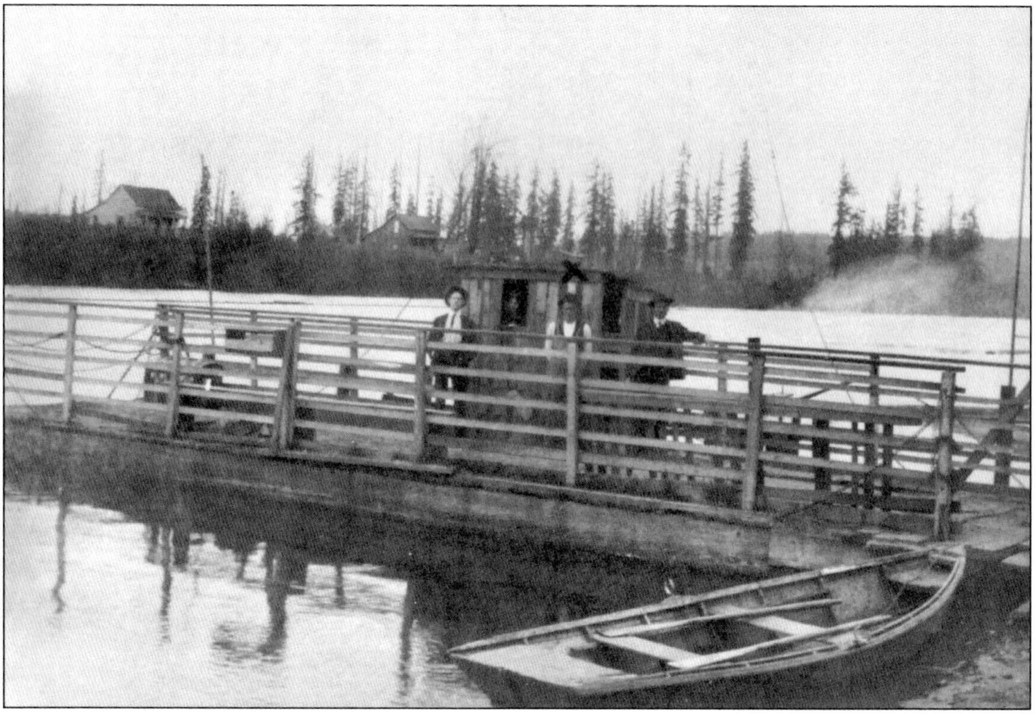

The first ferry at Castle Rock was owned by William Whittle and operated prior to the construction of the Eddy toll bridge. From the time of the destruction of the Eddy toll bridge in 1906, another ferry docked on the town side of the Cowlitz River at the west end of A Street. It was owned by Henry Powelson and operated by Parde Jackson. In this photograph of the second ferry, the riders are, from left to right, unidentified, Jackson, and Powelson. The boy looking out of the center window is Verle Powelson, Henry's son. The Powelson ferry operated until the construction of the high steel bridge in 1910.

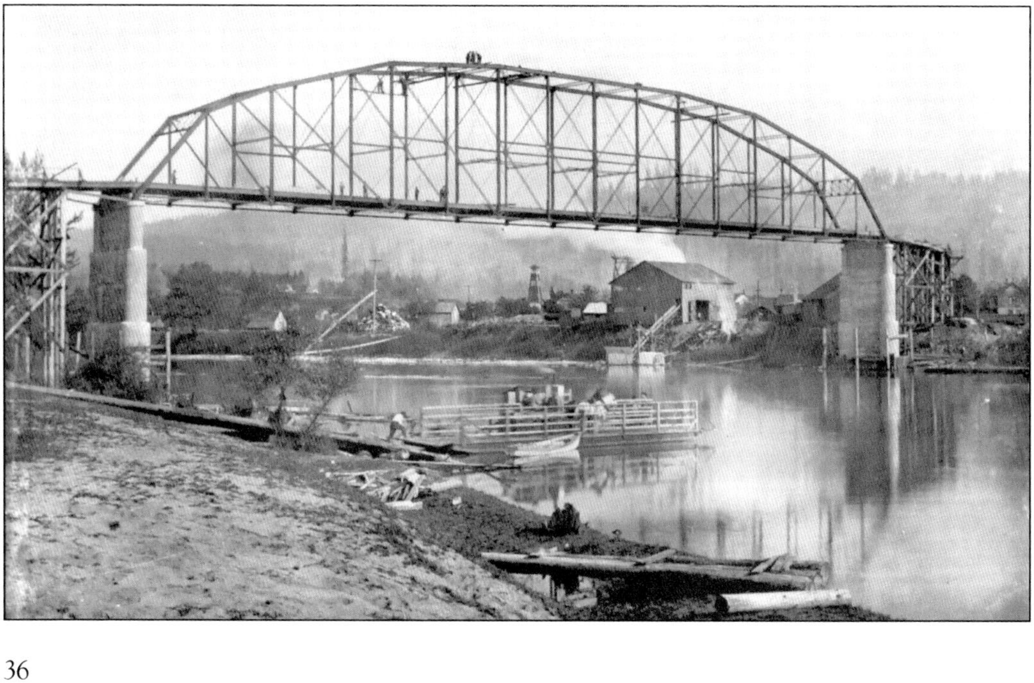

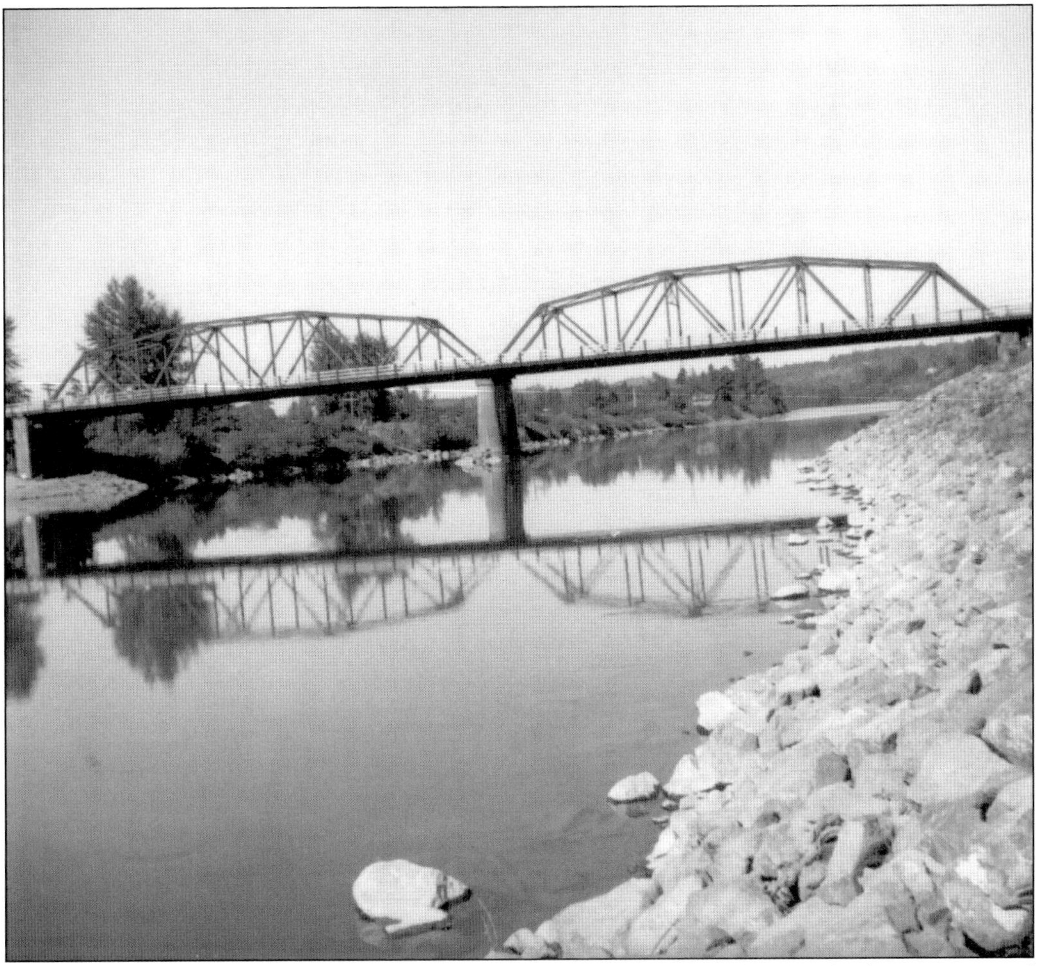

The Castle Rock Bridge stands over the Cowlitz River in 1957. The first bridge constructed after the destruction of the Eddy toll bridge was referred to as the high steel bridge, which was constructed of steel and concrete in 1910. It was 300 feet long and 60 feet high. It can be seen under construction on the previous page. That bridge was replaced by the second steel bridge, which was constructed over the Cowlitz River in 1926 and stood until the 1960s, when the current bridge was built. For many years, the Castle Rock Bridge was the only way across the Cowlitz River between Kelso and Toledo. In 2006, a bridge was built at Lexington that connects Interstate 5 with State Route 411, the West Side Highway. There is now a plan underway to create a walking and bicycling trail from Castle Rock to that new bridge.

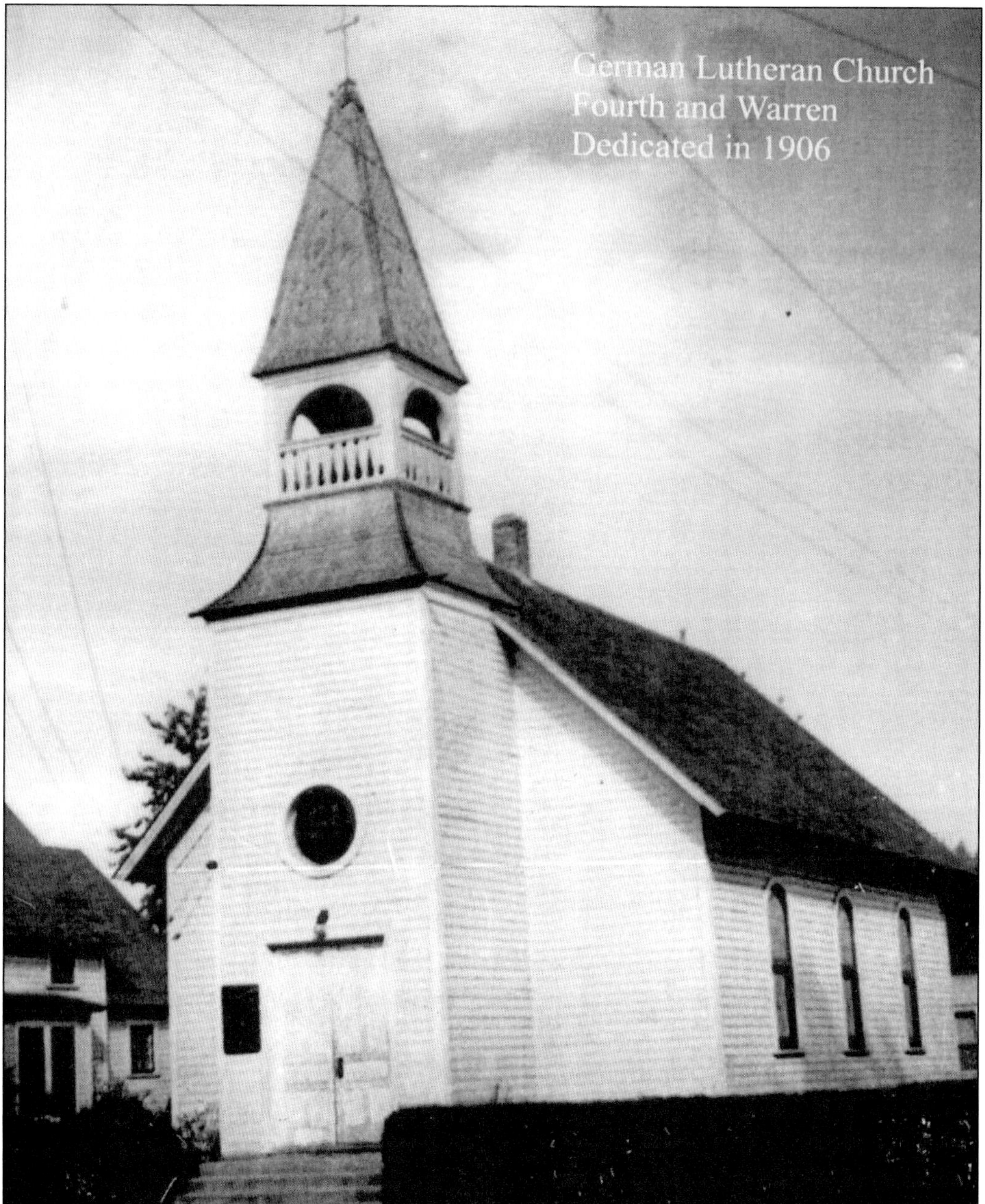

The history of Castle Rock is inextricably bound with the history of its churches. The German Lutheran church was dedicated in 1906. The first church services were held in the homes of the early pioneers, and the services were conducted in German. The first resident minister was Fred Meineke. Worship in German was discontinued in 1939. Among his other accomplishments, William Huntington was a minister and, in the early days, held services in his home. He was also instrumental in establishing the Christian church in Castle Rock. Capt. George Pyle was a lay Methodist minister, and Elisha Jackson was a minister and held services at the Jackson Inn.

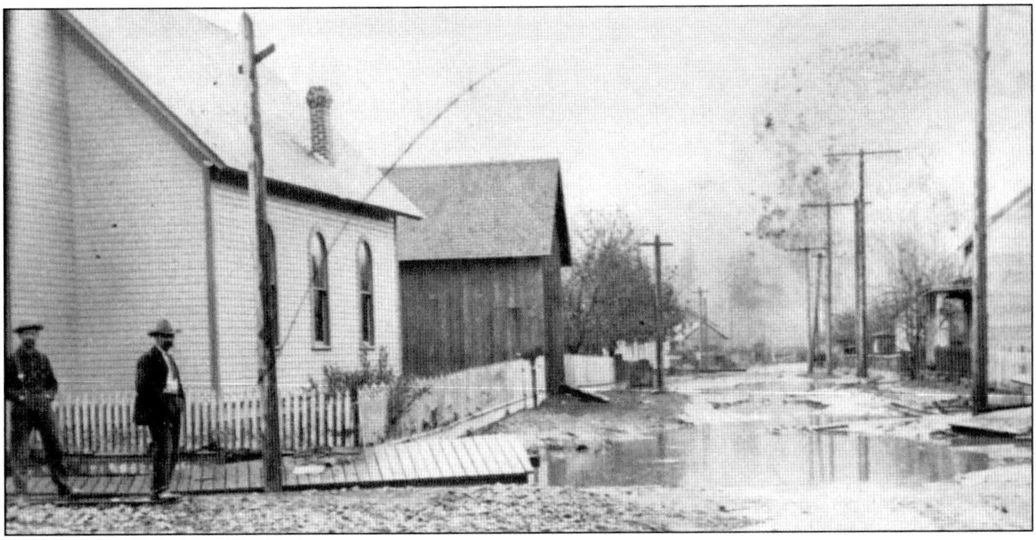

Another view of the German Lutheran church is at the left of this picture. The aftermath of the flood in 1916 has left the street full of water, and the boardwalk has twisted to one side. The current Lutheran church, St. Paul Lutheran, is at the corner of First Avenue and B Street SW. It was built in 1949 and held its first service on June 18, 1950. The congregation of this church continues to follow the pioneer traditions and is a strong force for good in the community. They host free lunches in the summer designed to provide low-income children with a good meal when they do not have access to school lunches; however, these meals are open to anyone and create a spot for community social contact for many other people as well. The food and serving duties are provided by all the town's churches and individual volunteers, too.

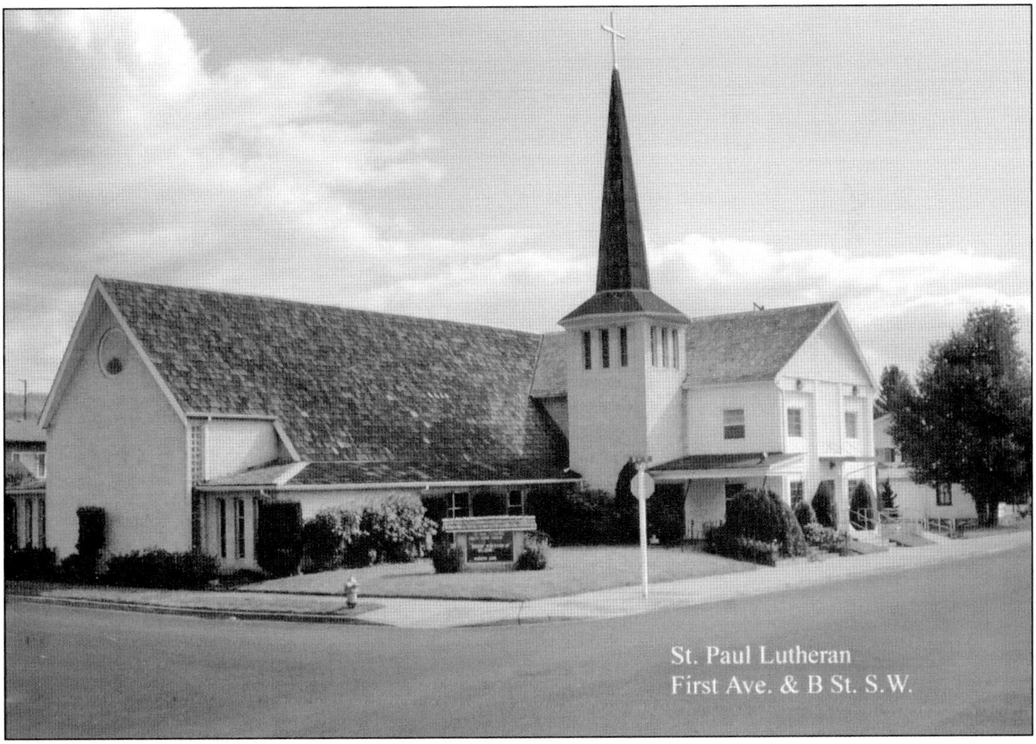

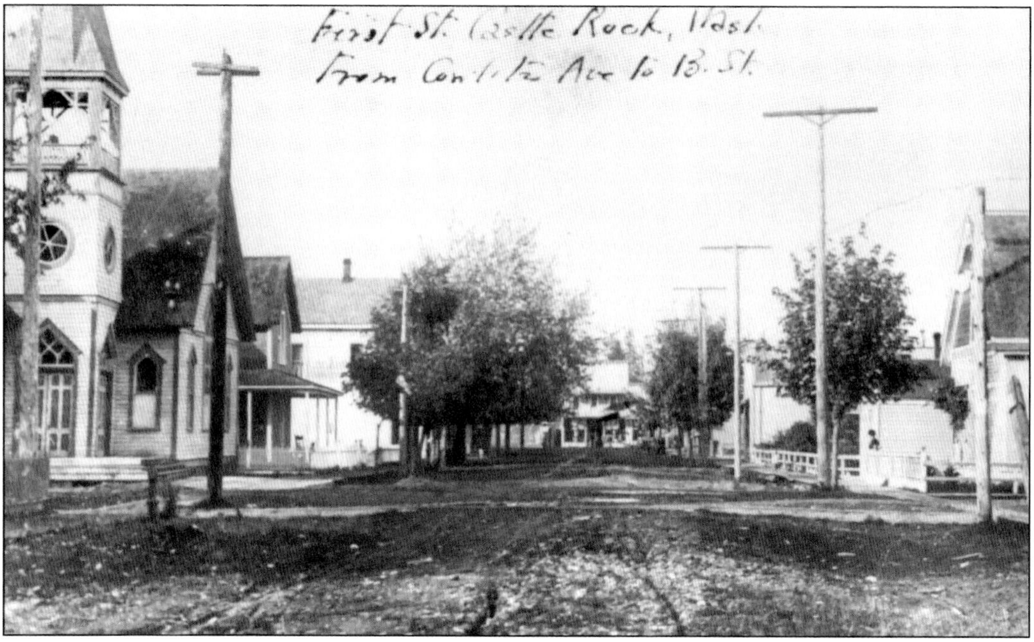

Taken prior to 1913, this early postcard shows First Street from B Street to Cowlitz Street looking north. Ruts from wagons can be seen in the street. The Castle Rock United Methodist Church, built in 1888, is on the far left; then the Lovering home; and the Boewer building. Just behind the trees, a partial view of the Savoy Hotel can be seen. At the end of First Street, on Cowlitz Street, just past the trees, is a hardware store. On the right side of the street is the Dahlman home, a dentist office (the small building), and an obscure view of the old bank building. The second photograph of the Methodist church was taken in November 1979, and the unusual snow makes it a Christmas card view. Though remodeled and added to several times over the years, this is actually still the original building.

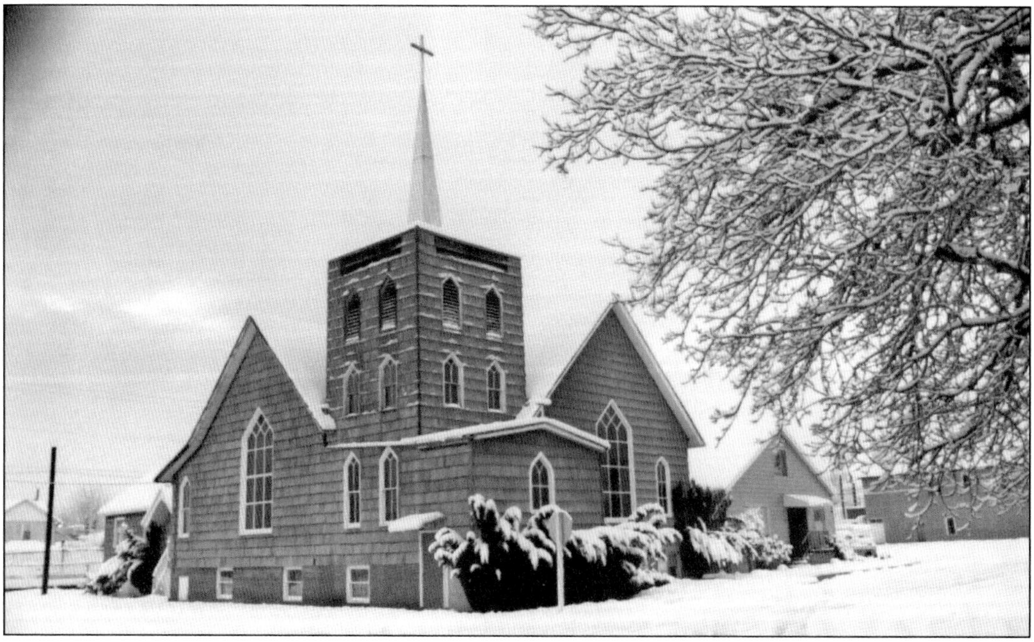

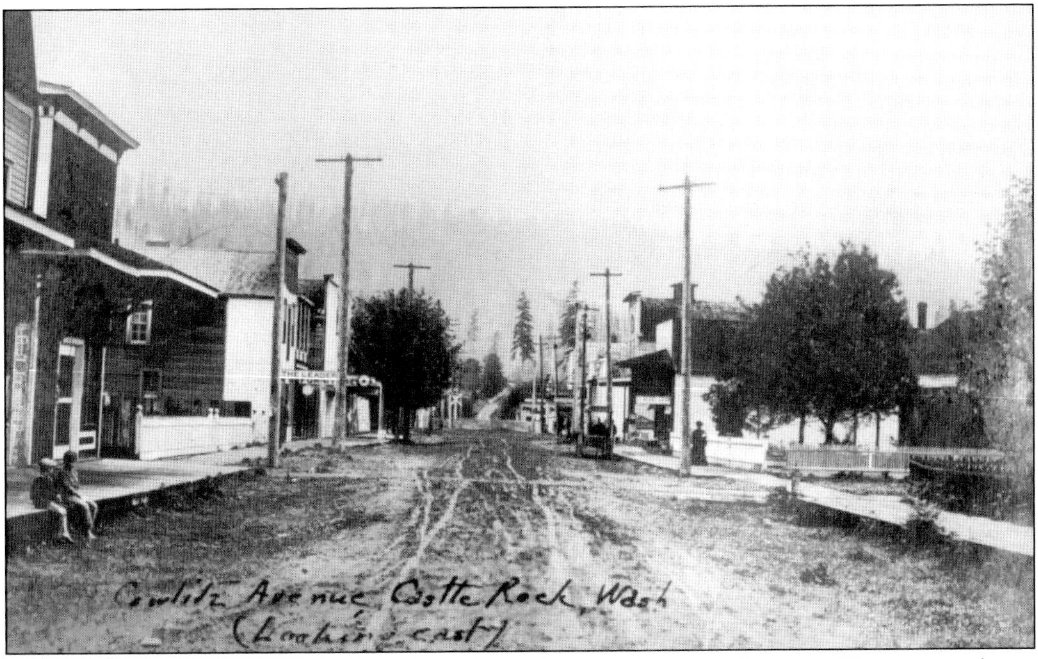

Many views of downtown Castle Rock have been photographed over the years. The picture above, taken in 1900, is looking east toward the railroad tracks, where Huntington Avenue is now. The white railroad crossing signs can be clearly seen. The street is not paved, and wagon tracks are visible. The sidewalks were built of wood and were called boardwalks.

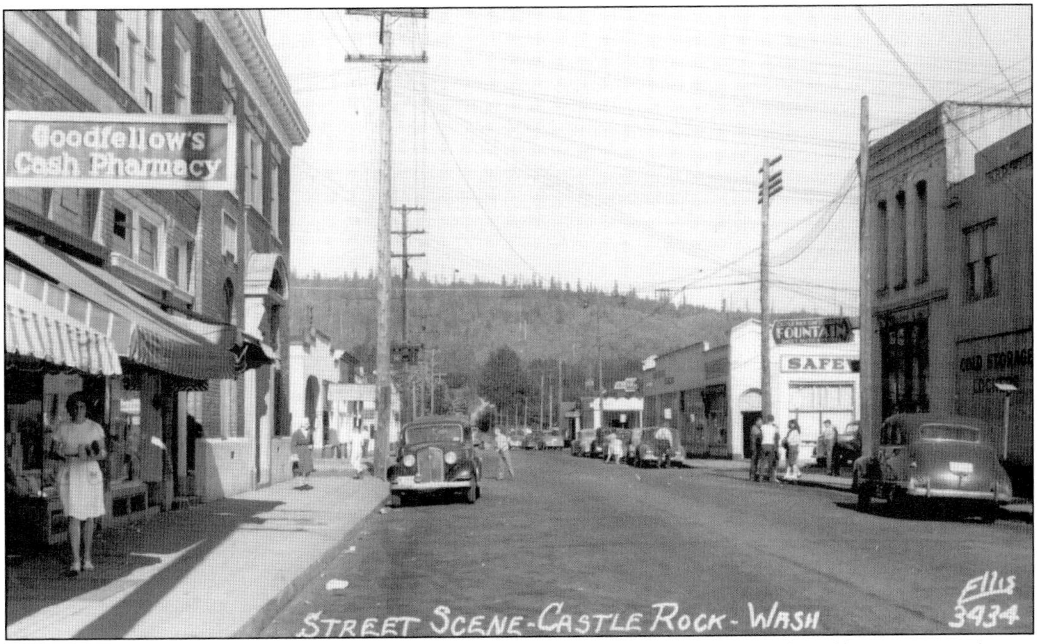

Fast-forward to the 1940s, and Cowlitz Street is paved and has cement sidewalks in many places. Many cars are seen, and the proliferation of telephones and electric power shows in the lines making veritable spiderwebs above the street. Fashions were for shorter skirts due to the lack of fabric available during World War II.

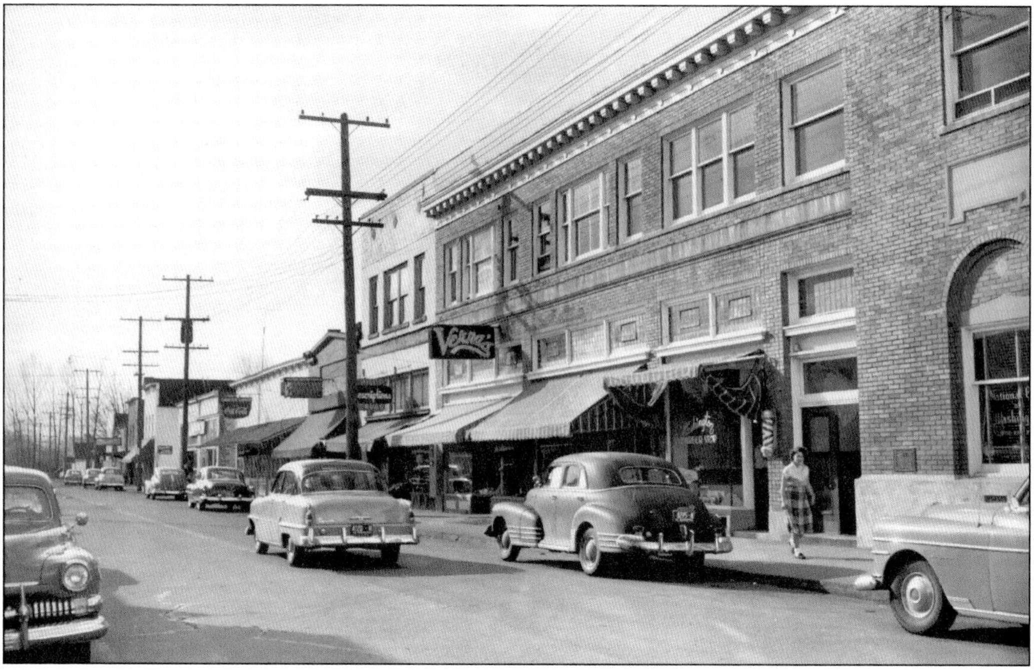

The picture above is a view showing Cowlitz Street looking west from Huntington Avenue in the 1940s. Cars line the streets, and the town is bustling. The building on the far left edge of the photograph is the old Safeway store, where Napa Auto Parts is now. Across Front Avenue from Safeway is White's Sweet Shop, which was a place to get ice cream, soft drinks, and hamburgers. Across the street on the northwest corner of First Avenue and Cowlitz Street is the bank building. On the northeast corner in the far right of the picture is the Ten Cent Store. The view below is also Cowlitz Street in the 1940s looking west but from Front Avenue, one block farther west. (Above, courtesy Judy Tinney.)

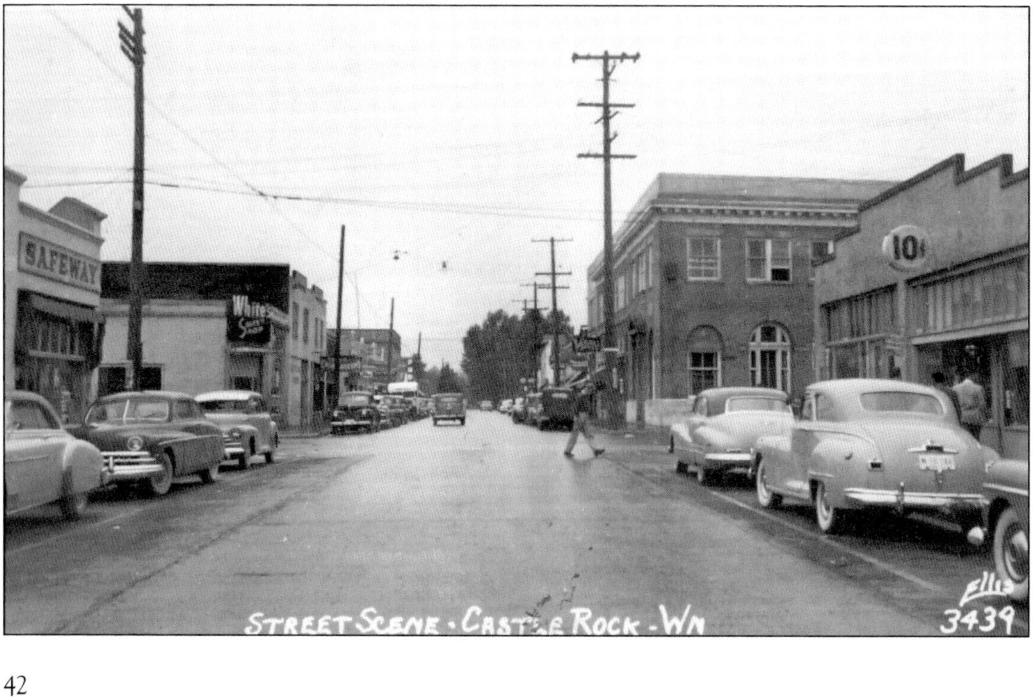

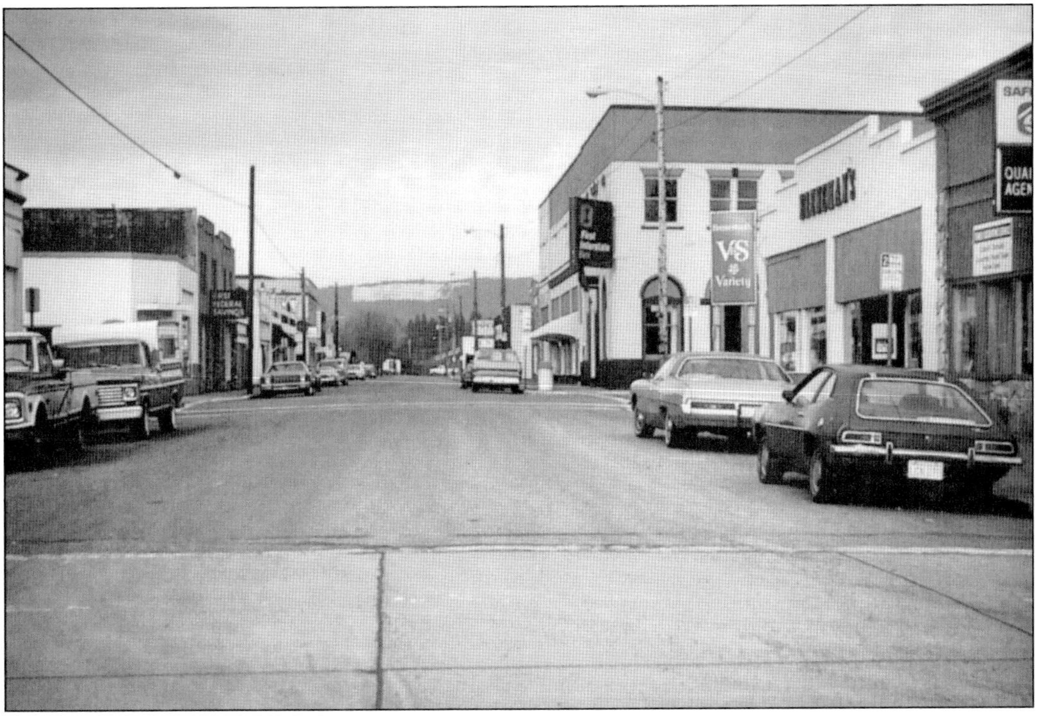

This postcard view is of Cowlitz Street looking west in the 1970s. The store on the far right has changed from the Ten Cent Store to Breneman's V&S Variety. The building on the northwest corner of Cowlitz Street and Front Avenue is still a bank but is now the First Interstate Bank.

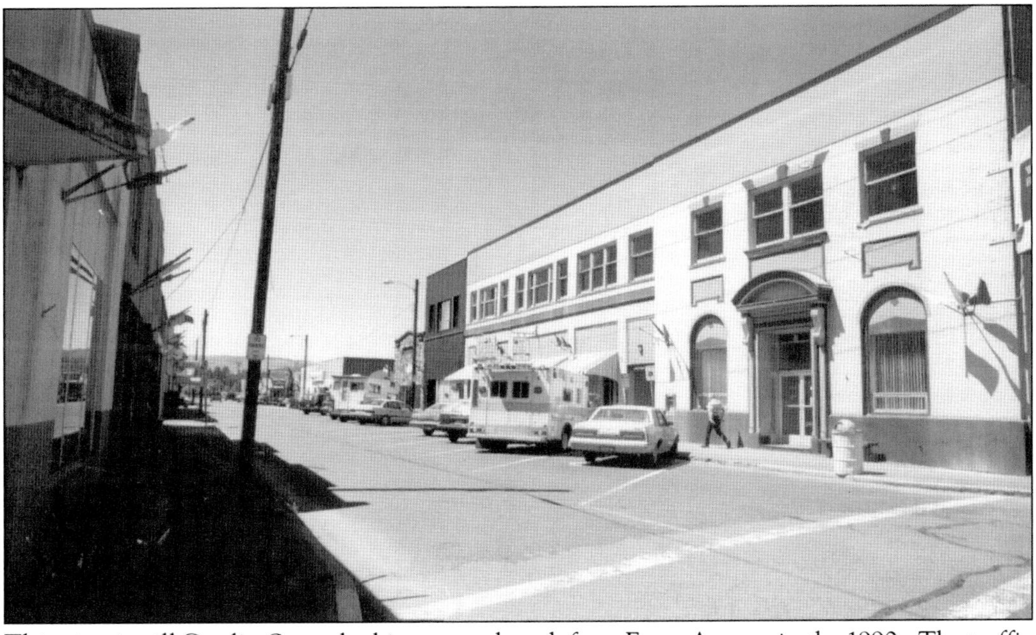

This view is still Cowlitz Street looking west, though from Front Avenue in the 1990s. The traffic flow has been changed to one way going west, and parking has been changed from parallel to the curb to front-in angled toward the curb. This change was instituted to increase the number of parking spaces on the street.

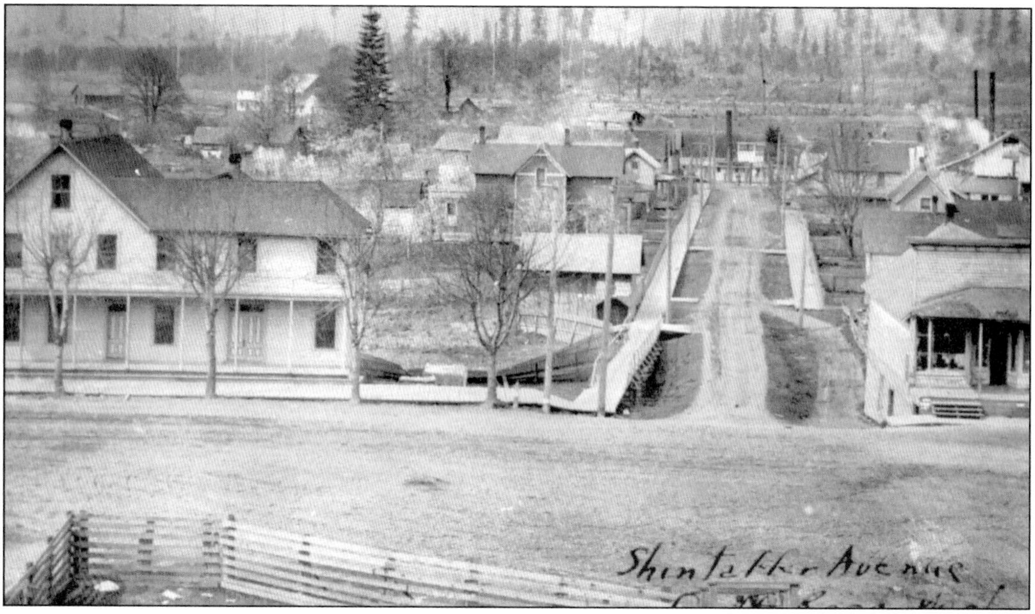

These are two very different views of Shintaffer Street looking west from Front Avenue. The photograph above was taken in 1900 and shows an unpaved street with boardwalks alongside. Shintaffer then was a business street with a dock at the west end on the Cowlitz River. The steamer *Northwest* is moored at the dock. In the foreground on the left is the Central Hotel. On the opposite corner of Shintaffer Street and Front Avenue is Ira Conger's store, which was a general store at the time. At the far west end of Shintaffer Street, on the north side, steam is emanating from the J. R. Robin and Sons shingle mill, one of the main industrial enterprises of the period. The photograph below is nearly the same view of Shintaffer Street looking west across Front Avenue in the 1970s. All the businesses have gone. Though the street is paved and has cement sidewalks, it is now a residential street. The yards of the houses have many well-grown trees and shrubs attesting to the age of the homes.

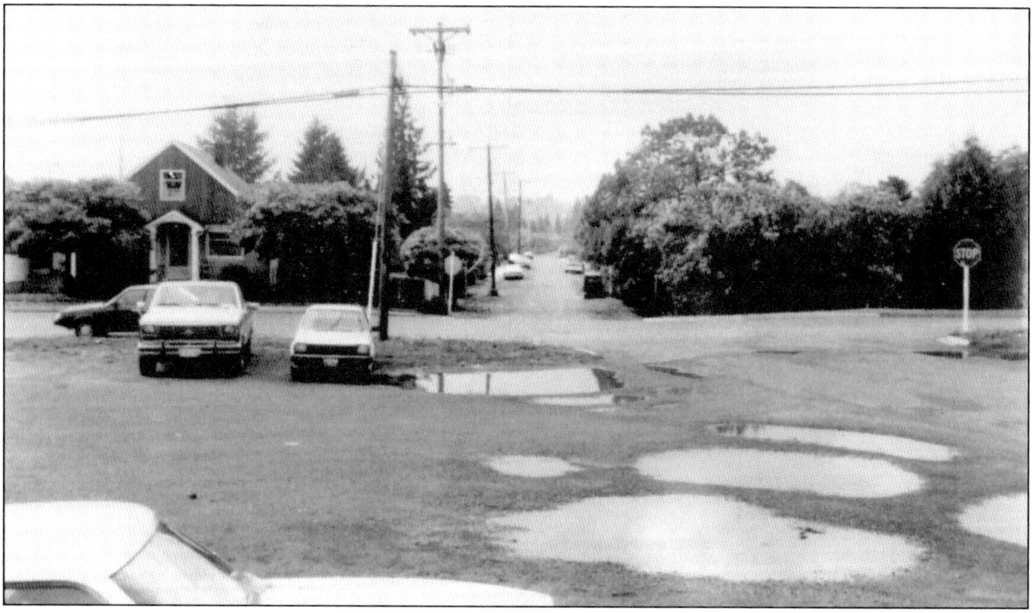

Three

Commerce and Industry

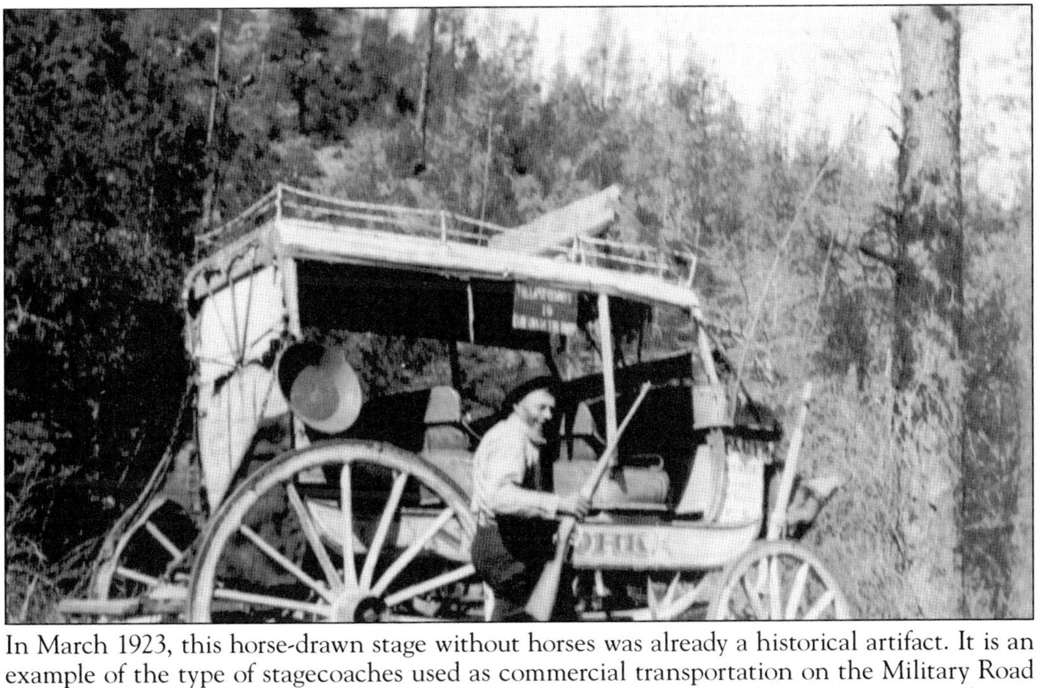

In March 1923, this horse-drawn stage without horses was already a historical artifact. It is an example of the type of stagecoaches used as commercial transportation on the Military Road between Vancouver and Olympia before the advent of steamboats or motorcars. Four to six horses pulled the stagecoach, the tires had metal rims, and the seats had no springs. This did not make for a very comfortable ride, especially since the Military Road was dirt with a swampy section covered by "puncheons made of trees not to exceed ten inches in diameter," as stated in the specifications for the road. It was not possible to swerve to miss stumps, ruts, or holes. On steep hills, the coach bumped along, often threatening to tip over. At times, the passengers had to get out and help push or pull the coach over rough hills or gullies.

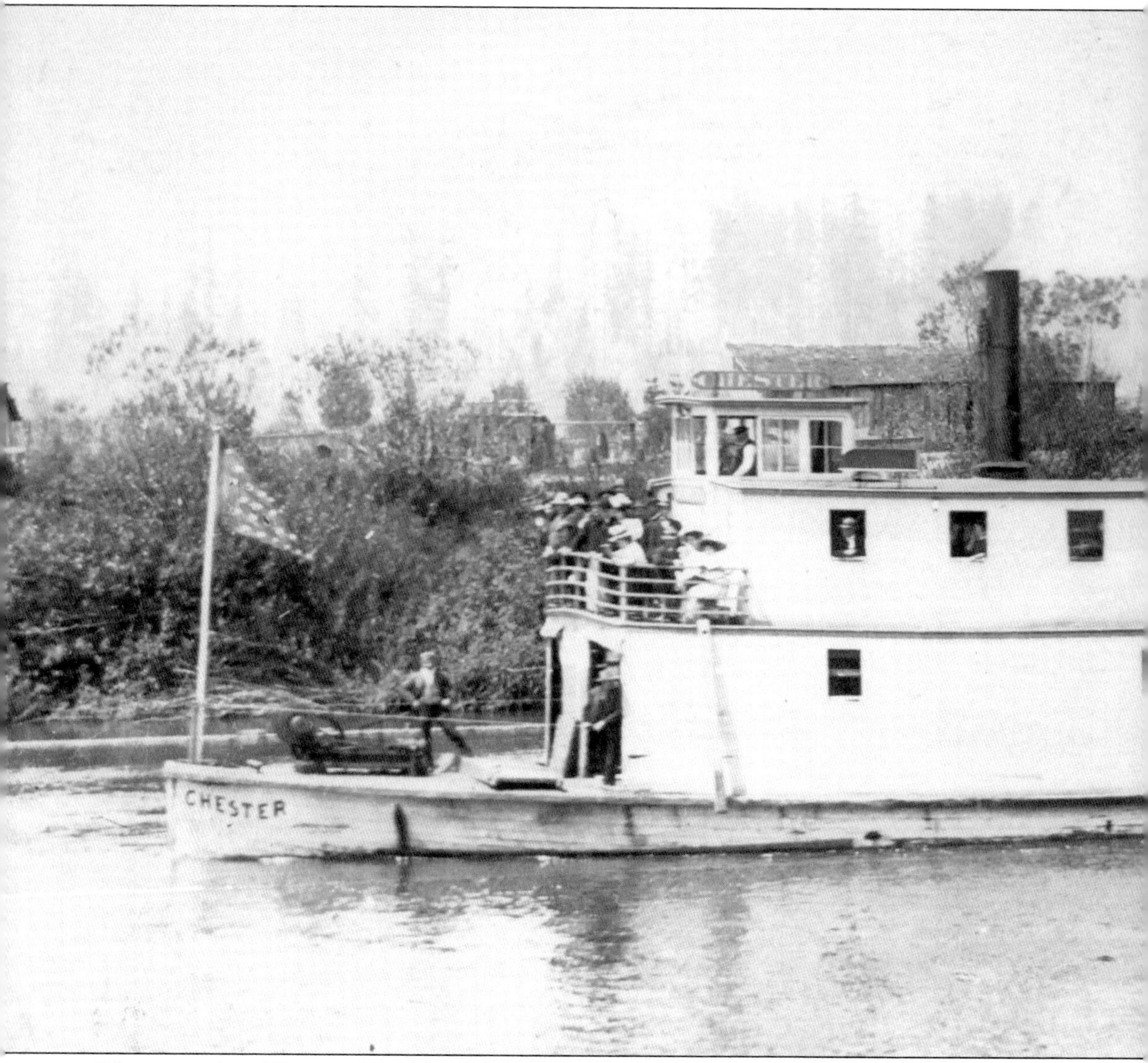

The steamship *Chester*, owned by the Joseph Kellogg Company, was launched in 1898. It was designed after a particularly dry year caused the river to be too low to operate earlier boats. The builders joked that the *Chester* could run on heavy dew. Low water was not the only hazard to be encountered on the river. Unexpectedly formed sand or gravel bars could trap boats. Debris and

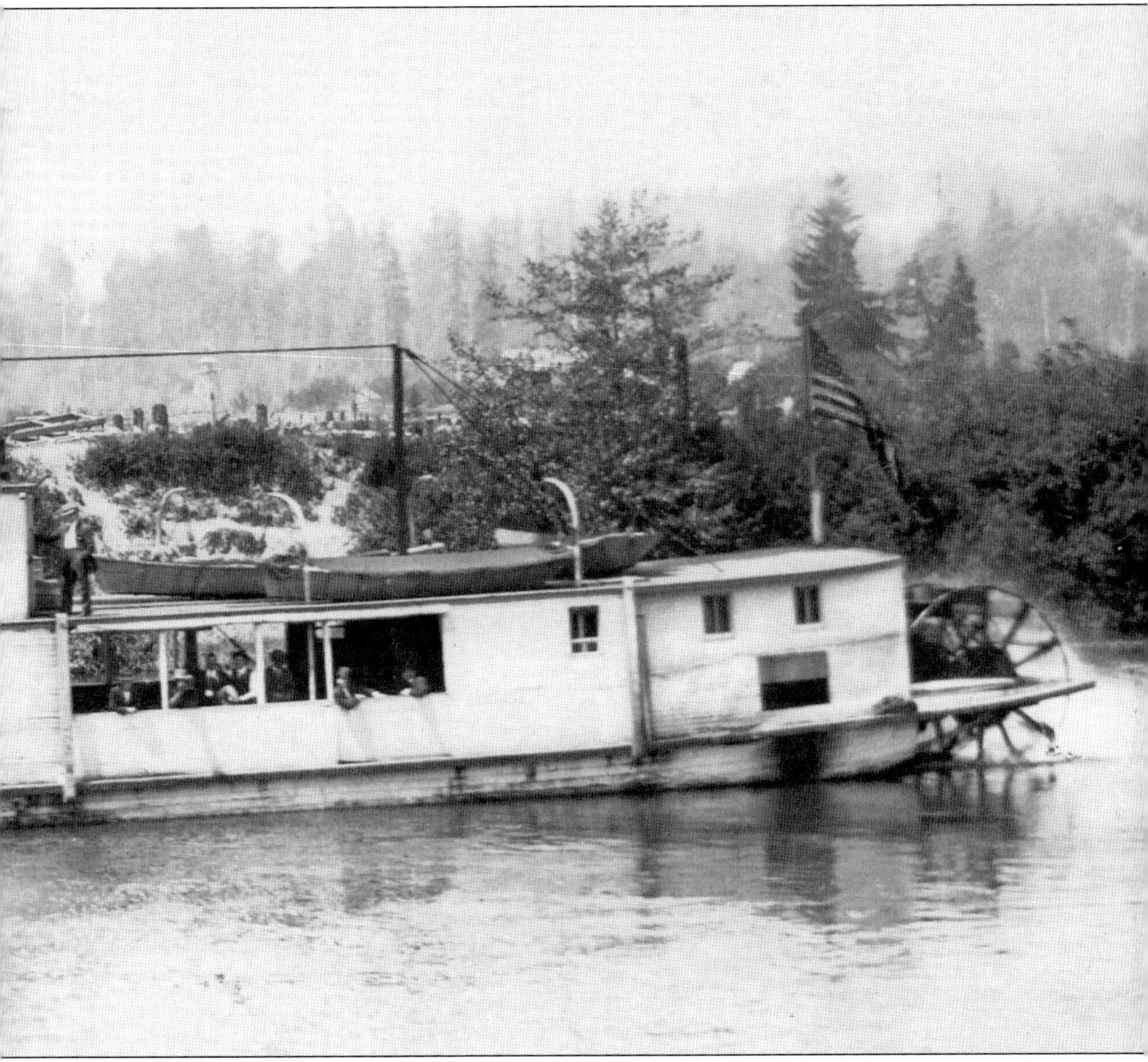

logs crashed holes into the bows and sides. Even tree limbs could jab in through the windows of the boats. At times, the water was so low even the little *Chester* could not move. Dredges were used to clear the river channel, but like the river of today, it kept refilling. Ultimately, dredging failed.

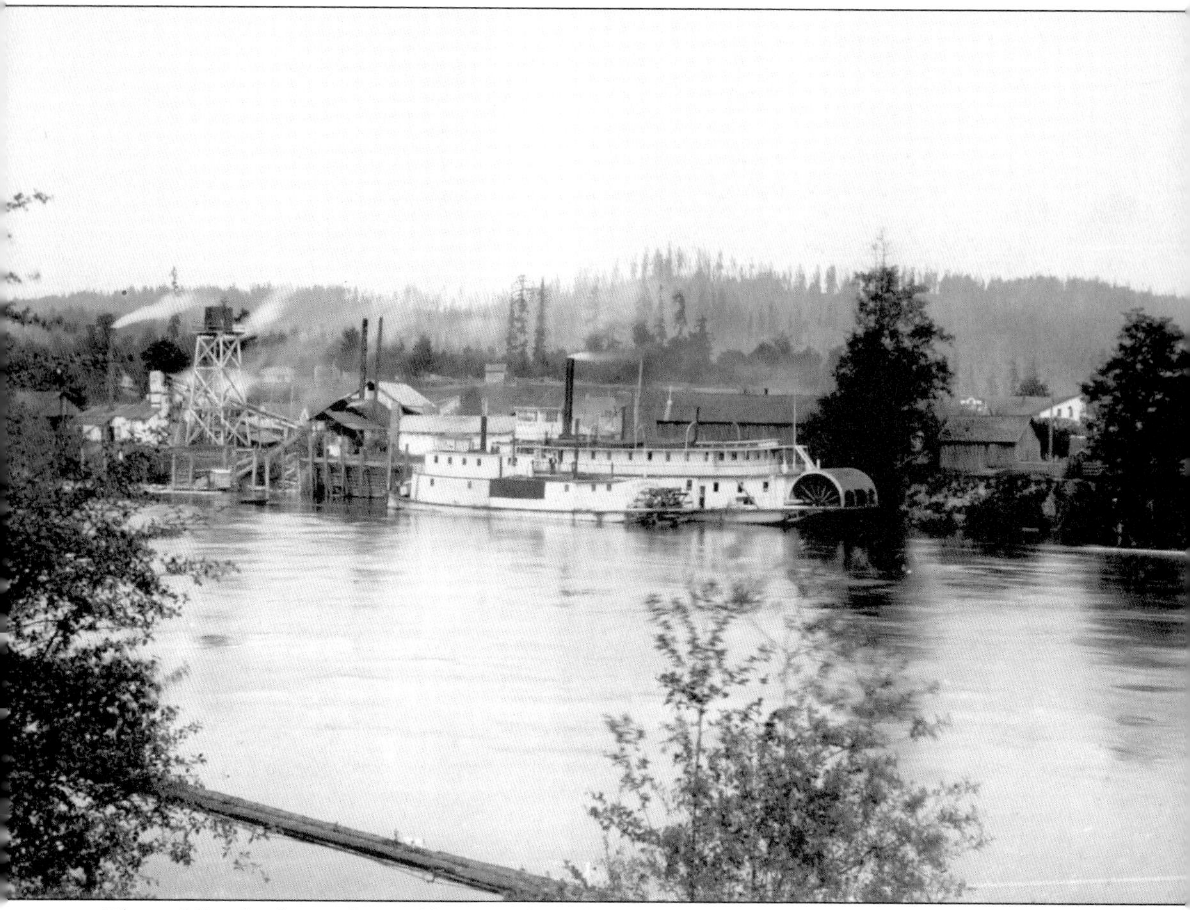

The paddle-wheel steamboats *Chester* and *Northwest* both belonged to the Joseph Kellogg Company, which also owned the dock on the Cowlitz River at the end of Shintaffer Street. The Joseph Kellogg Company held a virtual monopoly on steamboat service on the Cowlitz River. Other companies tried to compete, but the Joseph Kellogg Company improved its rates or schedules, and the competition ended. Also logging companies used the river to float log drives whenever they wanted. One time a log crashed a hole in the *Chester*, and she sank. Another time a raft of logs forced the *Northwest* out of the river channel. In attempting to escape, she struck a submerged tree, which punched a hole in her bow. After going to court over the issue, a compromise was eventually reached. The logging companies agreed to send the logs down the river at prearranged times, and the steamboats traveled safely. After the beginning of the 20th century, the *Chester* hauled equipment for the new transportation that would spell her end: cement for the new highway being constructed along the bottom of the Cowlitz River Valley. By 1923, users deserted the riverboats for land travel.

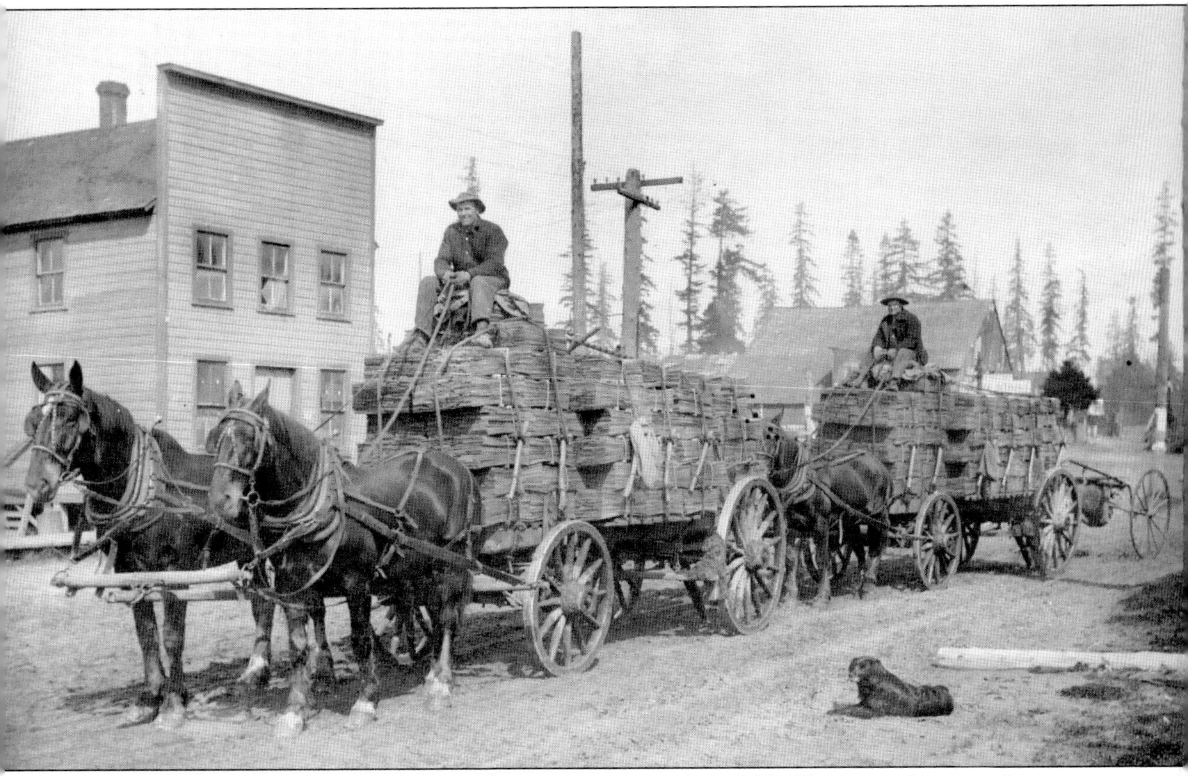

Bert Booth is in the driver's seat of the front wagon just after 1900. The second wagon driver is unidentified. The wagons are being used to haul shingles from Silver Lake, heading down Front Avenue in Castle Rock, to load onto the steamboats that docked at Shintaffer Street. Horses were still the main mode of land transportation, as evidenced by the stable sign that can be seen behind the second wagon. At this time, streets were still unpaved, though usually graveled. Wooden street crossings were an occasional luxury. Any sidewalks were still made of wood. Many residents kept horses, cows, chickens, and pigs because these were staples of life, even inside a town. Barns usually lined the alleys, and manure was piled in the alleys. Even with the advent of a piped water system, flush toilets were yet to make their appearance in most homes, and outdoor privies were the usual arrangement.

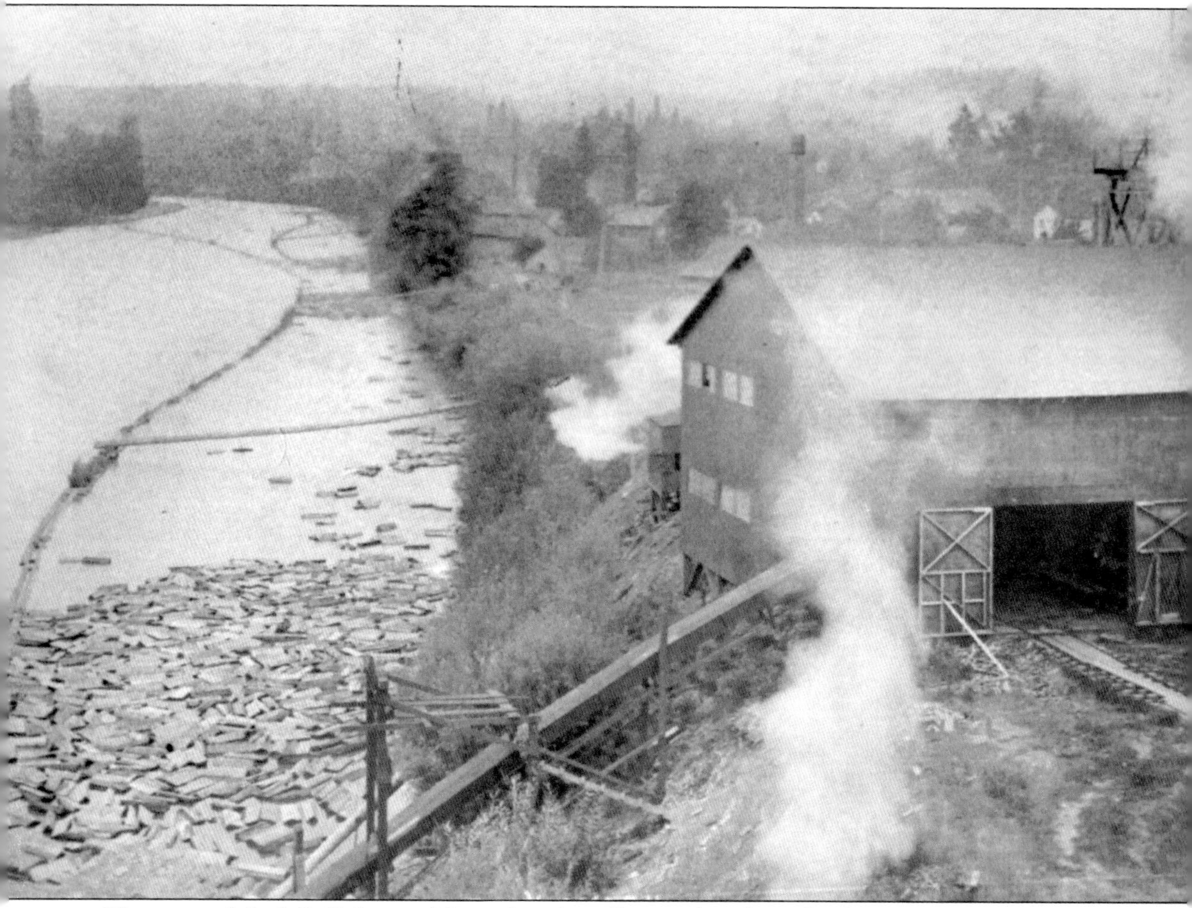

This view of the J. R. Robin and Sons shingle mill was taken from the deck of the high steel bridge in 1910. Cedar shingles were the biggest industry in early Castle Rock. The lower elevations of the river valleys and swampy areas made for a relatively heavy growth of western red cedar. This wood was ideal for the manufacture of shingles. Robin originally built a mill on the west side of the river, but after the entry of the railroad on the east side, he moved his mill to the end of Shintaffer Street, where his business was near the railway depot and next to the river and the newly constructed boat dock. It was reported in an early newspaper that "the output of shingles for Cowlitz County in the year of 1895 was about 107 million and, of these, about 75 million have been manufactured in and tributary to Castle Rock."

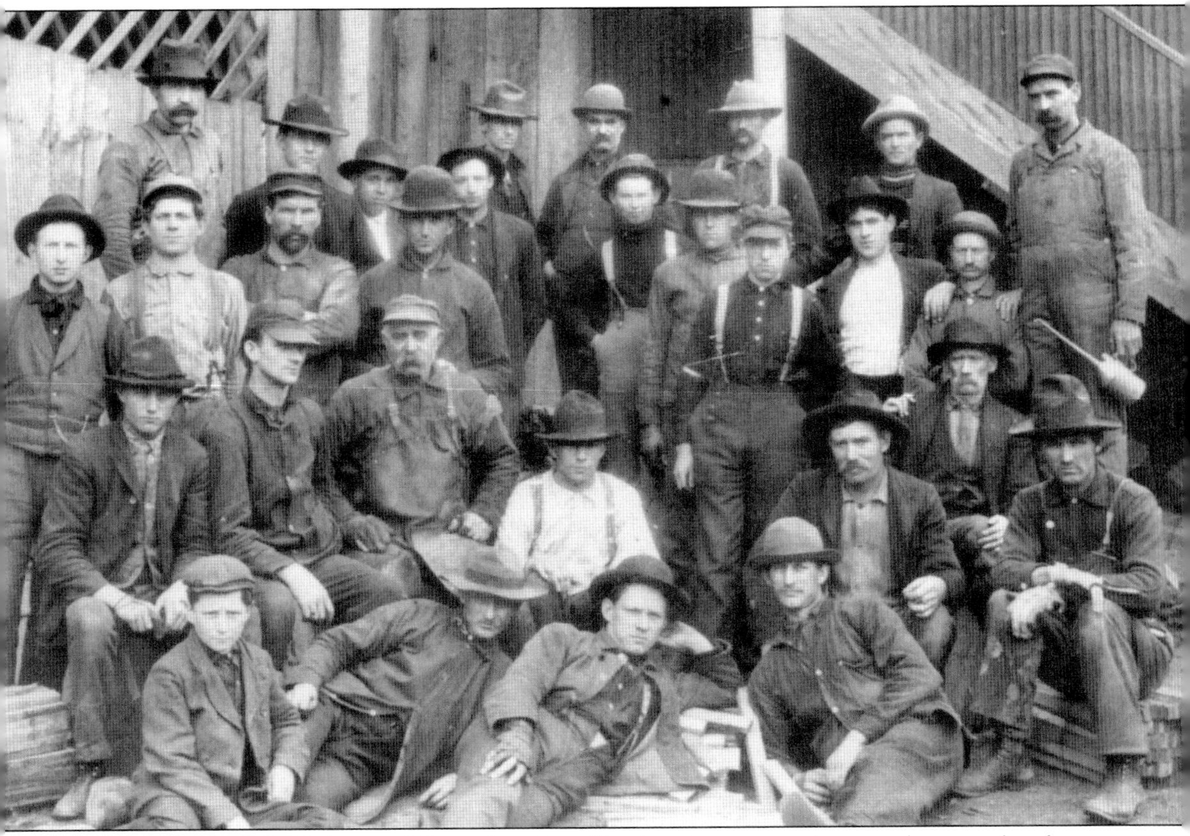

The crew of the J. R. Robin and Sons shingle mill takes time out to have a photograph taken in 1910. Most are unidentified. In the second row, third from left, the man with the moustache, cap, and leather apron is J. Bowen. In the third row, fifth from left, wearing a dark shirt, white suspenders, and a cap is Howard Huntington. In the middle of the back row, wearing a derby hat, is the mill owner, John Robin. This mill was an important part of the town as not only a source of jobs and income, but also powering the first source of electricity thanks to the steam engines that ran the saws. Townspeople tired of the smelly, smoky oil lamps rejoiced at having electric lights. The only drawback was that if the mill ran out of shingle bolts and shut down for a period, so did the electricity. In 1907, a boiler was installed for the electric plant to provide a steady supply of electricity to the town.

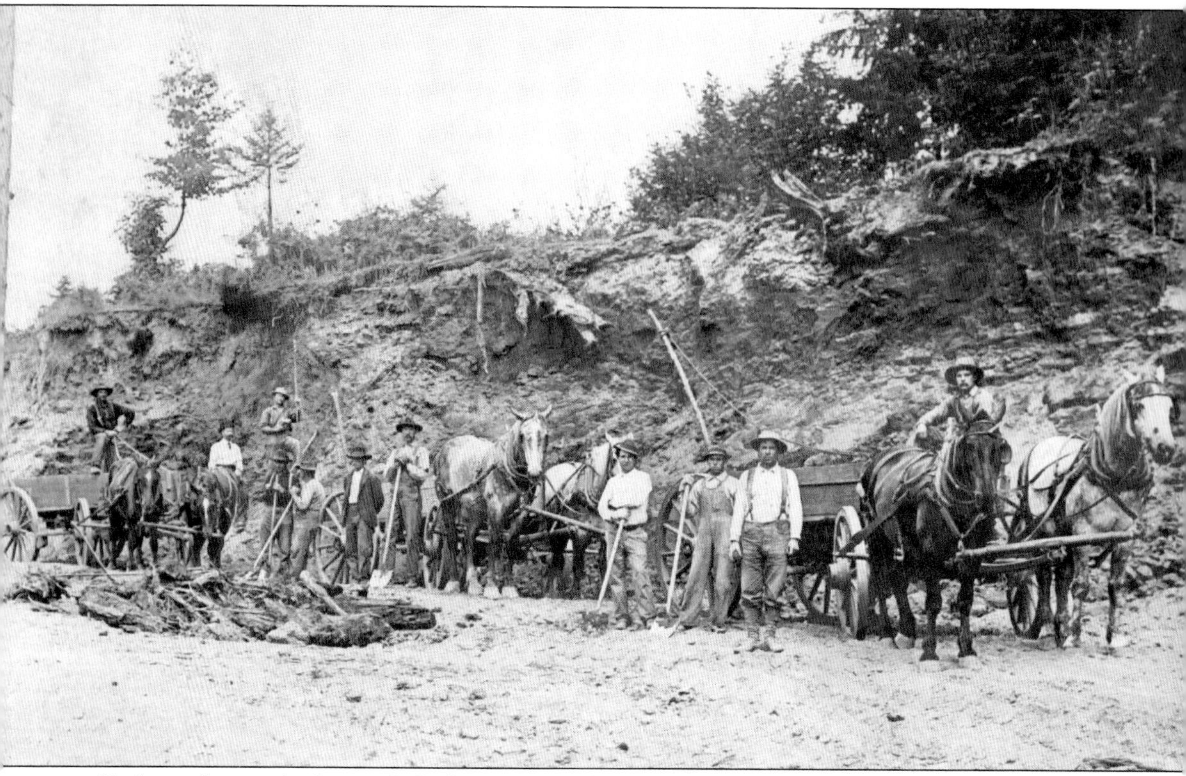

Early road crews had some help from teams of horses, but much of the work was done by hand. Roadbeds were dug out with shovels, as shown in this 1914 photograph of a Cowlitz County road crew. Excavating for roads this way was slow work. Trees had to be cut and the stumps removed from the roadbed before digging could be done. Sometimes huge rocks needed to be moved or blown up to get them out of the way. Often a road had to be constructed around a feature that could not be built over. Road surfaces were usually finished with gravel, but some were left as uncovered dirt.

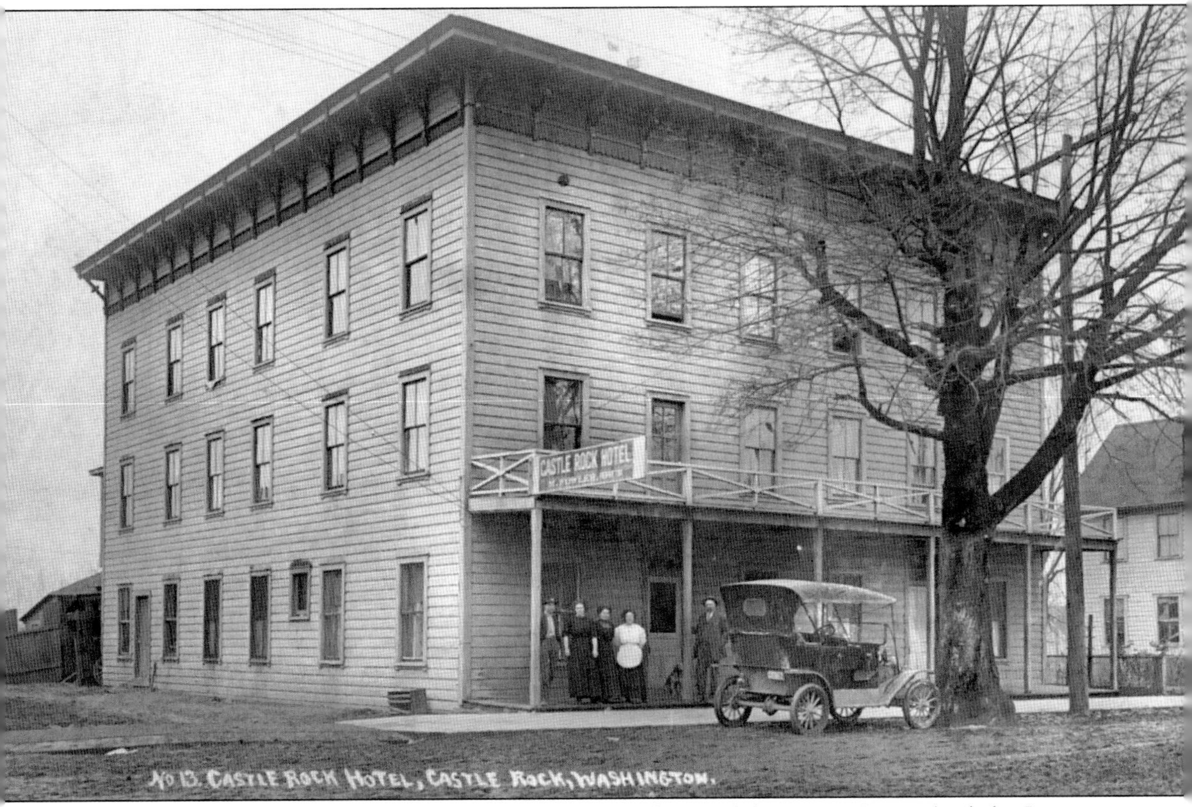

In 1918, the Castle Rock Hotel was one of the showplaces of the town. It was built by James Spencer and was originally known as the Spencer House. It occupied the land where the Castle Rock First Baptist Church is now. After it became the Castle Rock Hotel, it went through the hands of numerous owners and renters until its end. Its sign in the photograph states, "Jim Fowler, manager." Hotels were needed to cater to transients, newcomers, drummers (or salesmen), and laborers. There were as many as seven shingle mills operating in the area. Many of the mill workers, or shingle weavers, were what were called "short stakers." They moved frequently from place to place, taking jobs for a time and then moving on. The railroads, steamboats, and wagon teams were also bringing hundreds of new people seeking homes in the area.

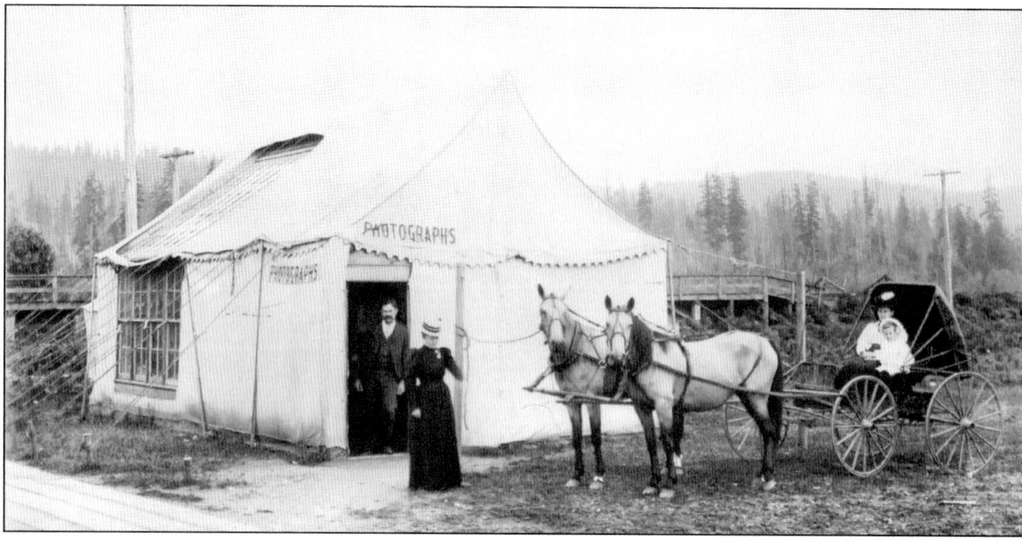

Itinerant photographers set up in a tent and stayed in Castle Rock for about a year. This was located in downtown because the Northern Pacific Railroad depot platform and telegraph poles along the railway can be seen in the background. The lady standing in front is identified as a Mrs. Graves and the lovely team of matched horses in harness to the buggy as her "steppers." The others pictured are unidentified. Good horses were prized possessions for their value as transportation. The St. Helens Livery Stable was a necessary business in Castle Rock until the advent and widespread use of the automobile. A livery stable not only cared for the horses of those traveling through or those belonging to rich townspeople who did not have their own stables, but it also provided rental horses and horse-drawn vehicles to those who needed them temporarily. (Below, courtesy CCHM.)

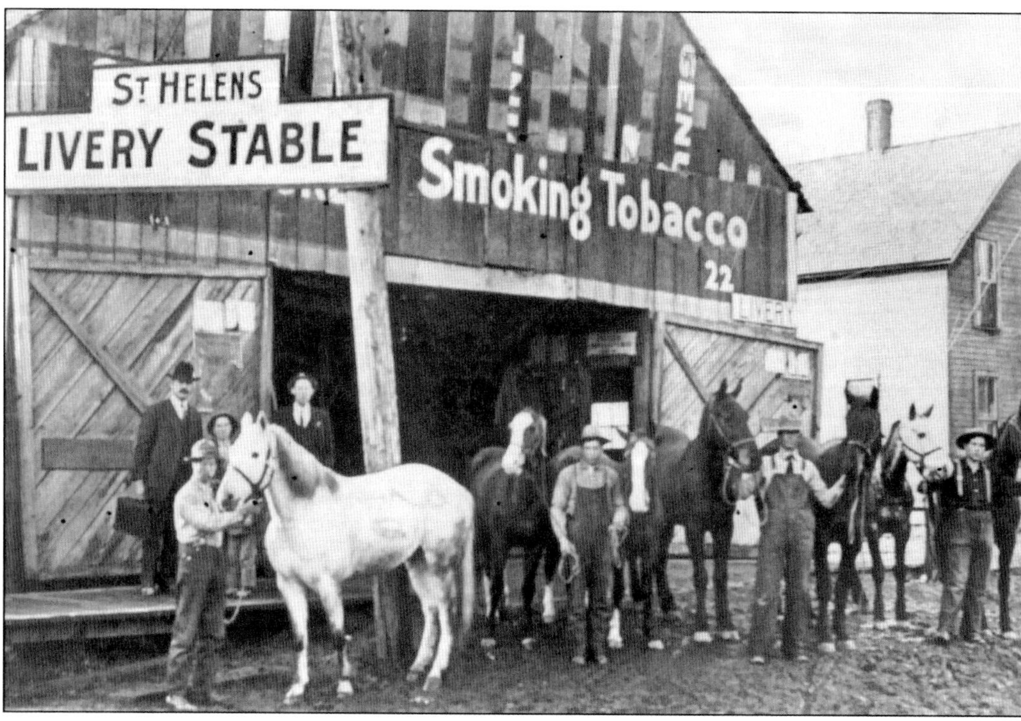

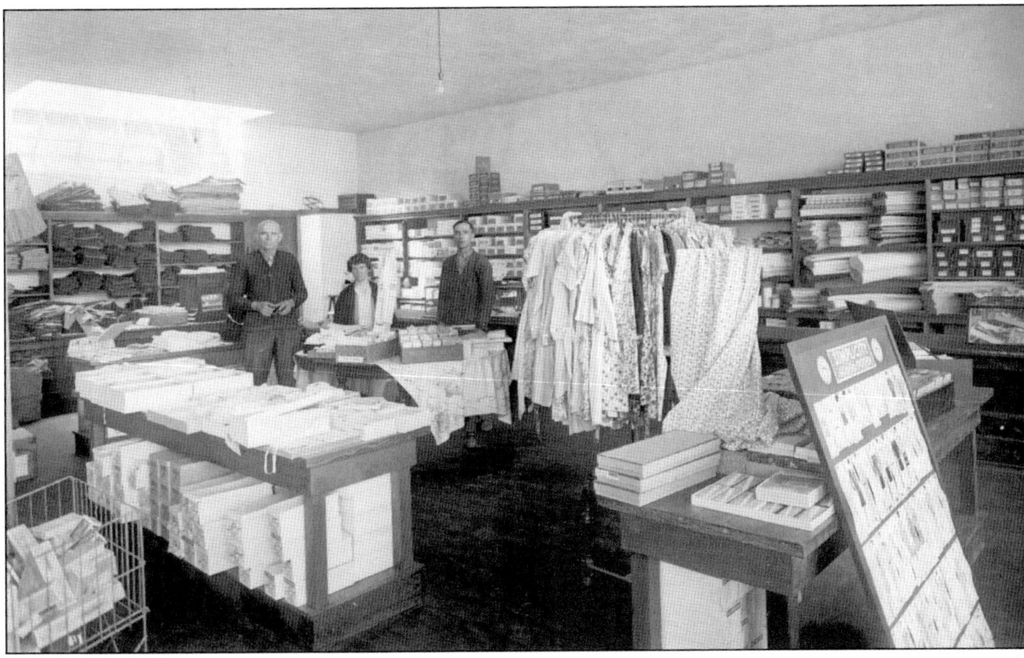

The Castle Rock Mercantile was originally a dry-goods and clothing store. Later it was more of a general and grocery store under the same name. Today the building is the location of the Castle Rock Public Library. The skylight on the left side of the photograph is in the storeroom of the library, though now it is boarded over.

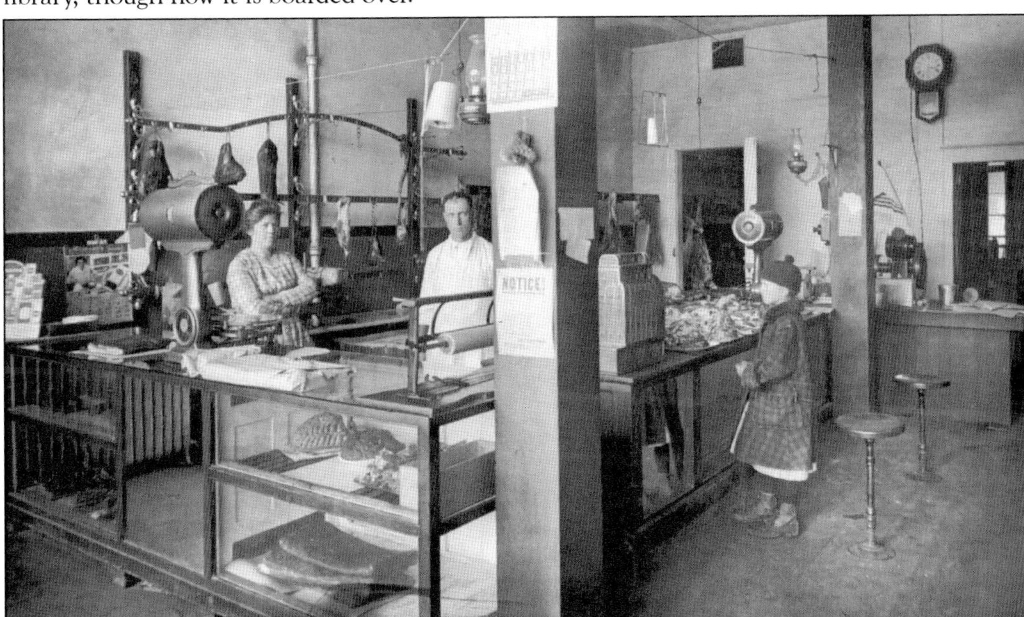

Grace Merrill McCormick and her husband, William McCormick, owned and operated a butcher shop in 1910. The child is one of their nieces but is unidentified. No refrigeration was available in meat shops, so the meat was hung in cool places, such as the back room. It was displayed in simple glass cases, and when sold, each order was hand-wrapped in the brown paper known as "butcher paper" and tied with string.

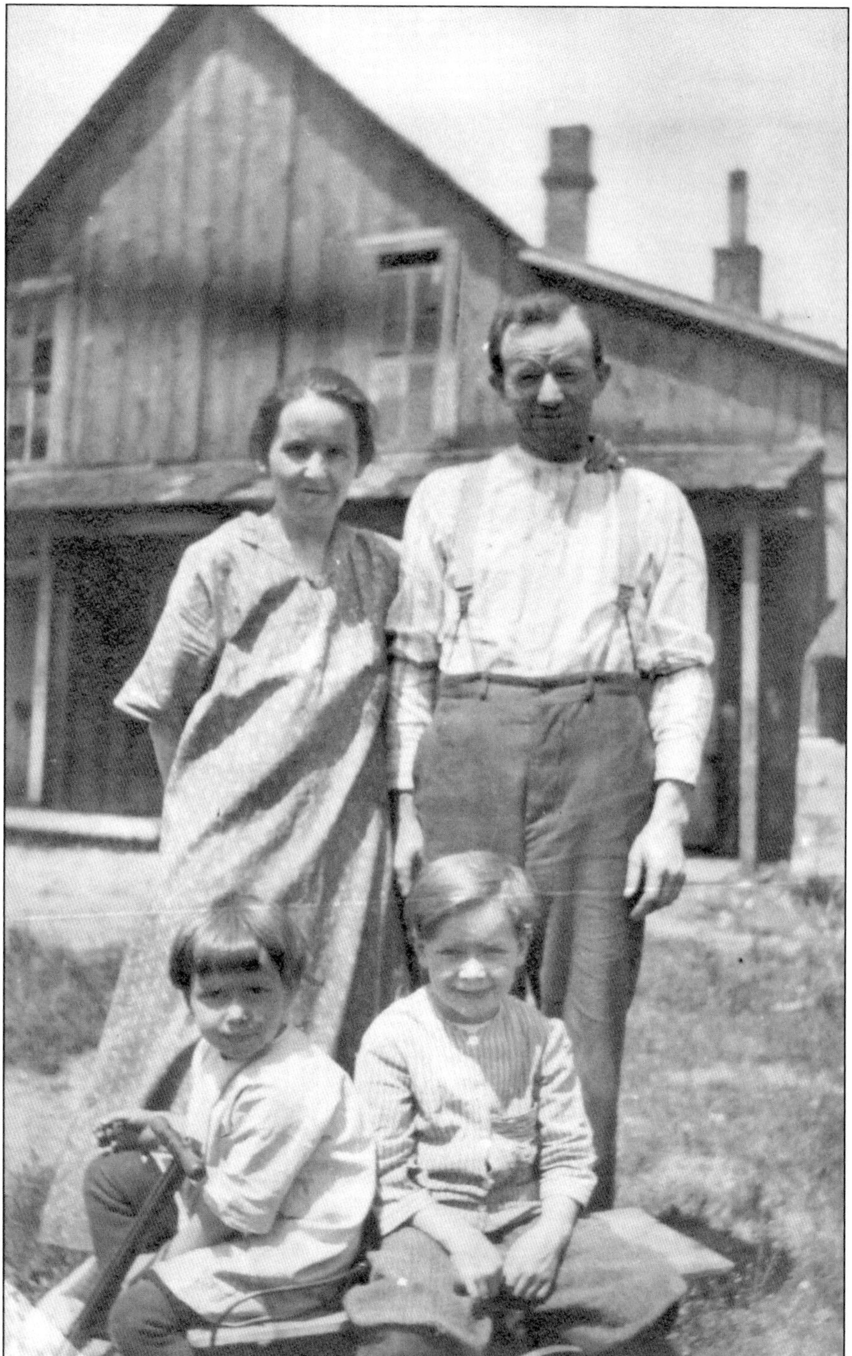

Ruth and Preston Moore had a confectionary store, or what would come to be called a "sweet shop" or "soda fountain," in downtown Castle Rock in the early 1900s. It was the bigger one in town and lasted many years. Here they are posed in the lot behind the store with their two children, ? Moore (left) and James Moore (right). The confectionery sold ice cream, which was stored in real iceboxes because refrigeration was not available, carbonated and non-carbonated soft drinks, candy and other treats, and cigarettes and cigars.

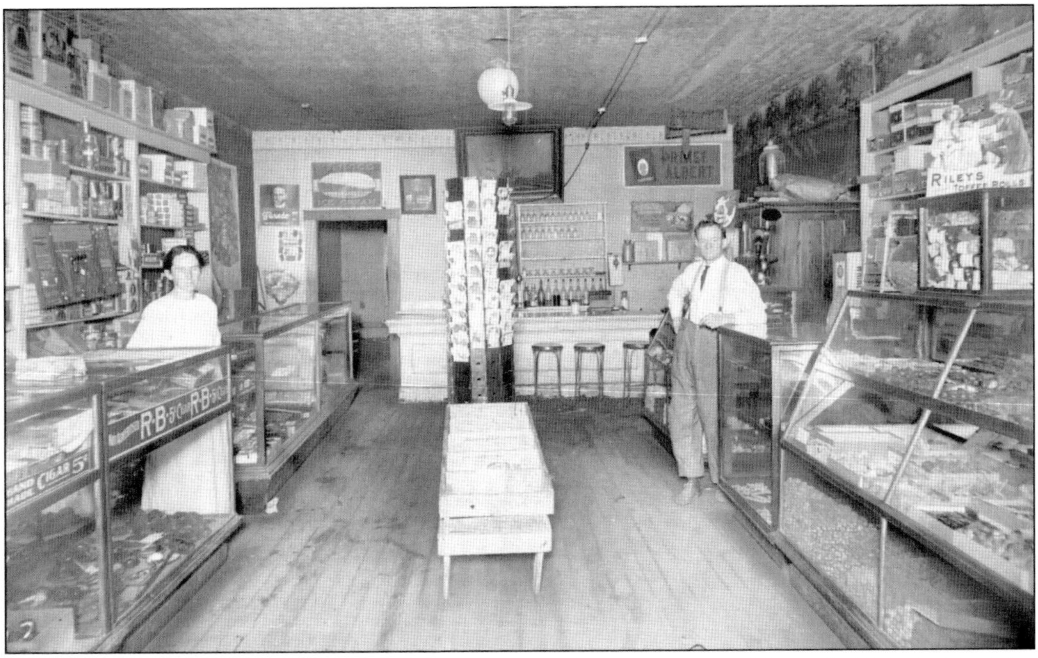

Ruth and Preston Moore greet customers in their confectionary store. The soft drinks behind the counter at the far end of the store were provided from bottles. This was before the soda fountain machine was affordable to stores in small towns. The candy counter is on the right, and the left side of the store was the cigar store.

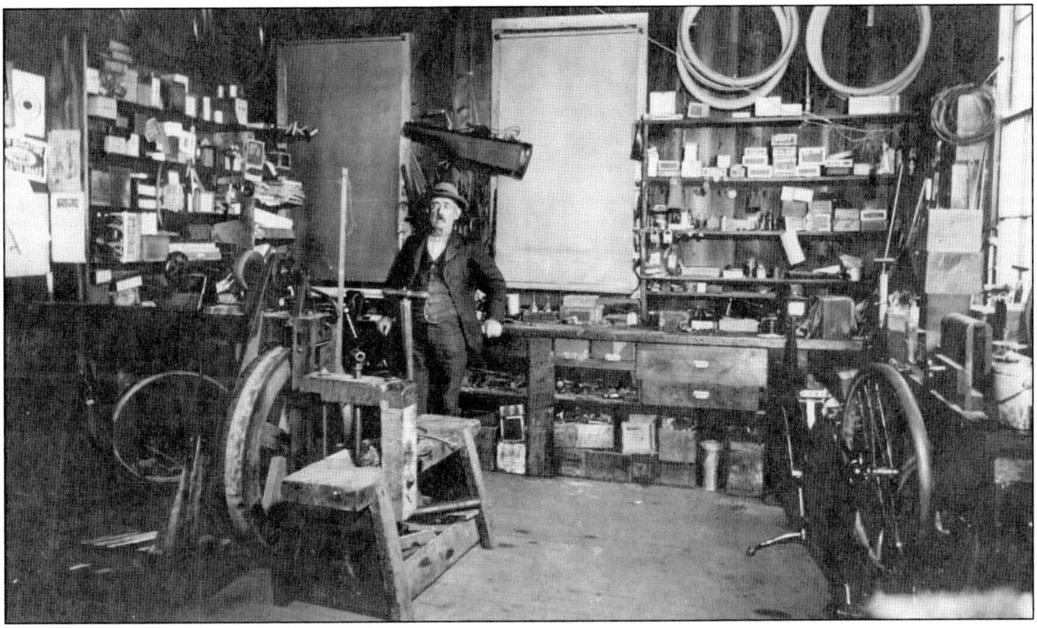

John Dickson poses in his bicycle shop. During the late 1800s and early 1900s, bicycles were a common form of transportation rather than a child's toy. Dickson was an important businessman on the Castle Rock scene. He constructed two buildings, one of which was occupied by his shop, and the other he rented to other businesses. Though his business was bicycles, he is known for purchasing and driving the first automobile in Castle Rock.

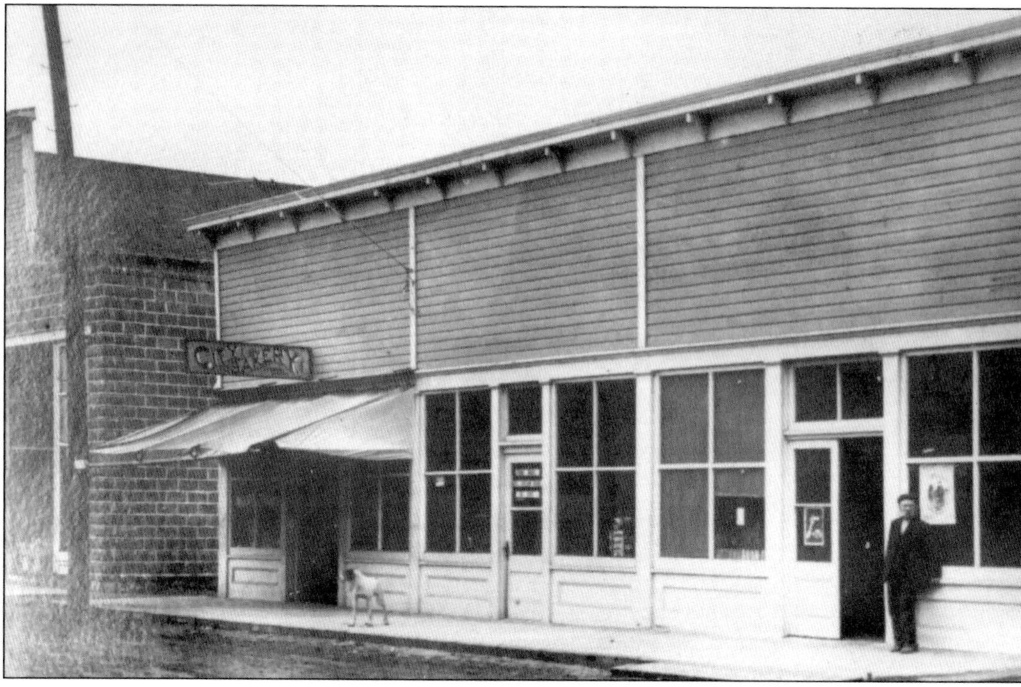

The photograph above is of John Dickson in front of his bicycle shop. He had his shop in one side of the building, and the City Bakery was next door, as shown by the sign on the left of the picture. In the photograph below, an unidentified young business owner poses in the door of his hardware store. This store can also be seen on the left side of the above picture. Dickson had both structures built, though the brick one was the newer of the two. Bricks were being manufactured by a brickyard locally at that time. Some of them were even made of clay taken from a quarry at the foot of Castle Rock. After his death, Dickson's widow married Otto Doering, and he became owner of the buildings.

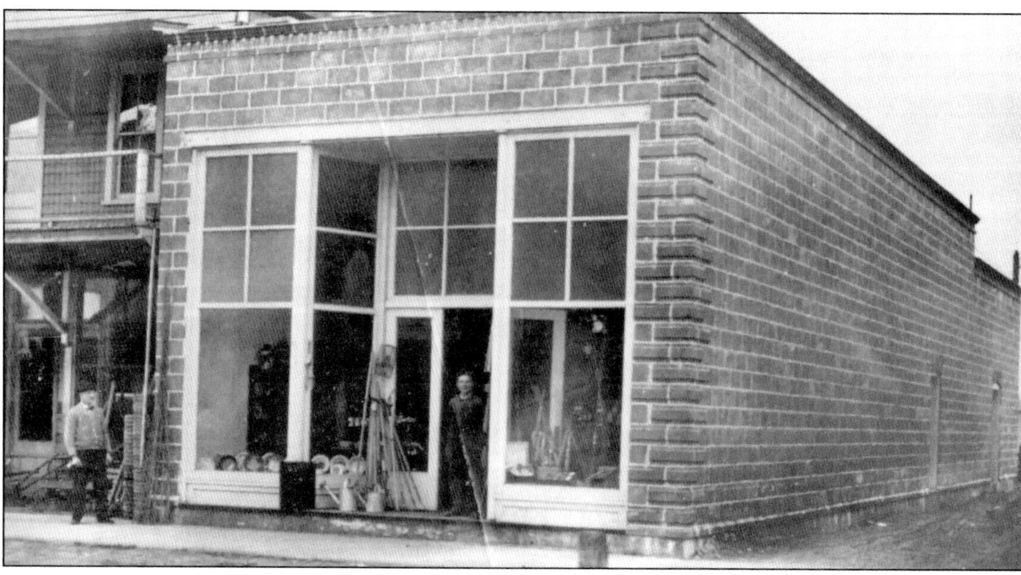

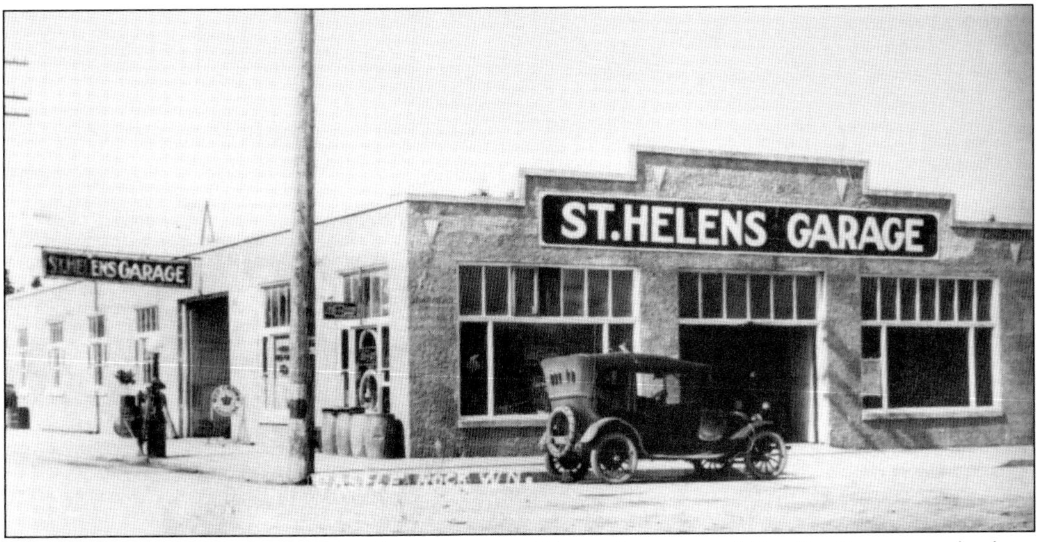

The St. Helens Garage, at the northeast corner of Front Avenue and Cowlitz Street, was built in the 1920s by E. L. Drew. By then, cars were becoming fairly common, but not everyone could repair or maintain them. This created a need for commercial garages with professional mechanics. This building still exists, though it has been through several transformations. The biggest change was sometime in the 1940s when it was remodeled from a garage into a store space. It became a 10¢ store, or what was commonly called a "dime store," the equivalent of today's dollar stores. By the 1960s, it had been sold and renamed Breneman's Variety Store, later Breneman's V&S Variety. Today the business in that structure is Grandma's Gallery, a craft supply and consignment store.

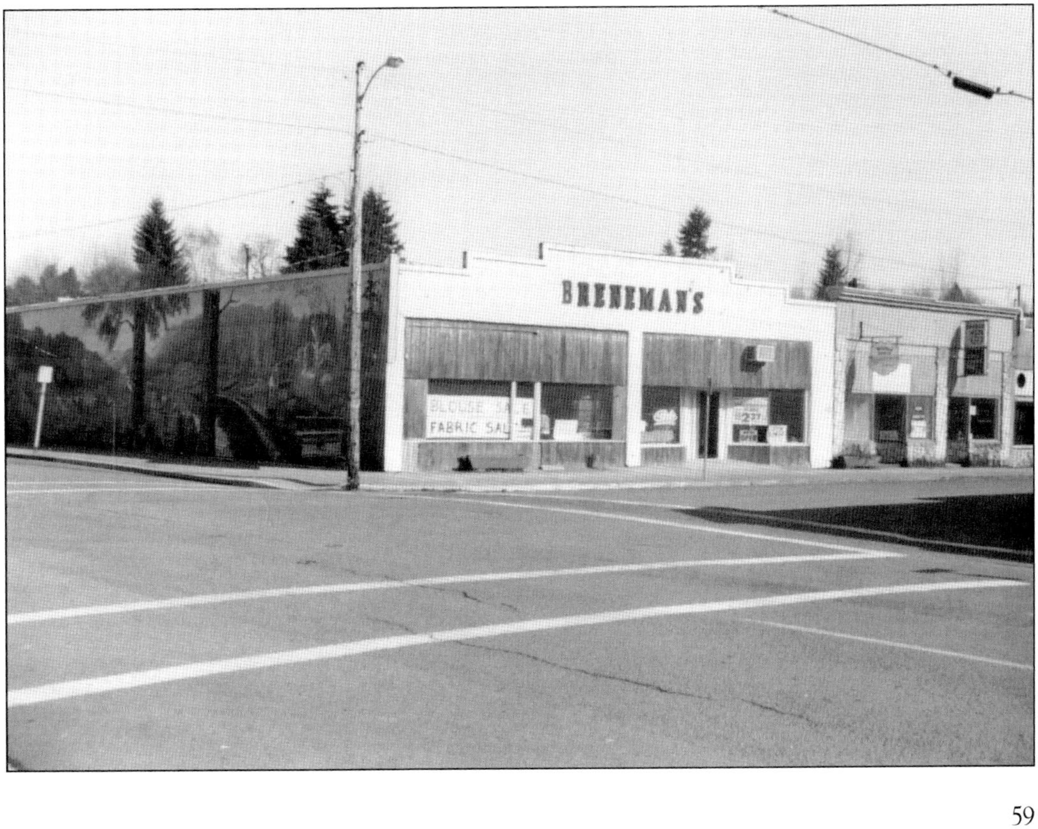

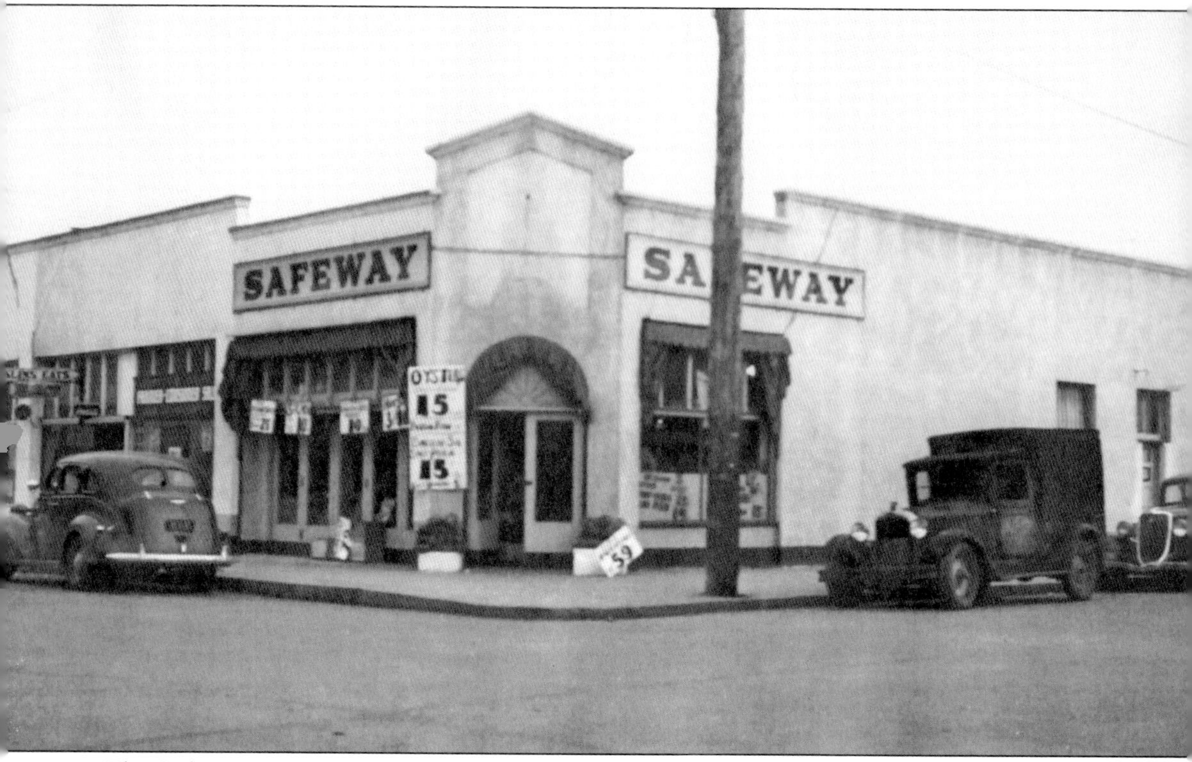

The Safeway store in Castle Rock was housed in a cement building on the southeast corner of Front Avenue and Cowlitz Street in the 1930s. One of the first chain grocery stores, it gave the locally owned stores some competition. Safeway was originally incorporated in 1914 in Southern California to operate a chain of stores. In 1926, Charles Merrill of Merrill Lynch began a series of transactions that led to the creation of the national Safeway chain of stores when he arranged the merger of Skaggs Cash Stores, a chain with operations in Northern California and the northwestern United States, with the Los Angeles–based Sam Seelig Stores. The Safeway business moved from its original building in Castle Rock to a new building in the 1960s. The building pictured here was then occupied by Rupley Chevrolet and is now a NAPA auto parts store.

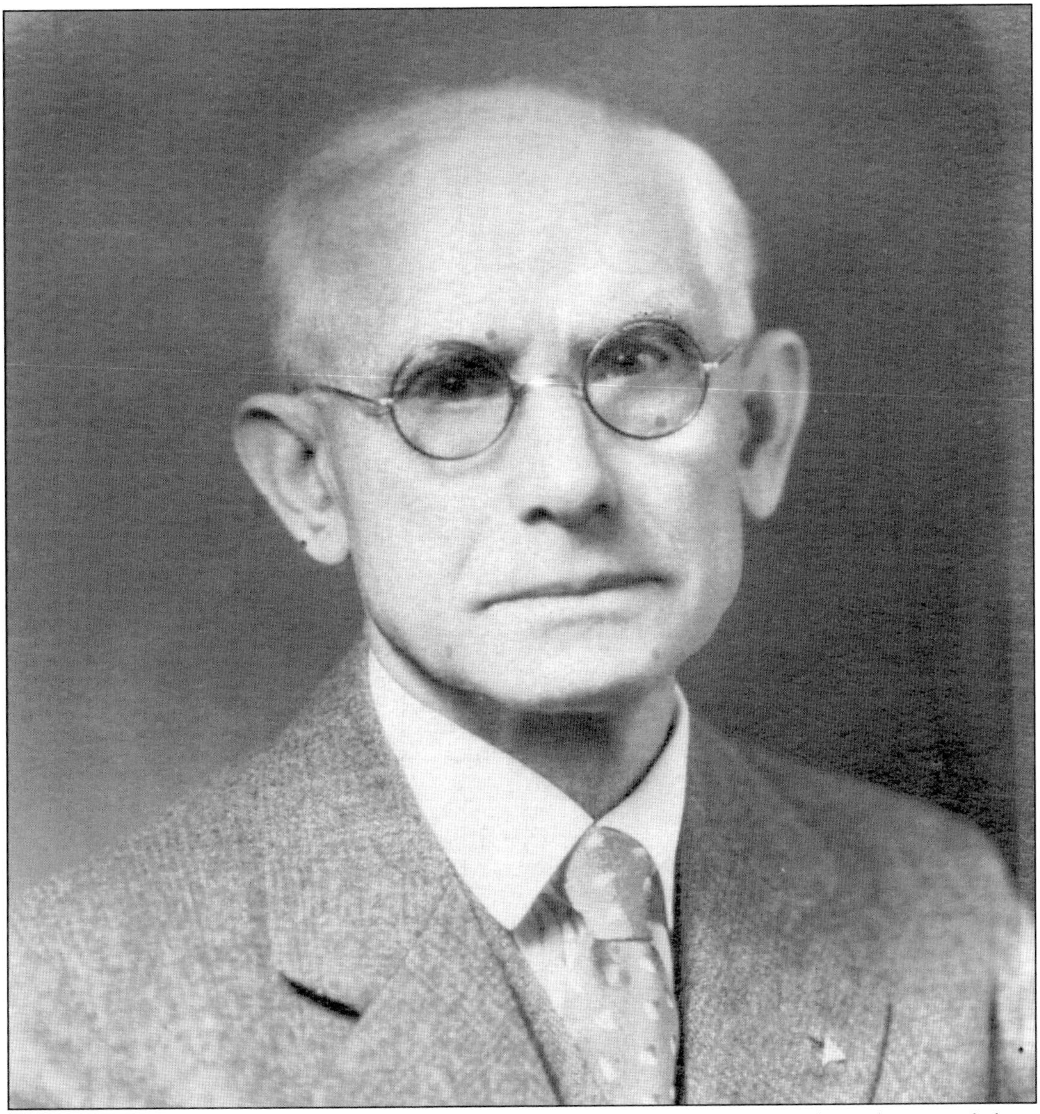

Samuel Roake was born in England in 1854. He was known by all as "Dad" to distinguish him from his son, Samuel C. Roake. Roake is the namesake of Roake Avenue, where his business was located. He was also an influential part of the history of Castle Rock in the 20th century. He started a business picking and selling cascara bark and ferns in the summer and evergreen boughs and wreaths in the winter, which became Green Mountain Evergreens. He was later active in the city government, was the mayor from 1919 to 1935, and was a volunteer fire fighter.

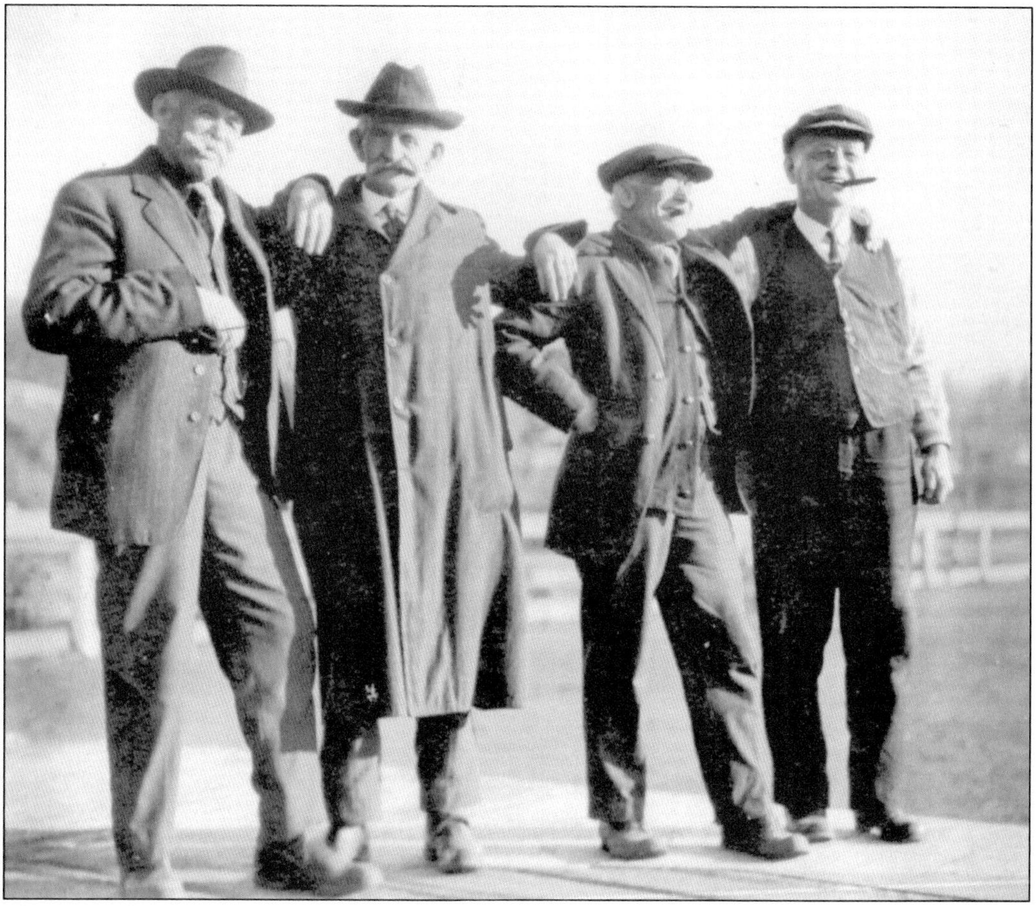

These city fathers, from left to right, "Dad" Berger, "Dad" Henderson, "Dad" Roake, and "Dad" Towree were photographed and labeled in a whimsical moment as a spoof on Samuel Roake's nickname. In the fashion of the early 20th century, men always wore hats in public. Ties and suits were also worn more often, unless the man was actually in a work situation where safety was against it. In a celebratory moment, all are smoking cigars.

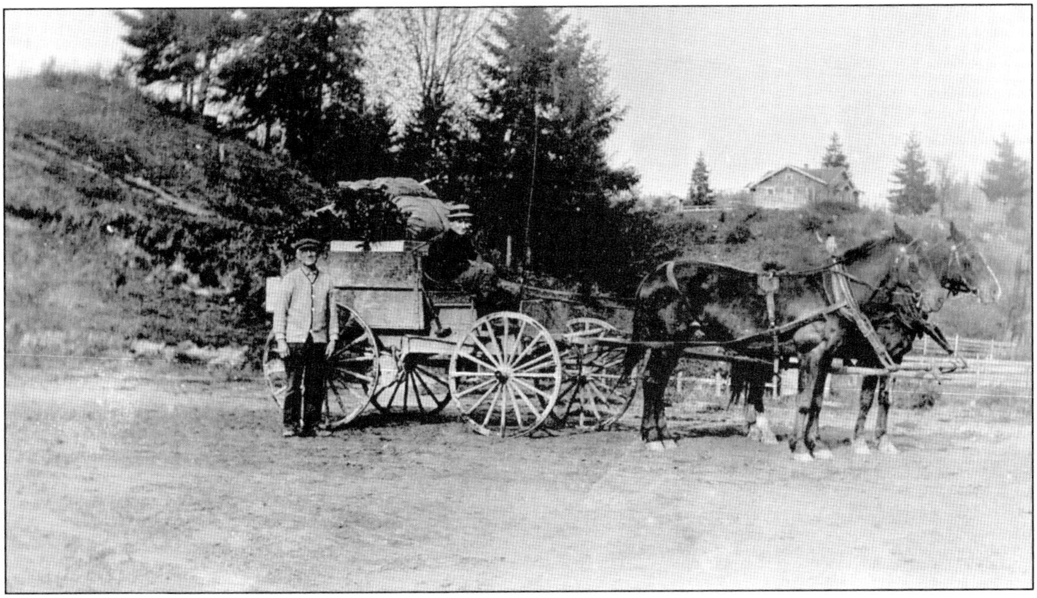

In 1913, Dad Roake is hauling bundles of cascara bark by horse and wagon. The business was originally known as Roake's Evergreens. Below, in the early 1920s in downtown Castle Rock, an unidentified man on crutches pokes the rubber tire of a new truck used for delivering boxes of evergreen boughs. The four men shown in front of the truck are, from left to right, two unidentified men, Samuel C. Roake, and Dad Roake.

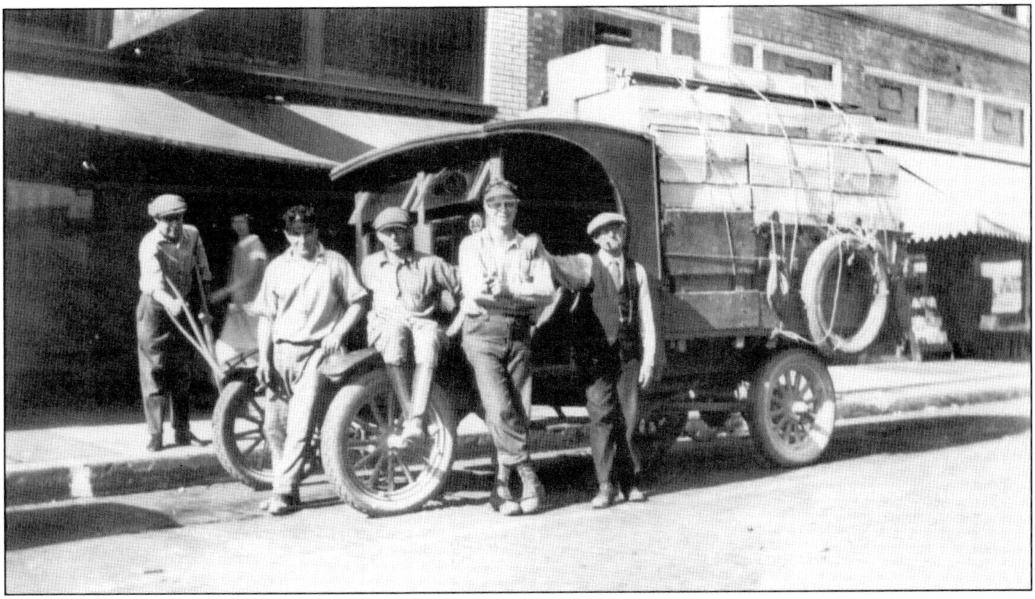

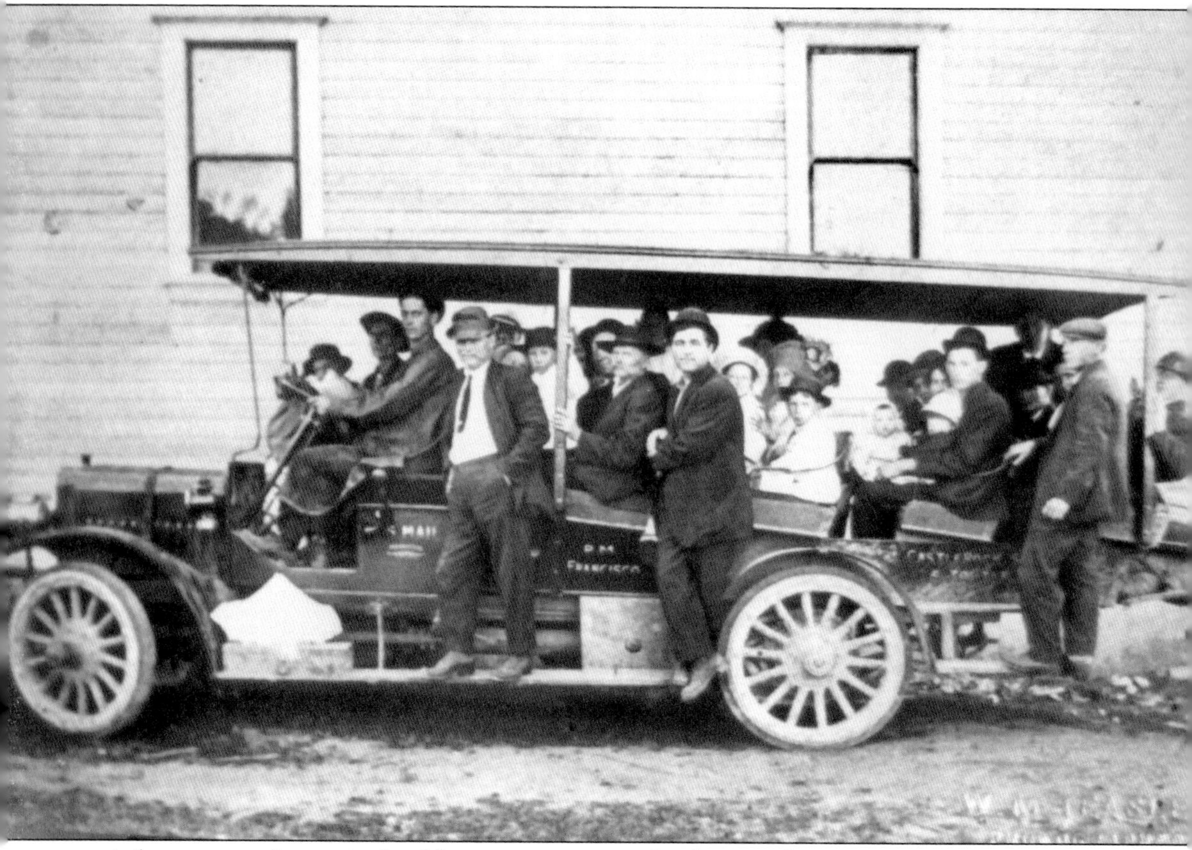

A forerunner of motorized public transportation, the first regular motor stage in town in 1914 was a Gram-Bernstine of unknown vintage and was owned by Friendly Francisco of Silver Lake. Actually, Francisco, known as a genius with tools, had taken a Gram-Bernstine chassis, added a Ford radiator and assorted other parts, and assembled his own contraption. It had hard rubber tires and a chain drive. Francisco is in the driver's seat of the vehicle. All the others are unidentified. The stage ran between Napoleon B. Gardner's store, located in Toutle, and Castle Rock. It had four rows of seats behind the driver that had some padding, but with rough roads and no windshield, it was not very comfortable. The men on the running boards are there for the photograph because it would not have been advisable to travel there, especially without handholds.

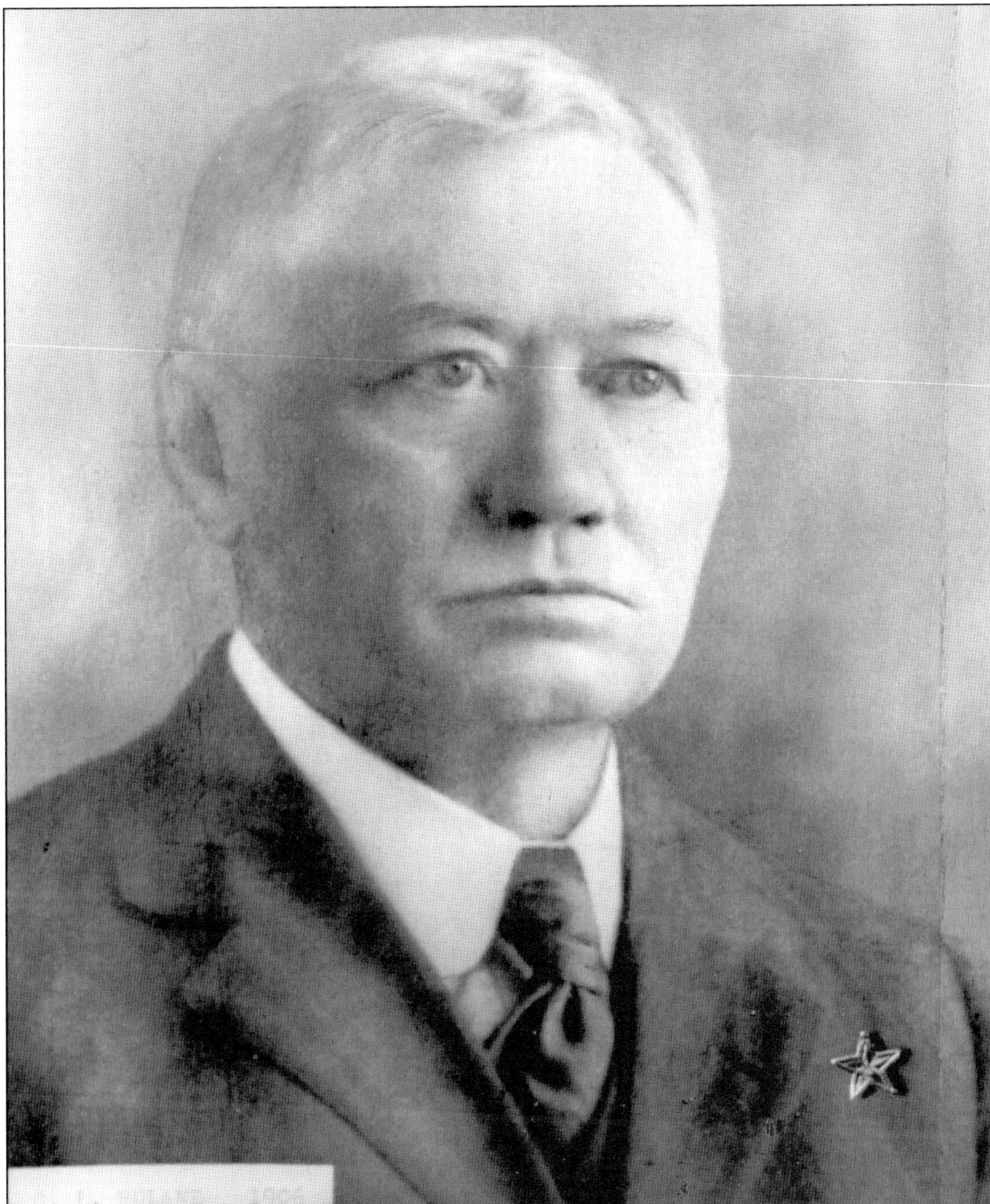

George L. Buland, one of the two owners of the Castle Rock Bank, was looking formidable in 1906. His was the second bank in town. The first bank was located next to the Northern Pacific Depot at the end of A Street. An advertisement in the *Advocate* in 1893 stated, "Bank of Castle Rock, Capital $25,000, doing a good banking business. Eastern Exchange bought and sold. Agents for the sale of Foreign Passenger Tickets and for Northern Pacific Railroad lands. Charles Erickson, President; Frank Hense, Vice President; Johnson Bragg, Cashier." Buland later purchased this business. Today the two sections of Buland Drive, at the edge of town, carry his name.

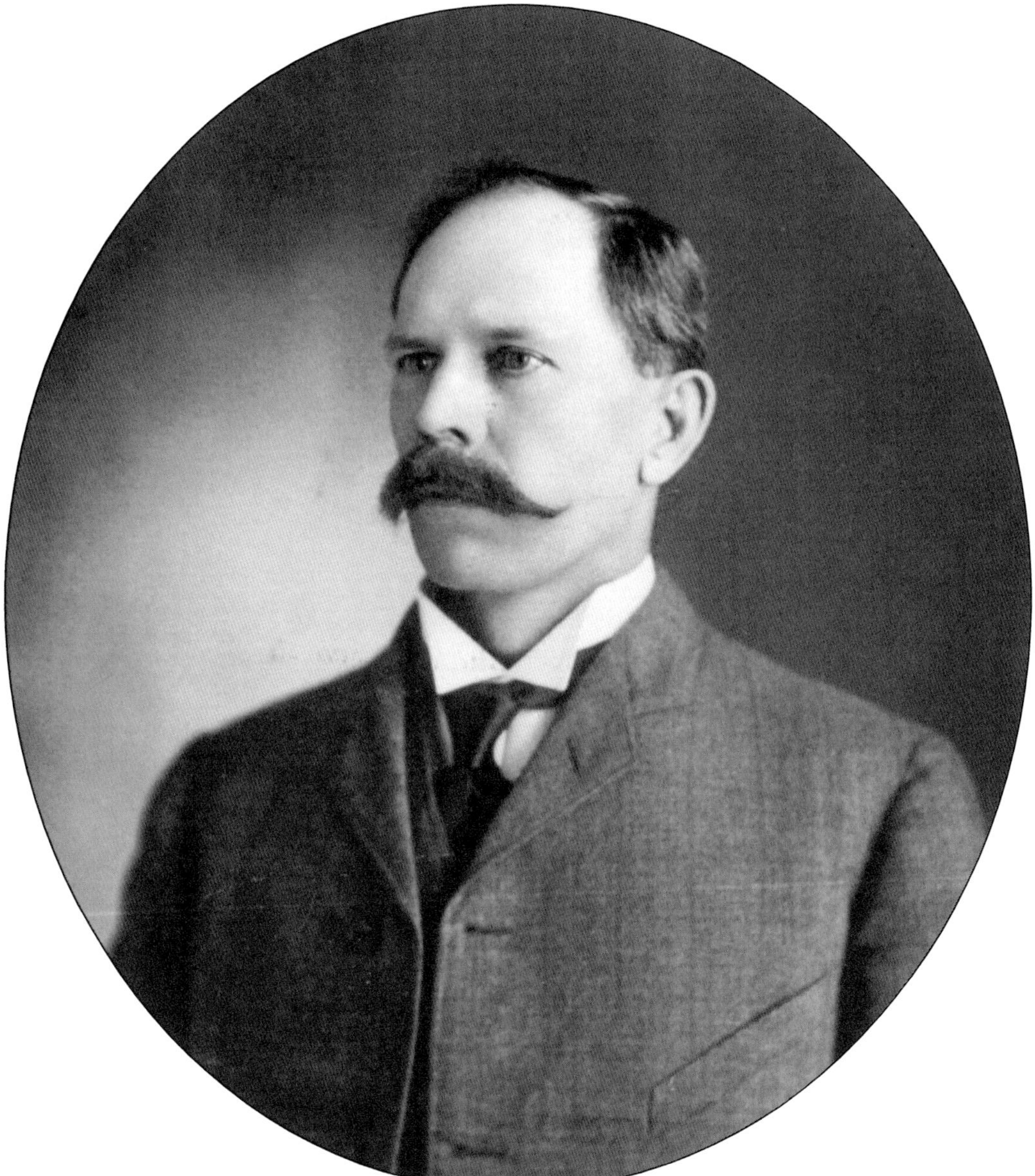

Milo P. Mason, partner with George L. Buland in the Castle Rock Bank, poses for a formal portrait in 1926. With his handlebar moustache, he was the epitome of the prosperous, fashionable businessman. In Longview, the Lumbermen's Bank and Trust Company failed, as did the Woodland State Bank after the stock market crash of 1929. The Castle Rock Bank and the Cowlitz Valley Bank of Kelso held on. They also lasted through the Great Depression of the 1930s.

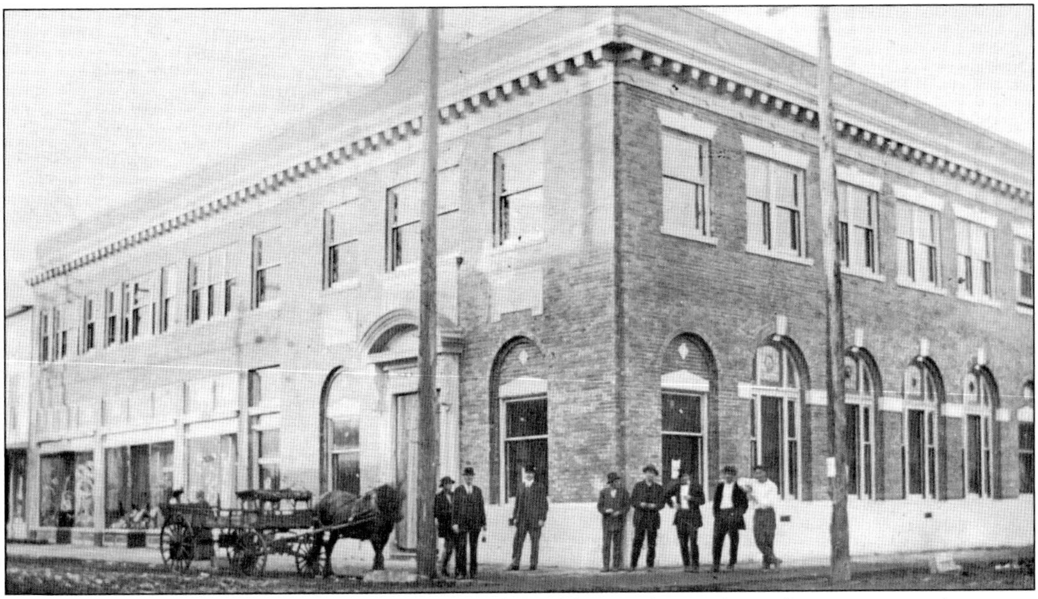

The newly constructed brick Castle Rock Bank building is shown from the exterior and interior on opening day in 1910. Below, in a view from the front entrance, from left to right, Milo P. Mason, one of the two owners, is standing; George L. Buland, the other owner, is at the cashier's window; and ? Huntington can just be seen behind the etched glass of the divider. The counters and floors were made of marble. There were lovely carved benches for patrons to use while waiting for service. Brass spittoons were provided for the use of the many men who used chewing tobacco at that time. The vault was located behind a strong gated grille at the back of the lobby. One impressed citizen wrote to a relative, "The new bank building has opened. It's a dandy!"

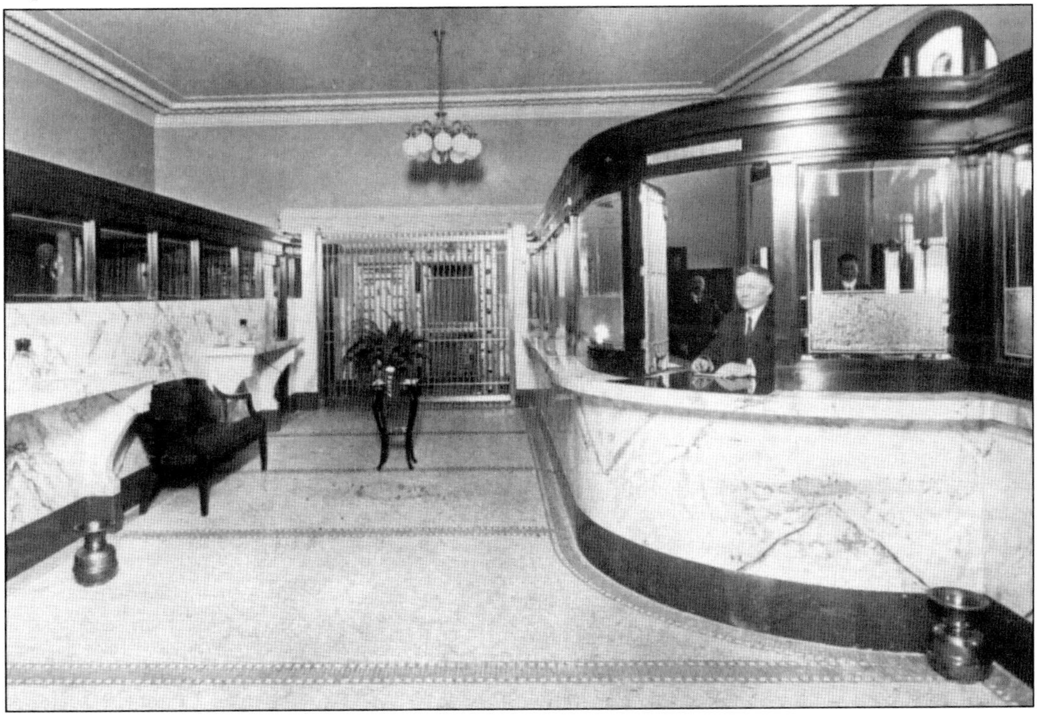

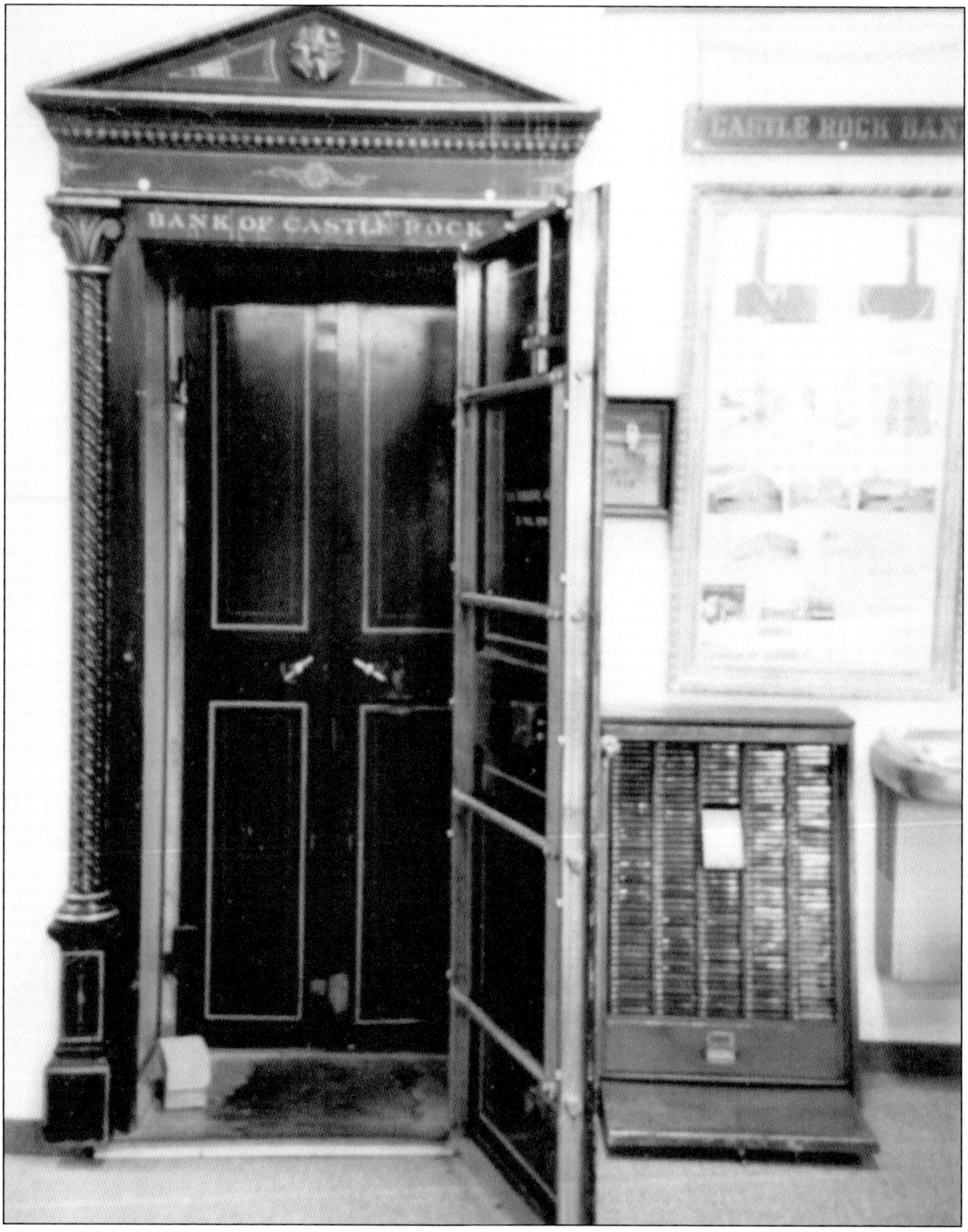

The vault of the Castle Rock Bank was installed in 1910 as a part of the state-of-the-art new bank building on the northwest corner of Cowlitz Street and Front Avenue. A most efficient and solid piece of equipment for its time, the outside of the vault was painted black with gold leaf decoration. The building was in continuous use as a bank, though it went through ownership by many companies and was operated under many names until it was finally left empty in the 1980s. After the building was purchased by Dr. Anwar Ayoub and remodeled for other business uses, the vault was considered too valuable and beautiful to just scrap. So it was uninstalled and moved to its present location in a special section of the Castle Rock Exhibit Hall and Visitor Center.

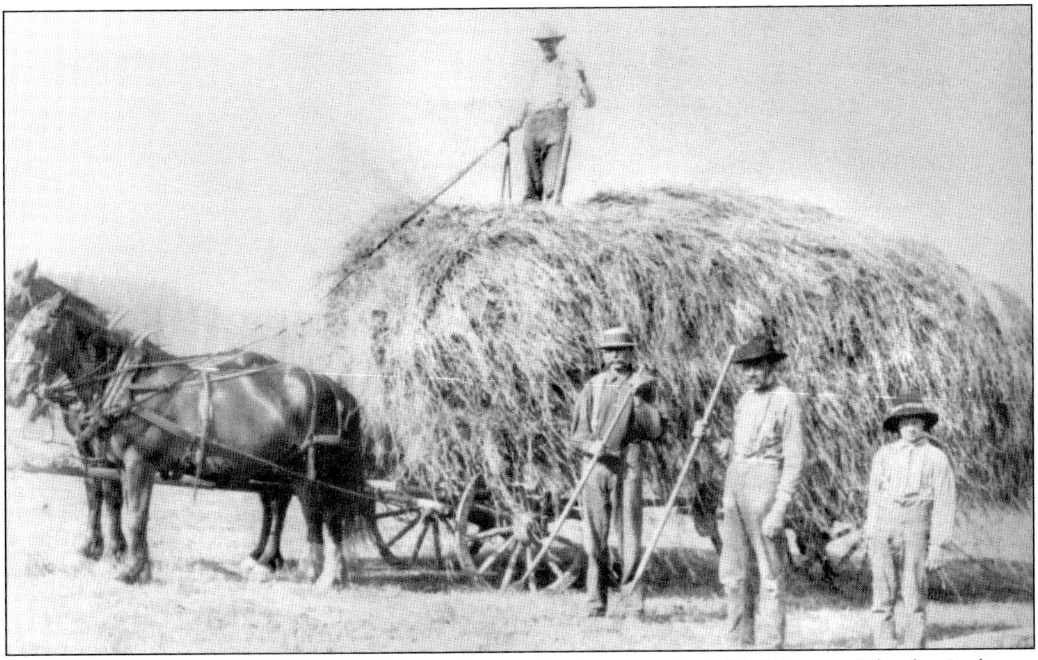

Henry Jackson (on the wagon) is leading a hay gathering crew in 1914. His son, Charley Jackson, is on the far right. The two men in the middle are unidentified. Hay was cut and dried in the field, and then loaded onto wagons to be taken either to be stored in a barn loosely or to be baled by a stationary horse-operated baler.

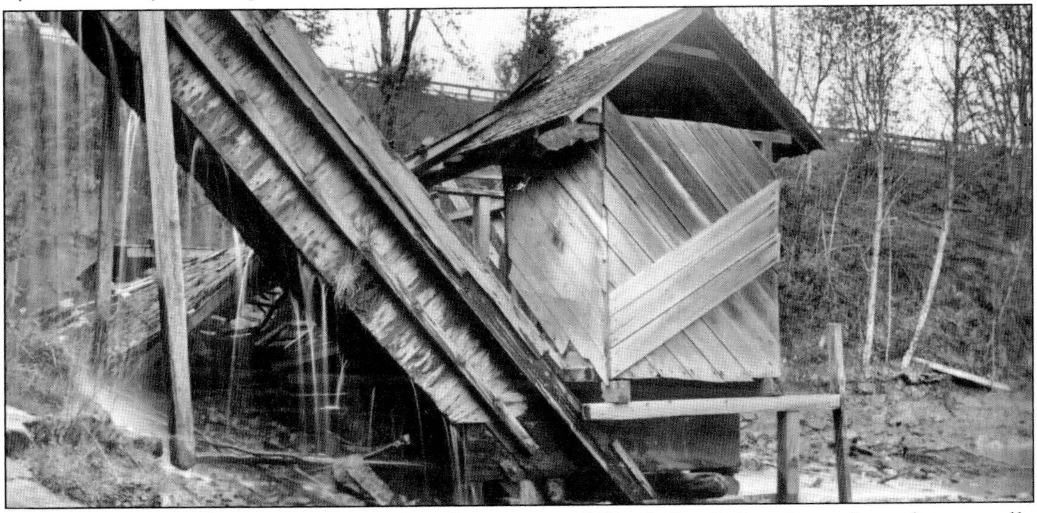

Mining is not as well known as an early industry around Castle Rock, but the early settlers actually built several mines. Though copper, quartz, and even a little gold were found around the base of Mount St. Helens, coal was the predominant product to be wrested from the ground in the lower valleys. The Red Ash Mine was built in the upper Delameter (then Arkansas) Valley. A tramway was built from the mine near Monahan Creek to the Cowlitz River, a distance of several miles. The track had rails of steel or wood strapped with steel. The cars were pulled by horses. There is only one published mention in the *Advocate* that stated, "On January 7, 1897, the steamer *Northwest* took a shipment of 275 sacks of Red Ash coal to Portland." There were undoubtedly many more shipments because the mine continued to operate for several years. (Courtesy CCHM.)

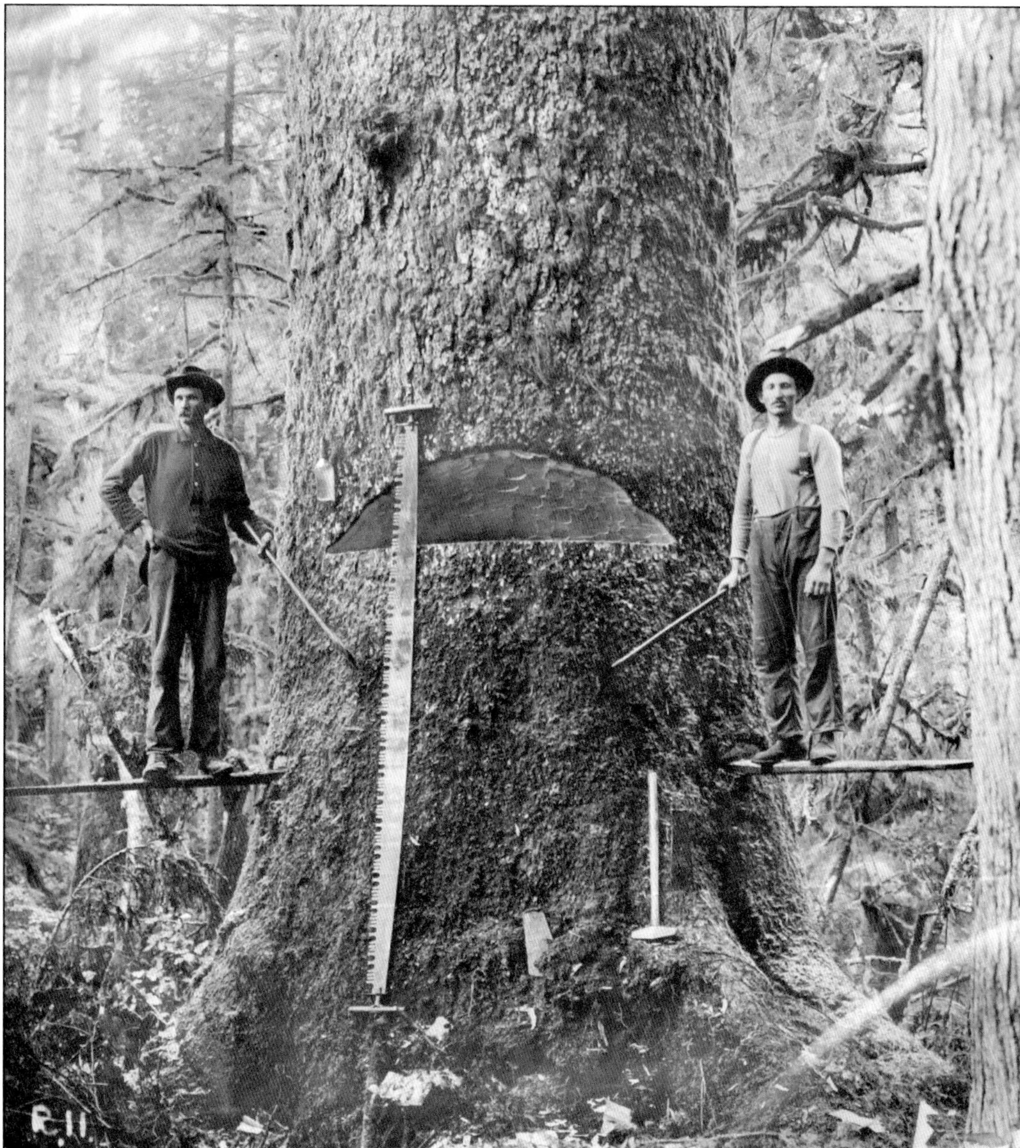

These two young men (both unidentified) pose on their springboards as they prepare to fell a huge tree. Notches were cut into the tree to support the springboards so the cutters would be even with each other. This allowed the timber fallers to cut the tree evenly and have better control over how it fell. The long, two-handed saw they are about to use is propped up in front of the tree.

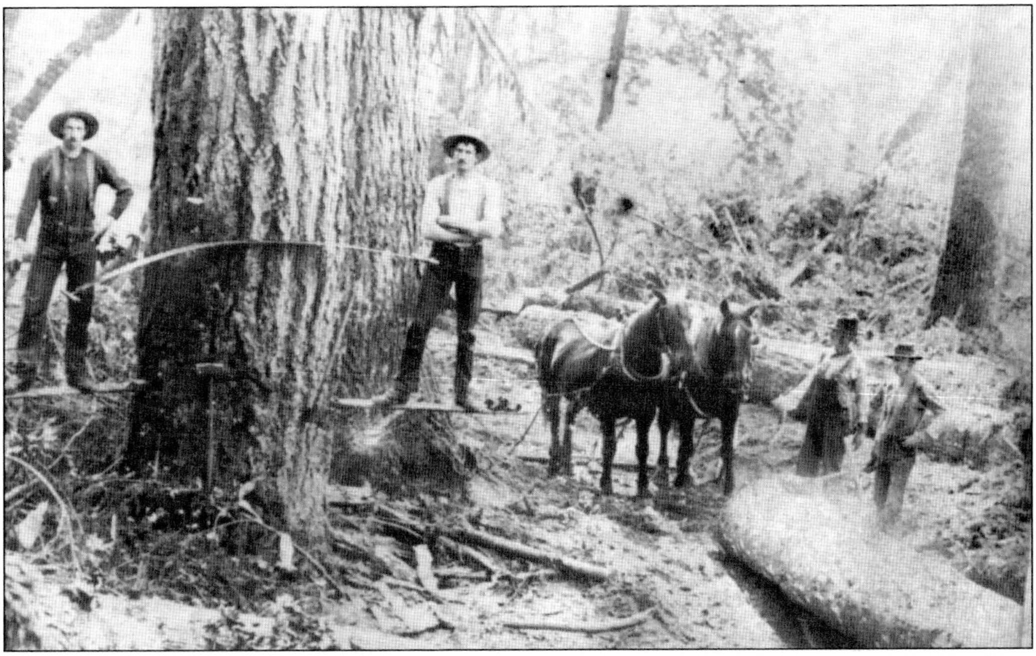

Horses were often used to pull the logs to the landing after they were cut by the fallers. These unidentified loggers are posing with their saw already in the cut on the tree as if they have just taken a break before really putting their backs into it. The two men to the right of the horses are also unidentified.

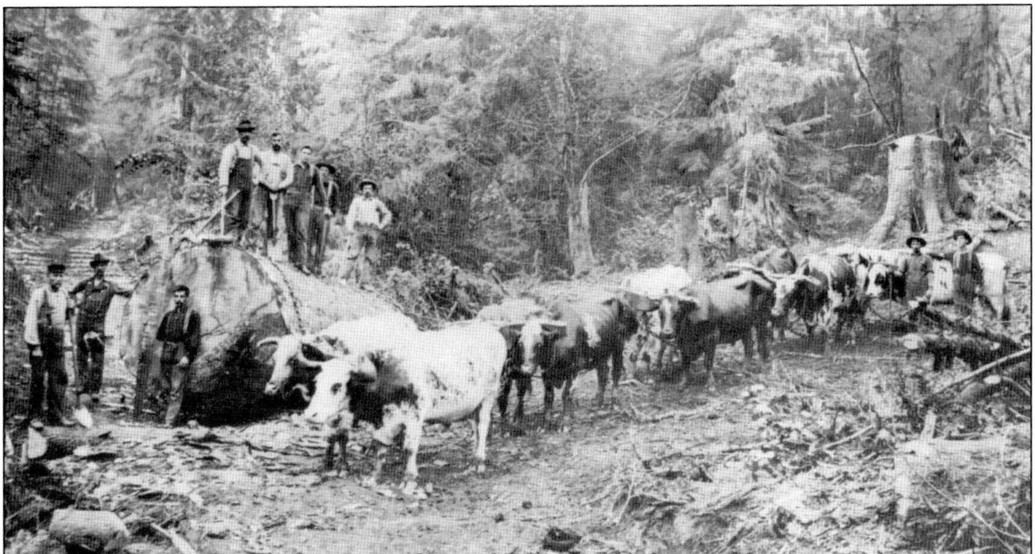

In the late 1800s, many logging operations used teams of oxen to drag the logs into place. These were referred to as "bull team" logging operations, though the oxen were not bulls but steers (castrated bulls). To haul the huge logs that were being cut down, teams of sometimes 10 or more oxen were required. Oxen were slower than horses, but their slow, steady pulling was better over rough ground. Many young boys wanted to grow up to be bull whackers or bull punchers, as the bull drivers were known.

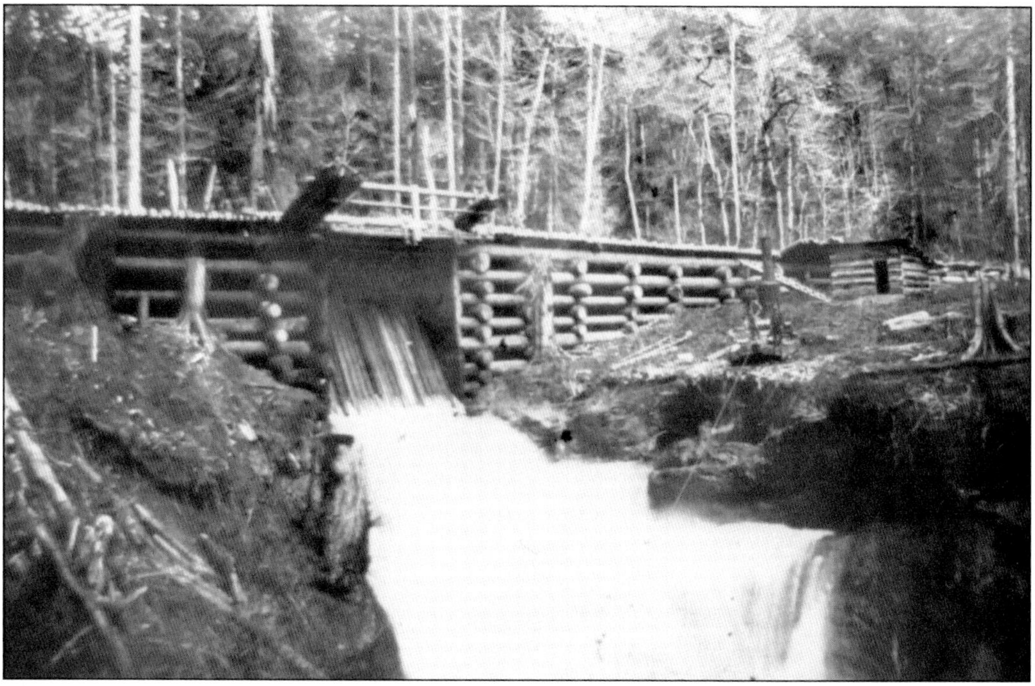

The Steve Paquette Splash Dam was on the north fork of the Arkansas Creek. Believed to have been built in the 1880s, its purpose was to collect water behind the dam to flush logs and shingle bolts down the creek and into the Cowlitz River.

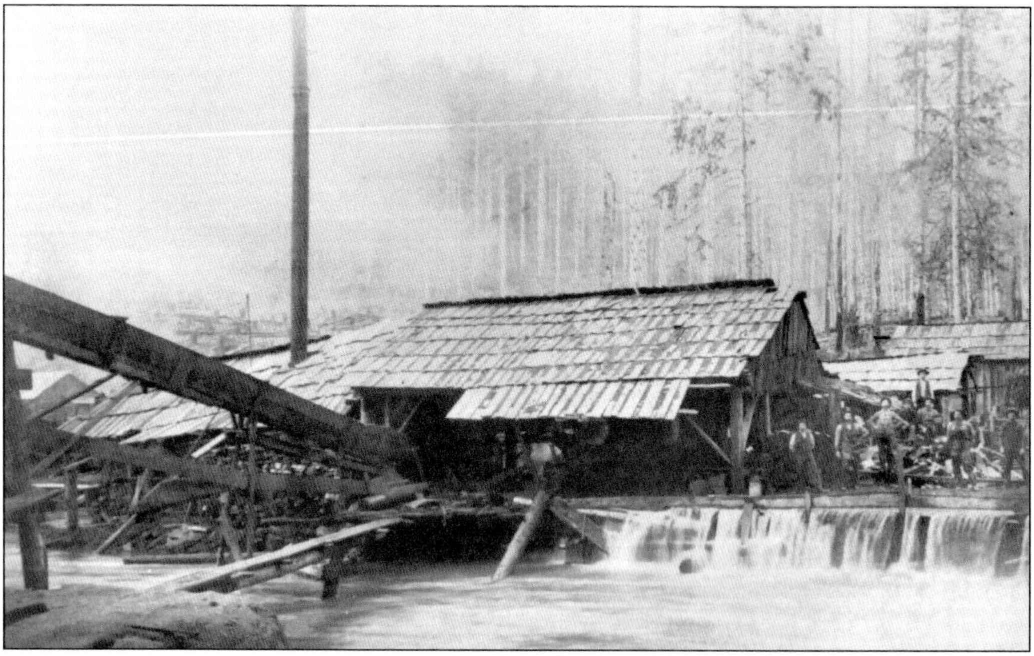

The Appleman shingle mill was located on Salmon Creek east of Castle Rock in the 1890s. The J. R. Robin and Sons shingle mill is better known due to its location next to the river and in the town. However, cedar was plentiful, and there were quite a few other mills in the valleys of the creeks that fed the river.

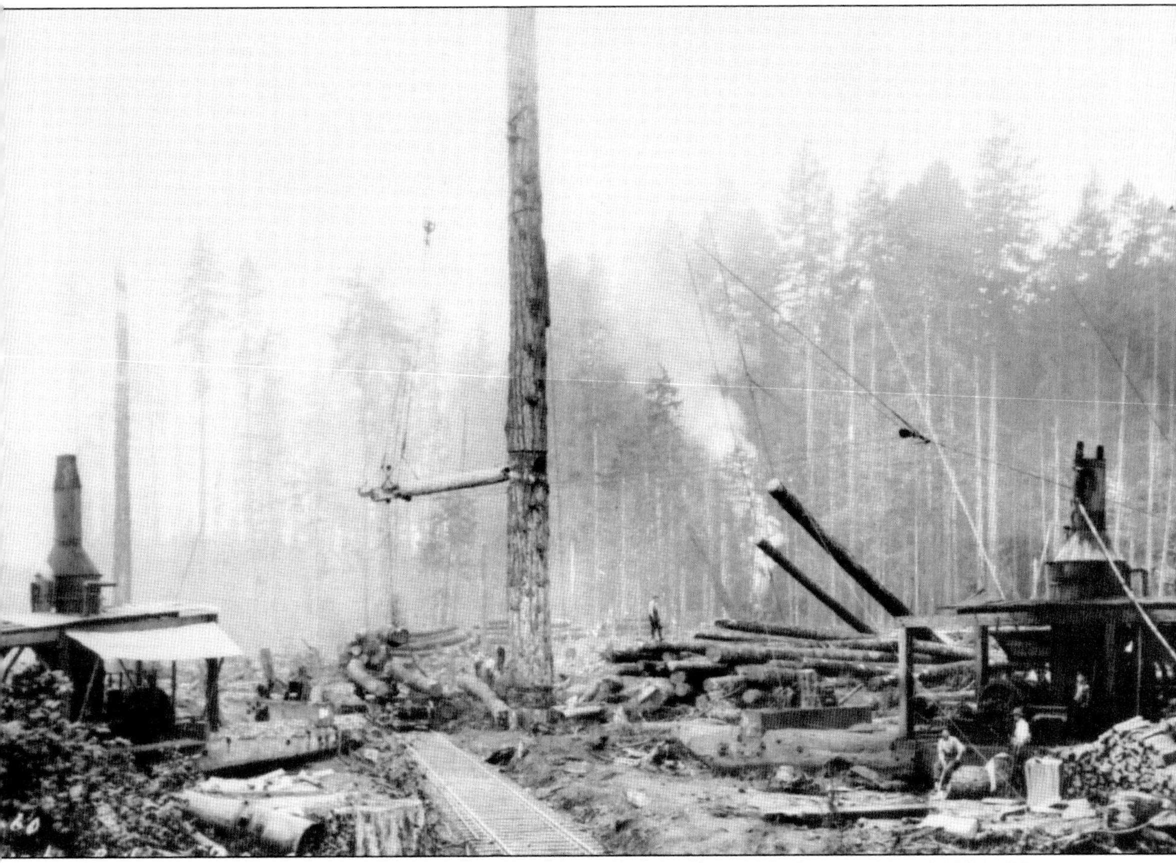

The Ostrander Railway and Timber Company was a big employer in the 1880s and 1890s. Here it is using a spar pole with a yardarm to lift the logs onto the railcars, which would be brought next to the yardarm on steel tracks. The mill owned by the Ostrander Railway and Timber Company became nationally famous for being able to mill extremely long logs, particularly valued as timbers for ships' masts. In World War I, there was a huge need for such timbers, and the mill worked day and night. Still, the workers could not keep up with the orders. The demand was so great that not enough flatcars could be in place to load the lumber once it was ready. In May 1917, the mill shipped seven masts to be built into Atlantic freighters. Each mast was 103 feet in height and 29 inches in diameter. One month later, the mill sent keels to Astoria.

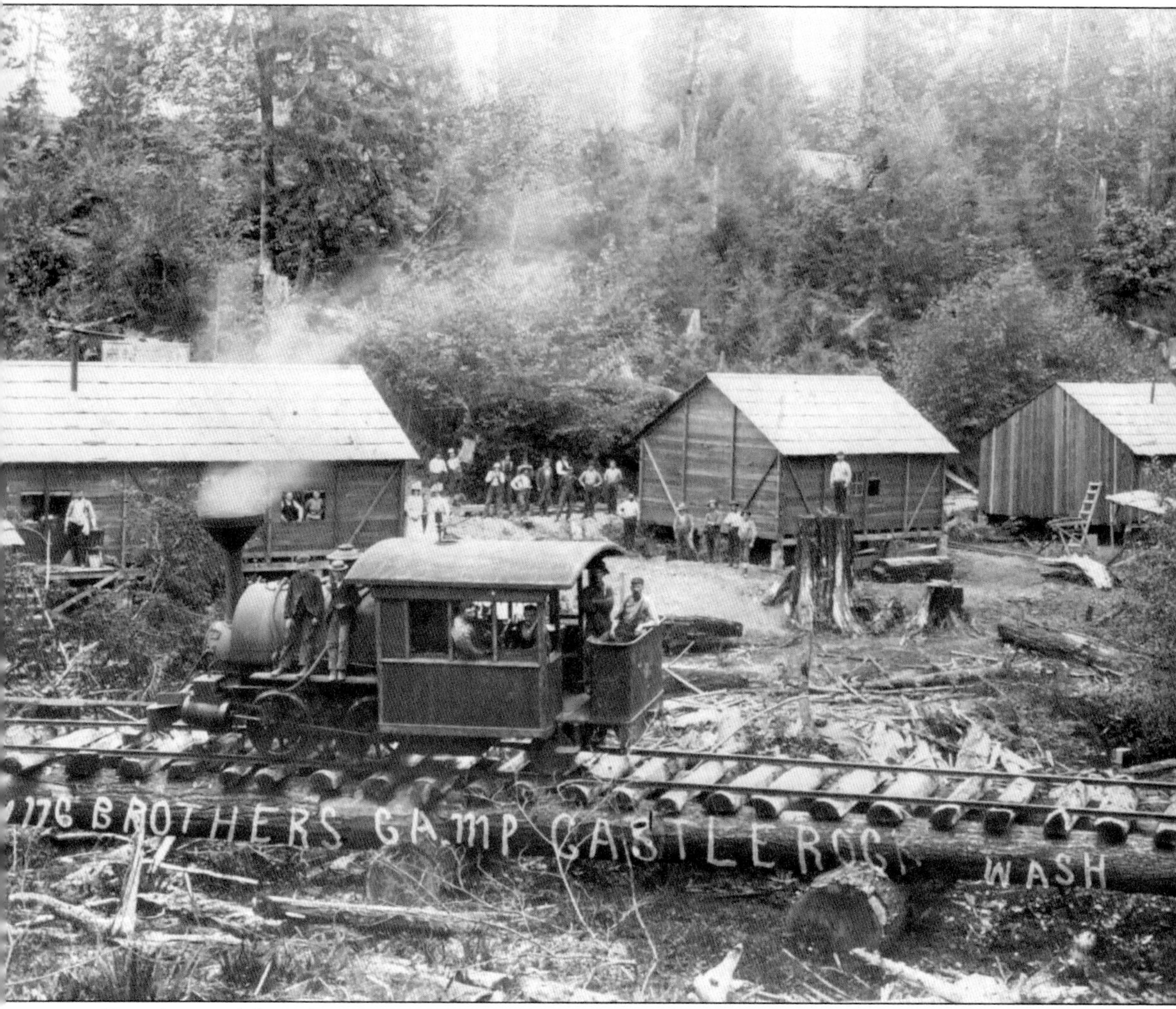

Travel to and from logging operations, more than a short distance from town, was too difficult and time consuming to be done on a daily basis. So logging companies set up camps, such as the Young Brothers logging camp. There were bunkhouses for the men to sleep in and a cookhouse for cooking and eating. Families sometimes accompanied the men to the camps. Cooking in the camps was one of the few ways for women to make money. Young Brothers was the first company known to have a steam locomotive. The business operated until 1902 with 3 miles of track and one rod engine. In the photograph above, taken in 1900, the couple in the window of the cookhouse is identified as Mr. and Mrs. Young and the young women in white on the cookhouse porch are, from left to right, Grace Merrill, Annie Merrill, and Mary Merrill. The engineer on the train is Bill Scott. All others are unidentified. The train engine is a saddleback Loki on a narrow-gauge track. (Courtesy CCHM.)

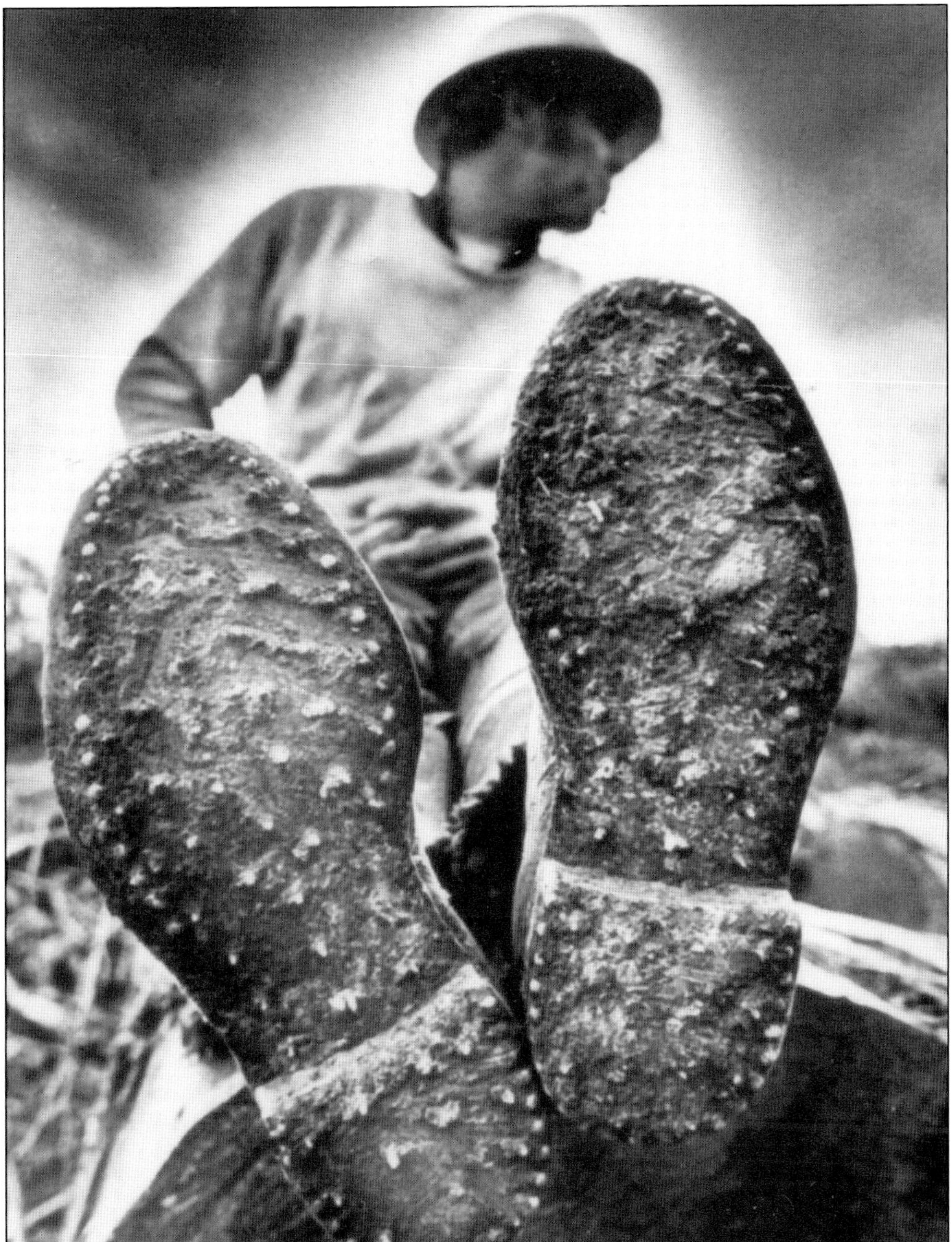

In the Pacific Northwest, the men who work "in the woods" are always called "loggers," never "lumberjacks." These men developed special clothing and equipment to fit their occupation. With the advent of metal hard hats, they became a vital piece of loggers' gear. Boots with the soles covered by small, metal spikes are called caulk (pronounced cork) boots. They are necessary to maintain traction when scrambling over logs to keep the logger from falling. After coming in from the woods, a logger sometimes stops to pick his mail at the post office or run other errands and forgets he is wearing this formidable footgear. There is still a sign in the U.S. Post Office in Castle Rock that reads, "Caulk shoes and roller skates prohibited."

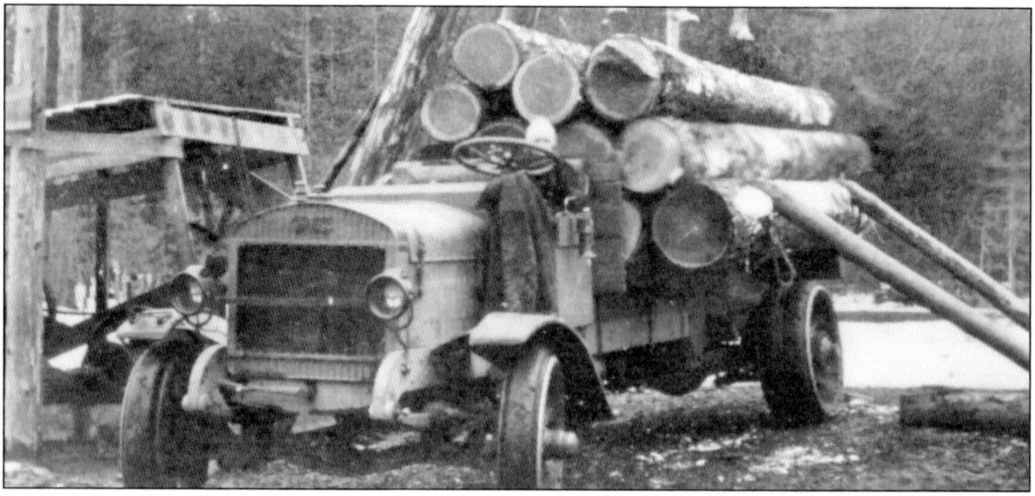

The advent of the gasoline engine was a gift to small-scale logging operations that could not afford to build railroads. Early logging trucks had hard rubber tires and no cab or windshield, though there were fenders on the front wheels to keep mud from being sprayed up on the driver. They often operated on plank roads constructed of rough-cut lumber. By the 1950s, separate truck cabs, or tractors, pulled trailers with four sets of two wheels clad in gigantic tires. Some old growth timber was still being harvested, and the logs were so big that one tree was an entire load, even on modern logging trucks.

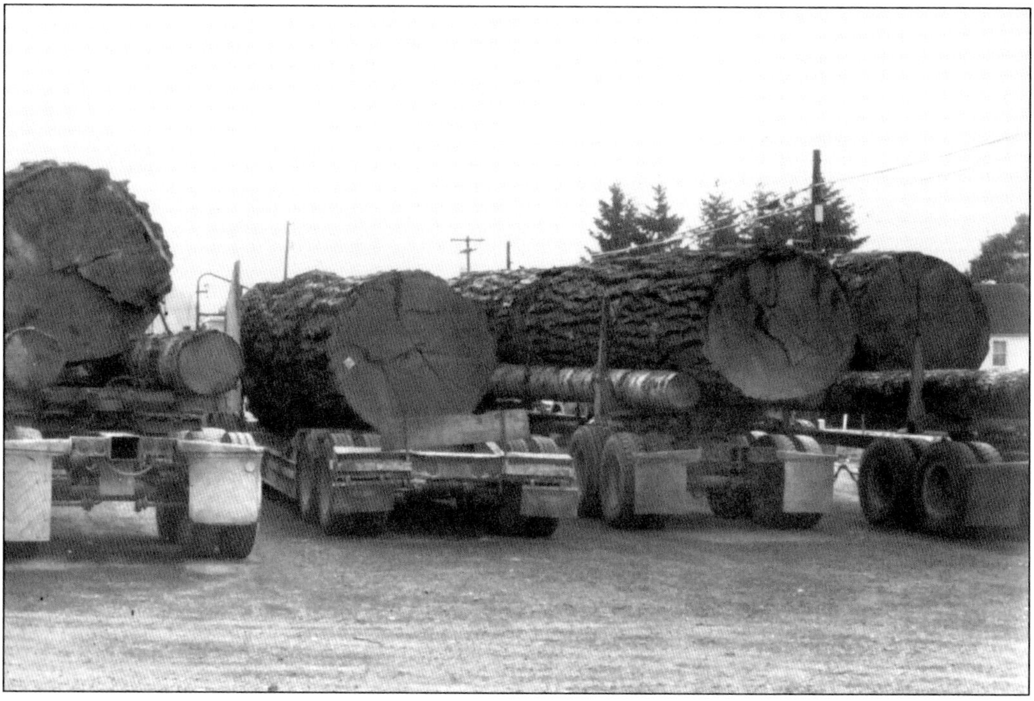

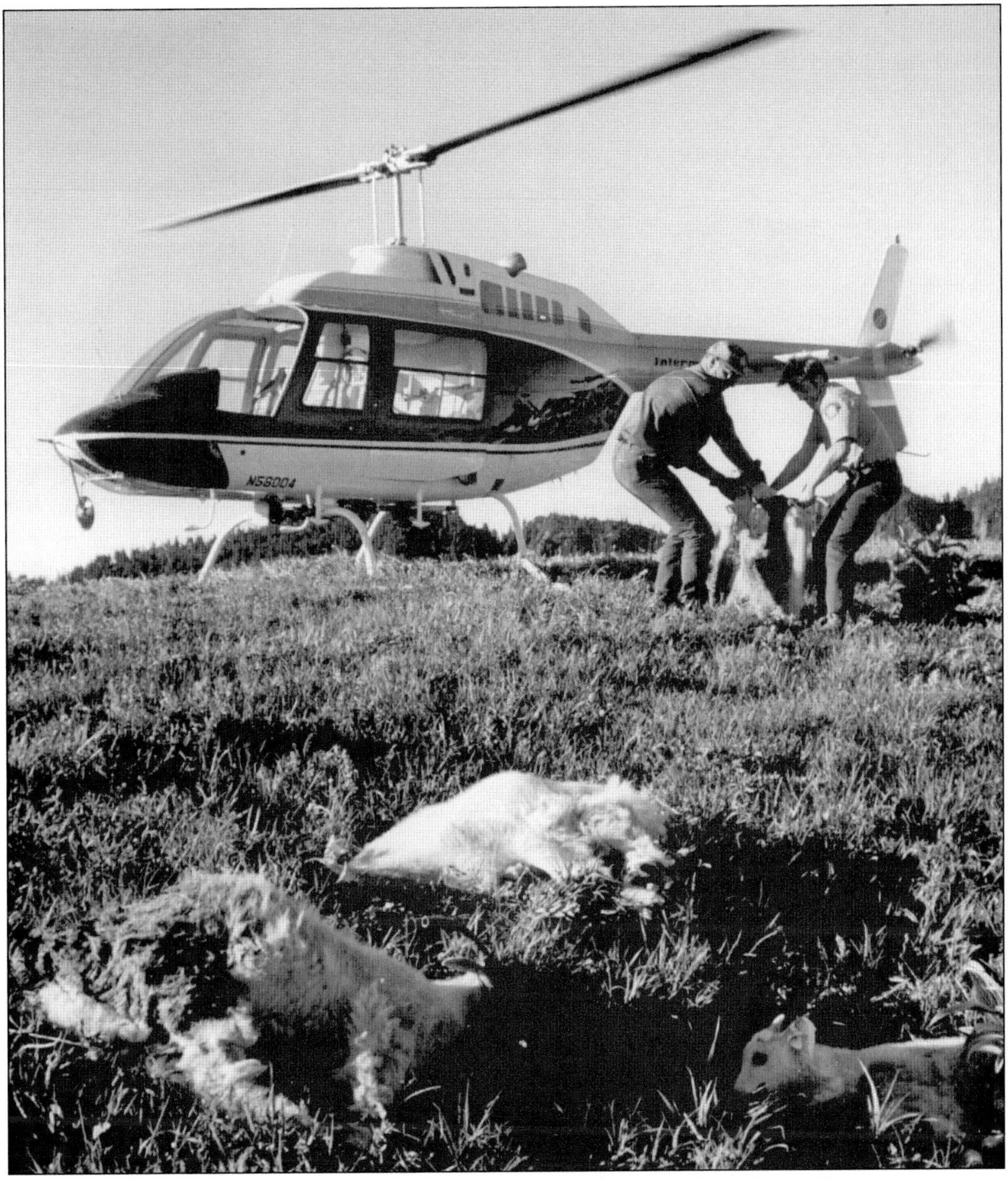

Pilot Ed Anderson (right) and Mike Christian of the Washington State Game Department move the last wild goat from a helicopter. Three other goats, previously airlifted to the site, are lying on the ground. They will all be released into the Mount Margaret area of the Gifford Pinchot National Forest near Castle Rock. In the latter part of the 20th century, helicopters were adapted to work in the woods. Sometimes used for thinning trees on steep hillsides, they are still not widely used for logging. Their use is almost universal in fighting forest fires, although airplanes are also used to fight fire from the air. Tank trucks and hand work are also used for controlling fires on the ground. Since the 1960s, Castle Rock has been the home of the southwest region headquarters of the Washington State Department of Natural Resources. This state governmental agency is responsible for the management of natural lands and resources, and the enforcement of regulations controlling them. (Courtesy James Hughes, U.S. Department of Agriculture Forest Service.)

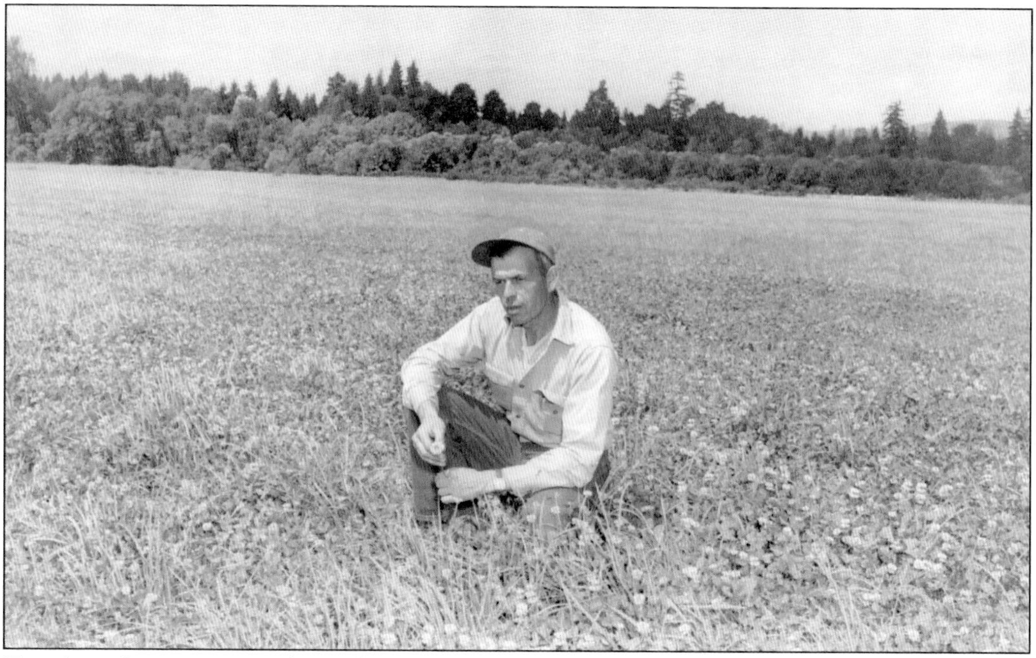

Two dairy farmers in Castle Rock in the 1950s were award winners at the state level from an association of farmers. Bill Larsen (pictured above) won the honor of "Grassman of the Year" in 1955; Ron Llewellen (shown below, right) earned the "Grassman of the Year" award in 1958. The award is given by the Washington Cattlemen's Association to the farmer who produces the best grass to nurture and increase production of his herd of dairy cattle. Larsen's farm was just south of Castle Rock in an area that is now inside the city limits. Llewellen's farm was just across the river on the west side of the West Side Highway directly across from where Castle Rock High School is now located. (Both, courtesy CCHM)

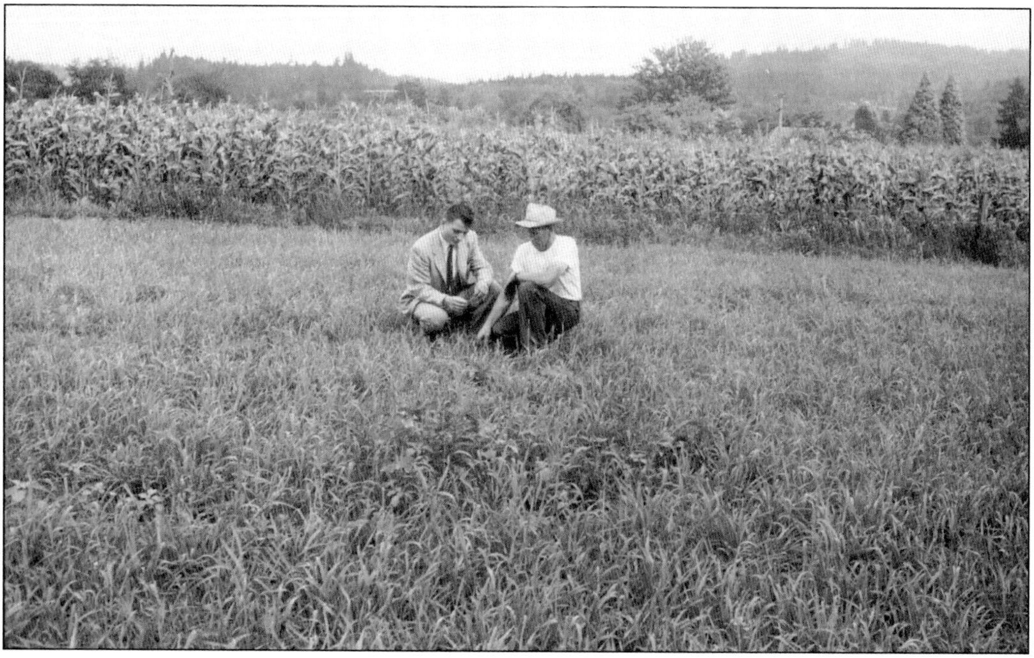

Four

COMMUNITY LIFE

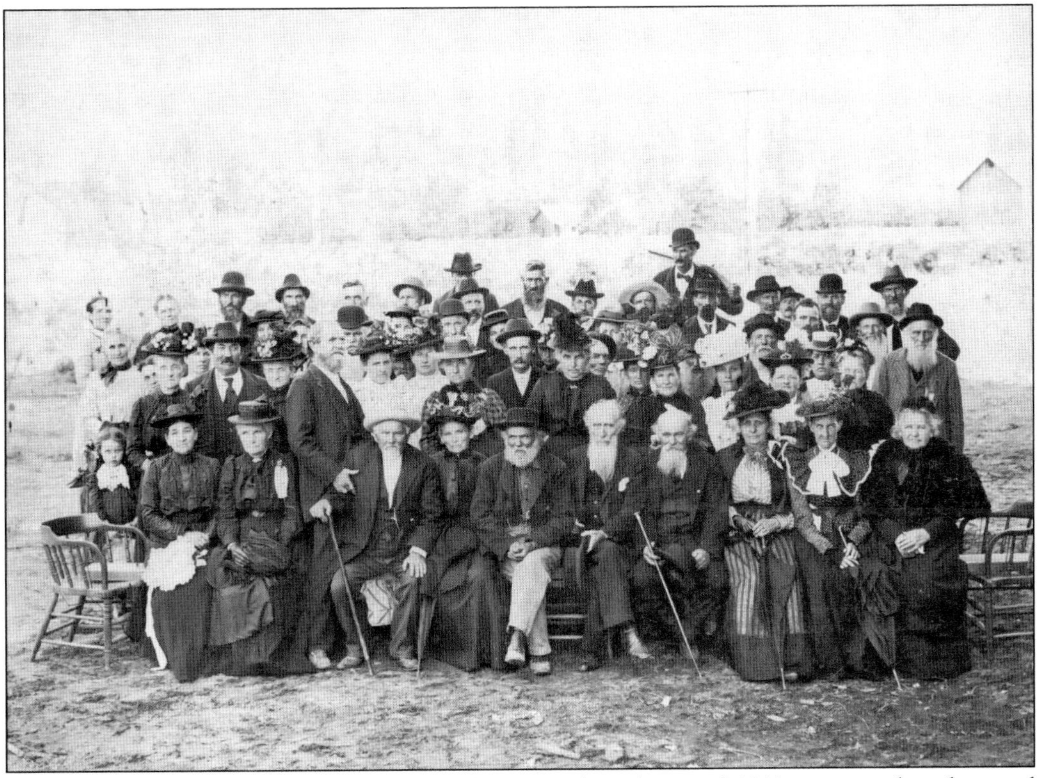

Many of the old settlers of the Castle Rock area gathered around 1910 to remember the good old days. Among the group are Ira Conger, John Robin, William Marshall, Pete Moore, Edwin Huntington, Hiram Jackson, Norman Burbee, James Spencer, Daniel Little, and John Plamondon. They are not individually identified. (Courtesy CCHM.)

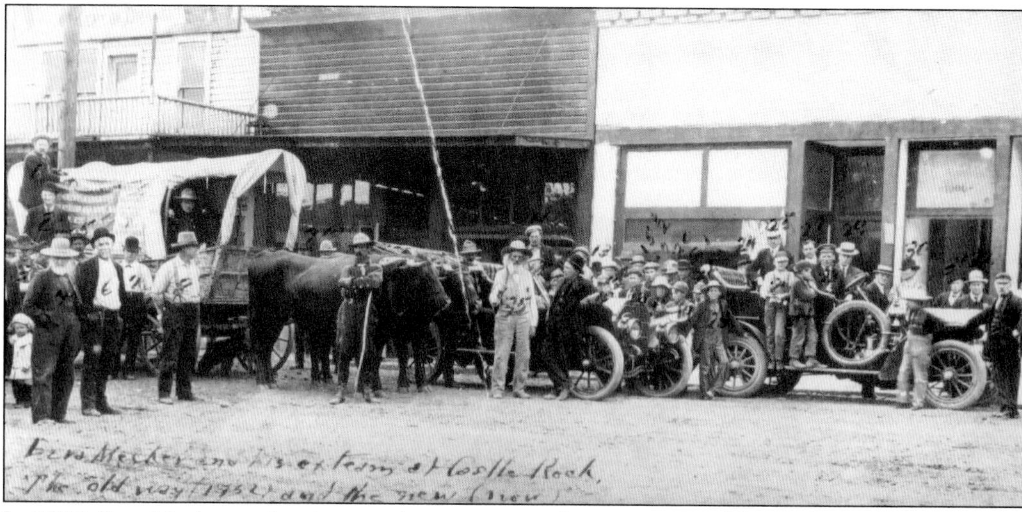

In 1906, Ezra Meeker took a journey by a wagon and ox team to publicize the Oregon Trail. He stopped in Castle Rock and posed for a photograph showing the old way of traveling beside the new. Meeker had settled originally at St. Helens, Oregon; moved to Kalama; and eventually made his home near Puyallup and ended his days as a hop farmer.

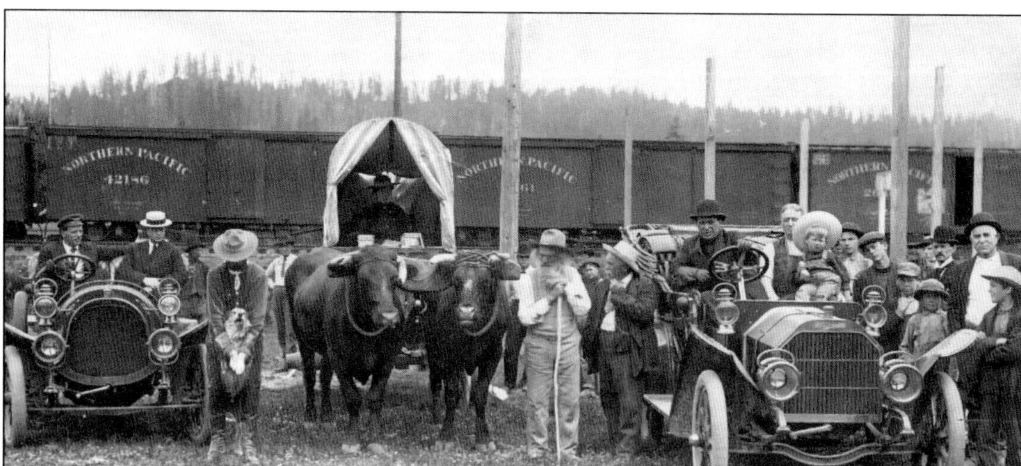

The photograph party moved to the railroad tracks and posed in front of a train to demonstrate three methods of transportation. Apparently, John Dickson was not available with the first motorcar in town. The car on the left is the second car in town, which was owned and driven by Nick Mansel. Ezra Meeker is at center with his ox team and wagon, and the car on the right is the third automobile in town. It was owned and driven by Windsor Robin.

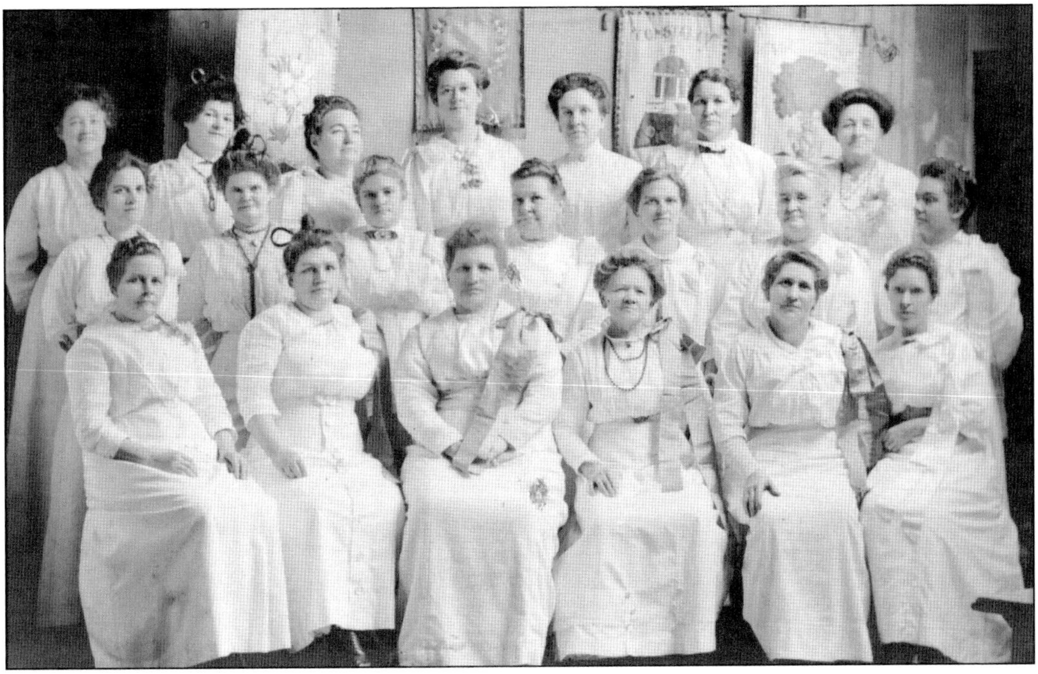

The 1800s were a time of social change, and many social, cultural, and religious organizations were founded. Most were either men's or women's groups. The Degree of Honor in Castle Rock was one of the oldest women's lodges in the state of Washington. Above, from left to right, are (first row) unidentified, ? Merrill, unidentified, Mrs. Charles Schotz, and two unidentified; (second row) all unidentified; (third row) three unidentified, Mrs. Elmer Huntington, unidentified, Mrs. A. Crowe, and a Mrs. Parker. The Knights of Pytheus was an early men's lodge. Shown below, the first and second rows are unidentified. From left to right are (third row) unidentified, C. "Chancy" Davis, unidentified, Fred Booth, unidentified, and Ted Becker. The man standing on the upper left is Sidney Ott. The man standing on the upper right is unidentified.

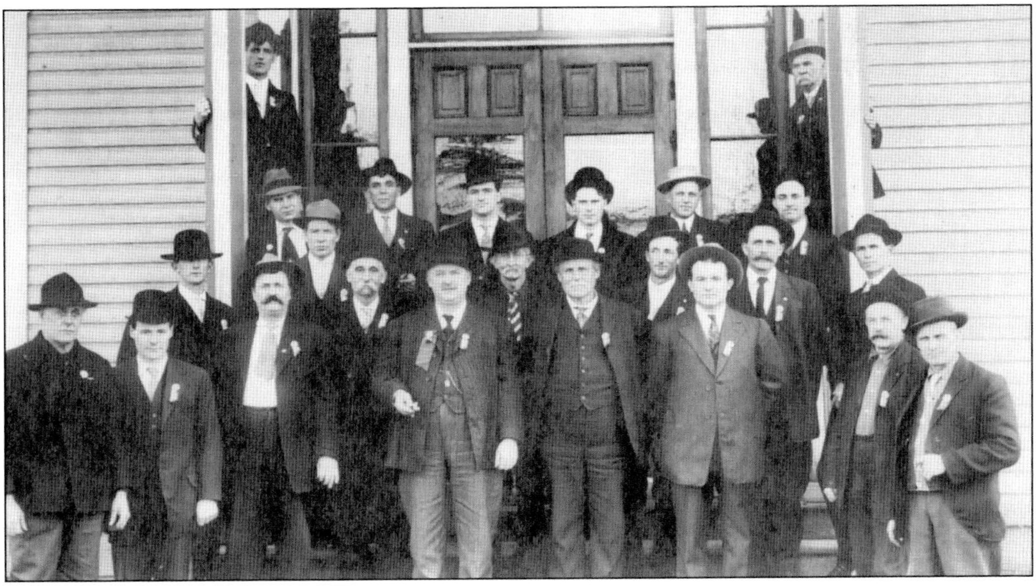

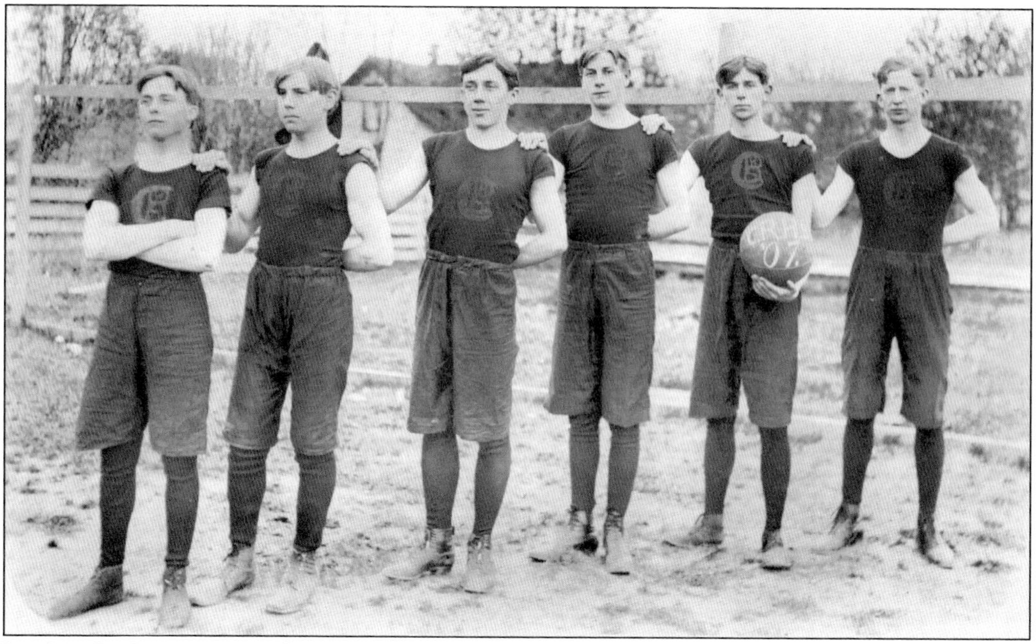

In 1891, Dr. James Naismith, a Canadian physical education professor from McGill University in Montreal and instructor at the Young Men's Christian Association (YMCA) School, invented the game of basketball. Peach baskets were used until 1906, when just the hoops were used. Basketball quickly became the ideal interscholastic sport because of its modest equipment and personnel requirements. The first photograph of a Castle Rock High School basketball team is dated 1907–1908 and shows that the uniforms exposed very little skin. The only identified member of the team is Eugene Powellson, holding the ball. Not to be outdone, the girls of the class of 1907–1908 also fielded a team. Below, from left to right, are (first row) Virginia Keatley, Dorothy Keatley, and Tressie Huntington; (second row) Lottie Shartle, Orville Robin, Crystal Cook, ? Sater (the manager), and Tracy Huntington.

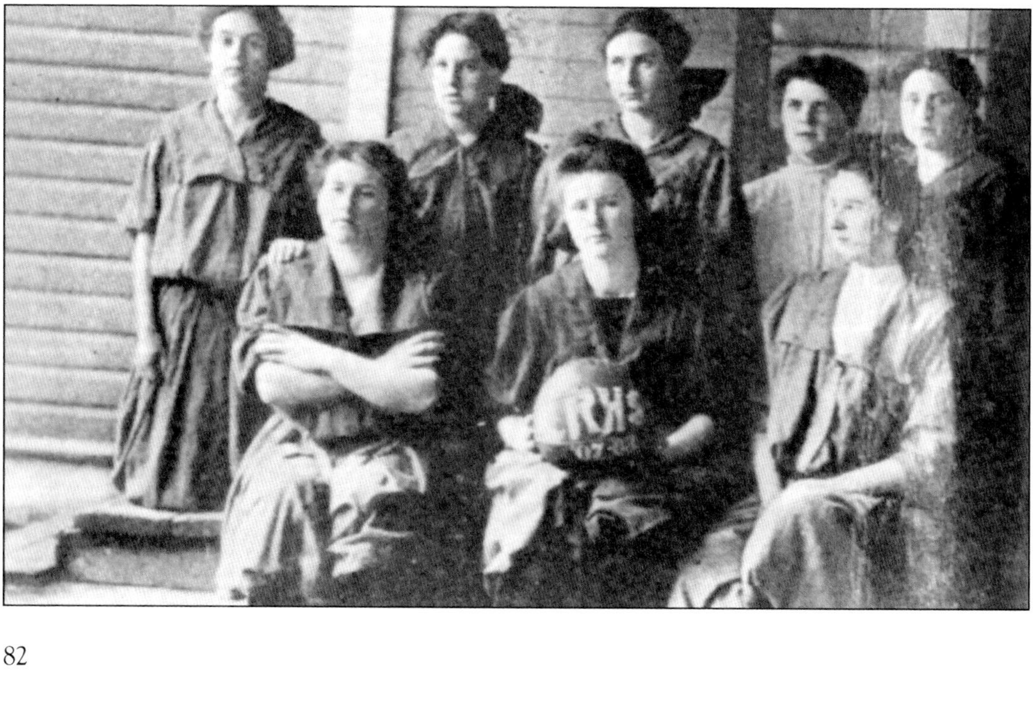

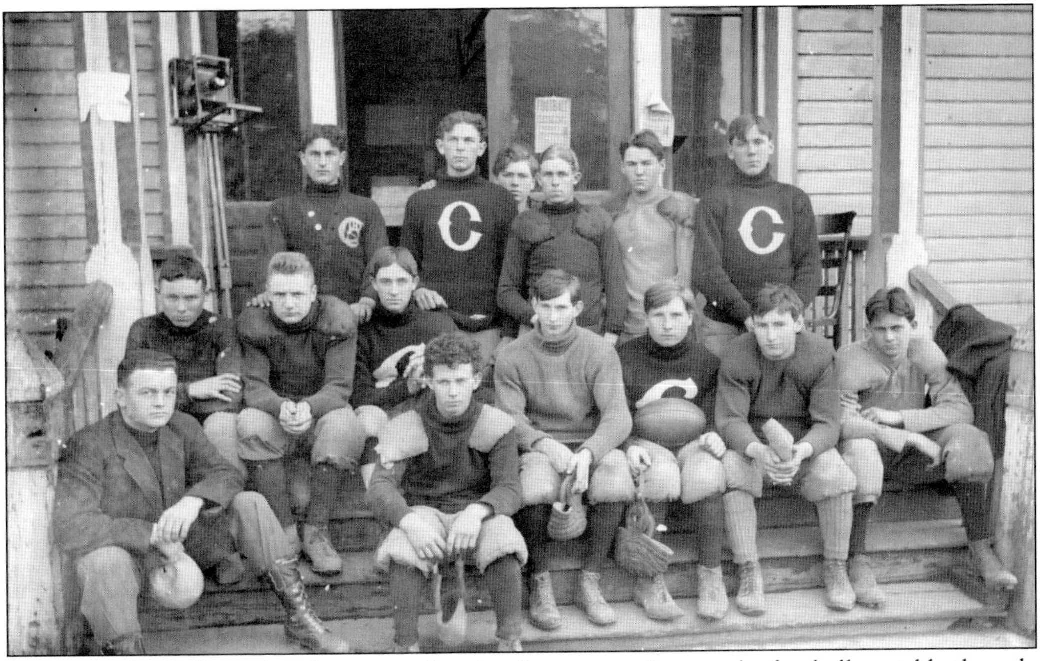

American football resulted from several major divergences from rugby football, notably the rule changes instituted by Walter Camp, considered the "Father of American Football." In the late 19th and early 20th centuries, game play developments by college coaches helped take advantage of the newly introduced forward pass. High school football dates back to the late 1800s, when it developed along with college football. High school football and basketball games became centers of community interest and activity, particularly in small towns. Above, Castle Rock High School (CRHS) football team players of 1910–1911 are all unidentified except for those in the third row, who are, from left to right, unidentified, Everett Powellson, Jason Little, and two unidentified players. Below, CRHS basketball team members of 1910–1911 are all unidentified.

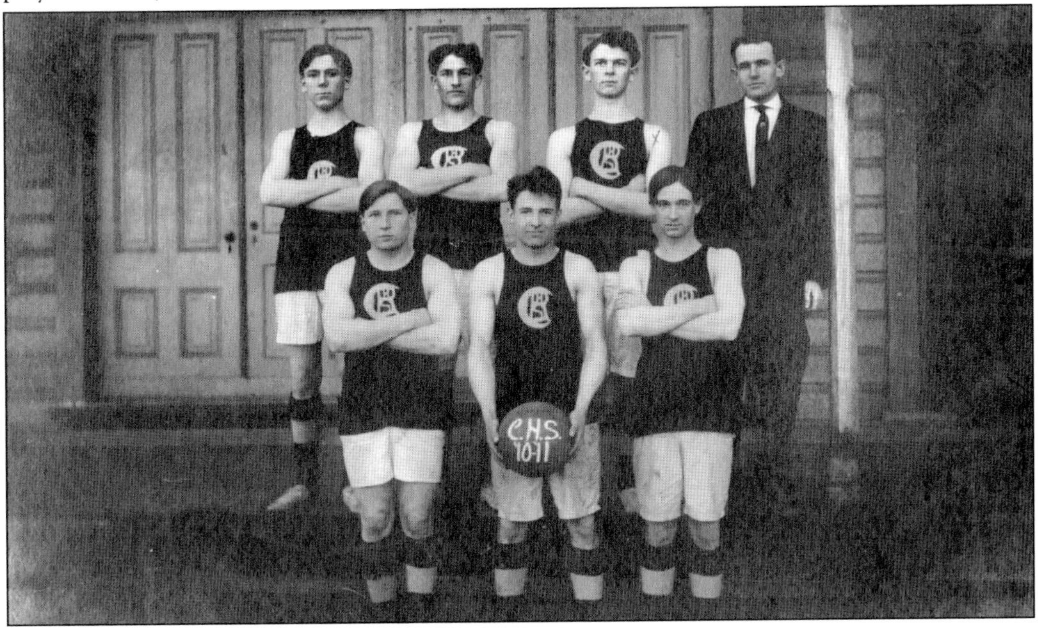

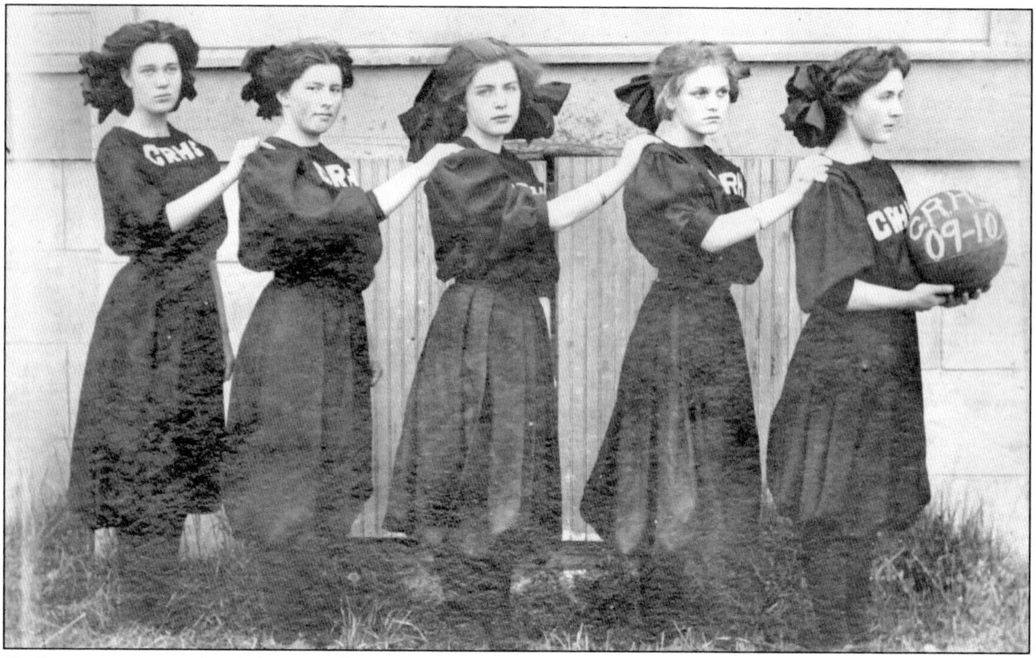

Girls were not to be left out of the development of basketball. In 1892, a physical education teacher at Smith College, Senda Berenson, modified Dr. James Naismith's rules for women. Her rules were first published in 1899. Pictured above, the Castle Rock girls' basketball team of 1909–1910 consisted of, from left to right, Mae Imboden Black, Virginia Keatley Rowe, Hazel Jackson Van de Griff, Mary Hanson Neil, and Crystal Cook Powellson holding the ball. Everett Powellson coached the teams. The photograph below shows, from left to right, Crystal Cook Powellson, Mary Hanson Neil, Mae Imboden Black, Virginia Keatley Rowe, and Hazel Jackson Van de Griff. The team name was Bloomerines.

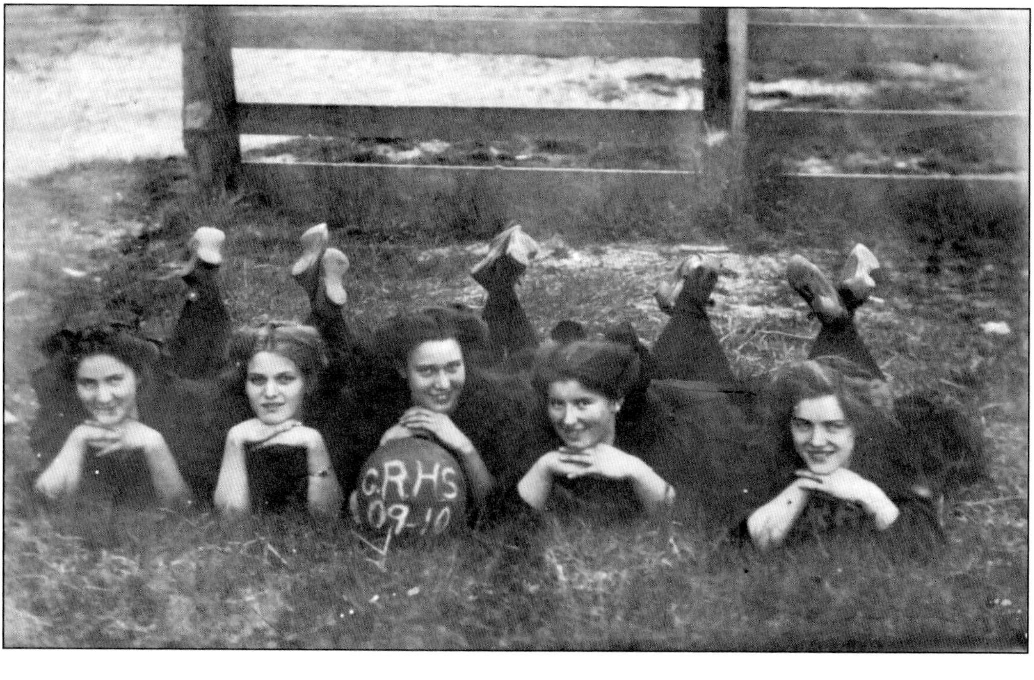

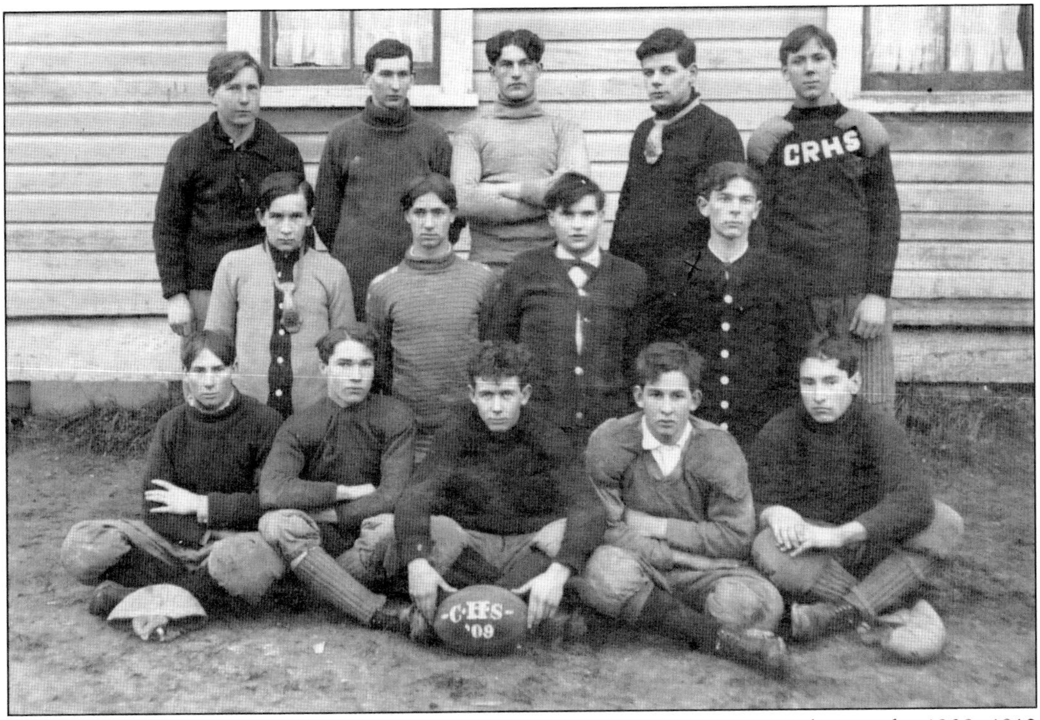

The earliest photograph of a Castle Rock High School football team was taken in the 1909–1910 school year. None are identified except Everett Powellson, who is in the second row, far right.

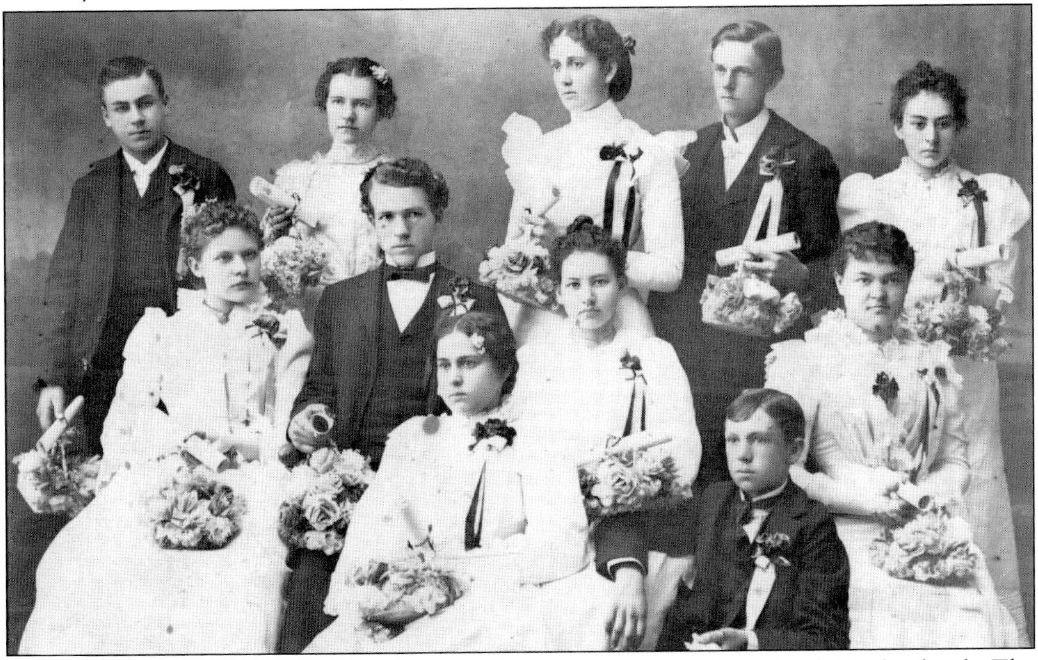

On May 23, 1885, the eighth-grade class was the first to graduate from Castle Rock schools. The graduating students are, from left to right, (first row) Eva A. Huntington and Howard Huntington; (second row) Mable Brewer, Arthur Studebaker, Nellie Pauly, and Eva M. Huntington; (third row) Raymond Cook, Ella Studebaker, Leona Longlin, Amon Foster, and Lizzie Pauly.

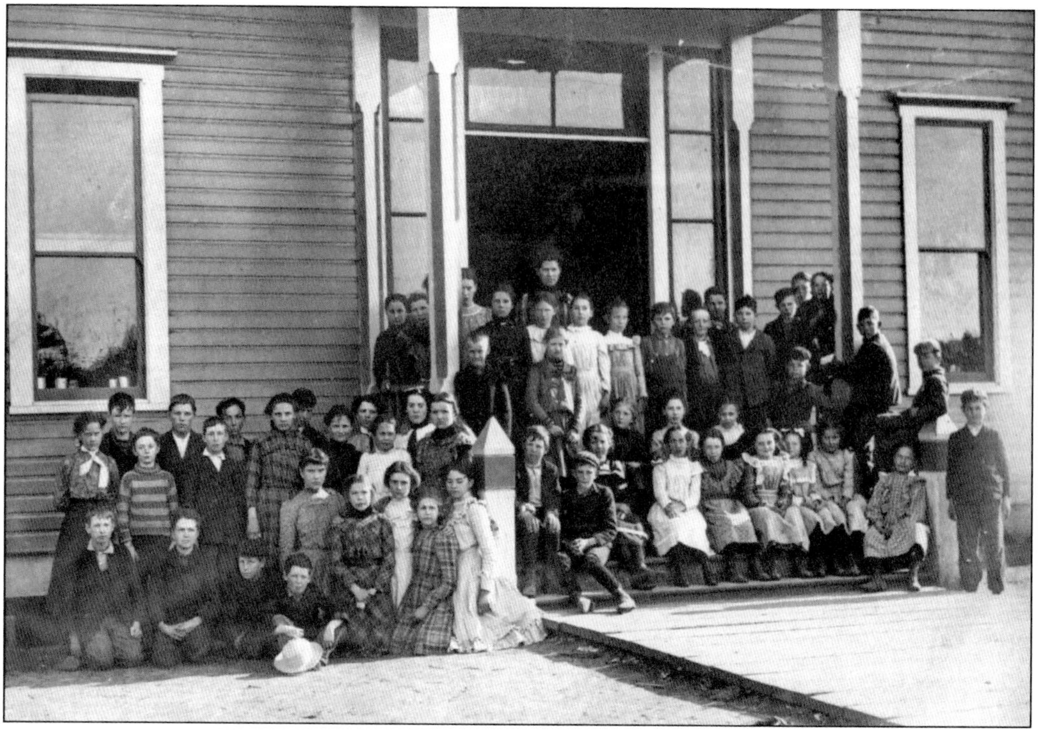

Combined fourth and fifth grade classes in the Castle Rock Grade School in 1900–1901 were taught by Bessie Shephardson (standing in the doorway above). In the photograph below are Castle Rock High School classes in 1911. As the town grew, so did the school student body. The first high school in 1900 was only two grades. Students would leave school and go to work at age 16.

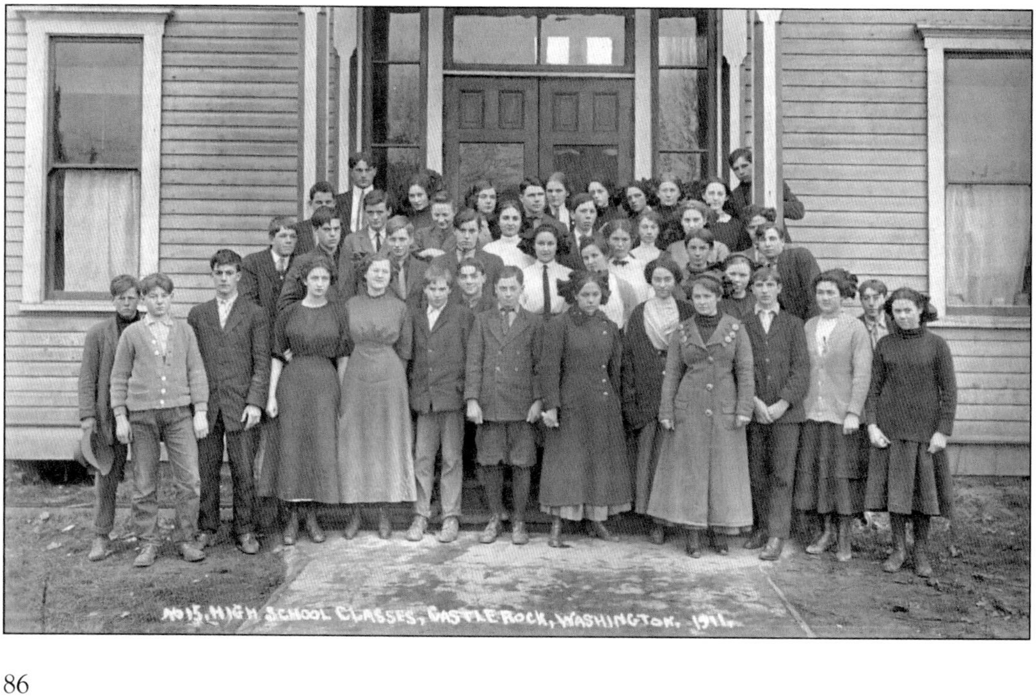

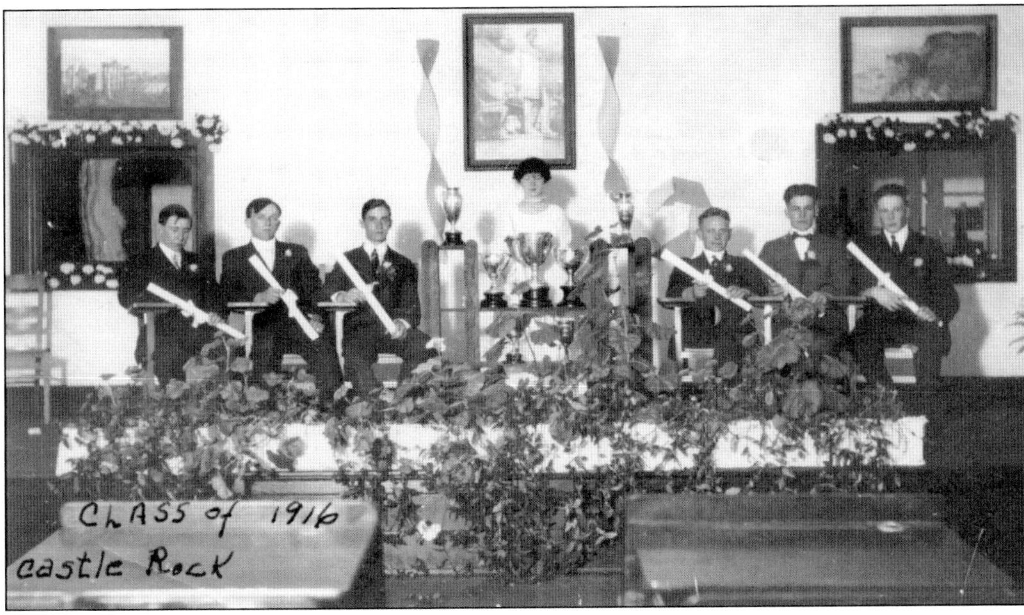

Above is the high school graduating class of 1916 with all unidentified except Seth Leaming (second from left). Below, students in Ted Goodwin's Sunday school class at the Castle Rock Christian Church in 1921–1922 are, from left to right, (first row) ? Wooster, Arnold Pomeroy, Jesse Moore, ? Drew, Fredy Studebaker, Oscar Anderson, ? Watkins, Albert Anderson, and Roy Welsh; (second row) Clyde Dale and Clare Holten; (third row) two unidentified, Wendell Wooster, Phillip Watkins, William Anderson, Wayne Wooster, Bud Watkins, and Lawson Watkins; (fourth row) Ted Goodwin.

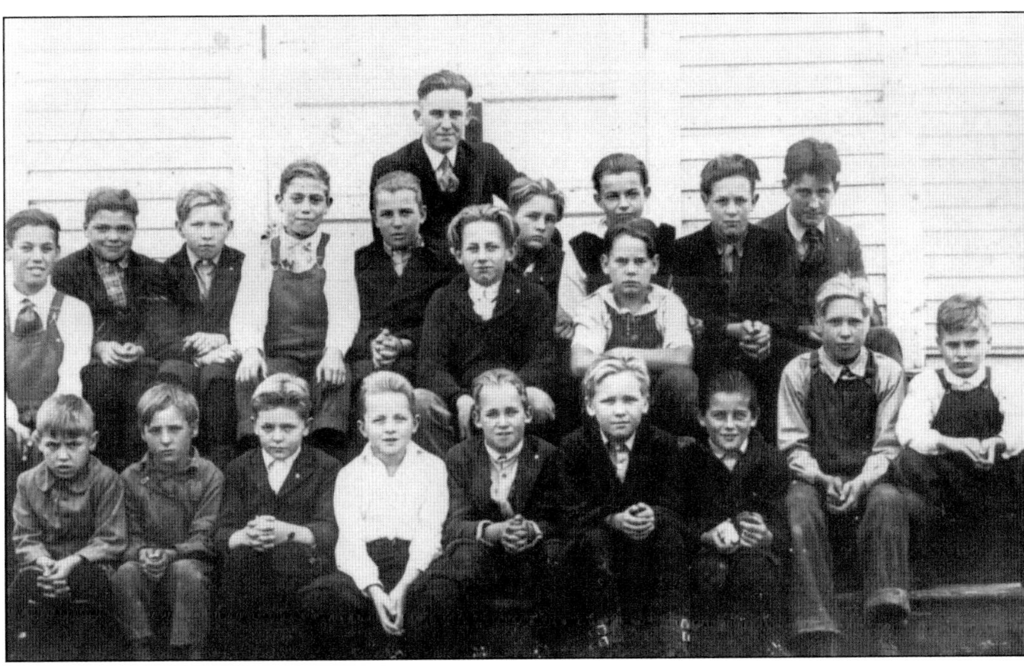

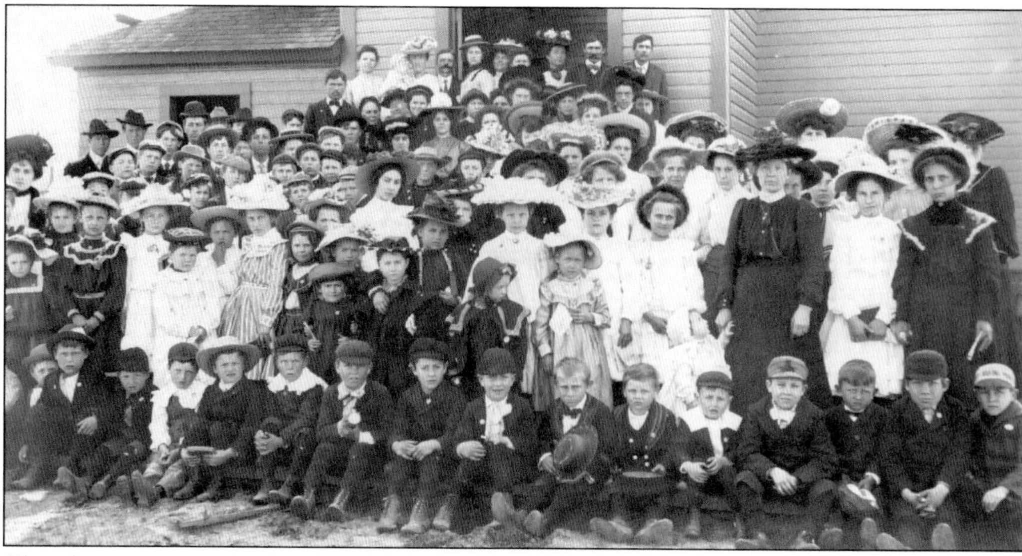

Churches were an important part of community life. Above, these members of the Castle Rock Christian Church appear to be dressed in their Easter finery in 1910. The only ones identified are first row, sixth from right, Jesse Moore, and ninth from right, Fredy Studebaker. Before radio, television, and recorded music were available in every home, many people learned to play instruments and kept it up their entire lives. In fact, playing music and singing was one of the major forms of entertainment whenever people gathered, either formally or informally. In 1911, Harvey Richardson, owner and operator of a jewelry shop, formed this mandolin club (shown below), though some members played other stringed instruments, such as banjo and guitar. Members of the group were, from left to right, (first row) Everett Powellson, Orlo Stevens, Bessie Ott, Myrtle Richardson (Harvey's wife), unidentified, and Clarence Dougherty; (second row) unidentified, Harry Hubbard, Harvey Richardson, Helen Argyle, Mina McNeil, Fred Berkenstock, and Chauncey Davis.

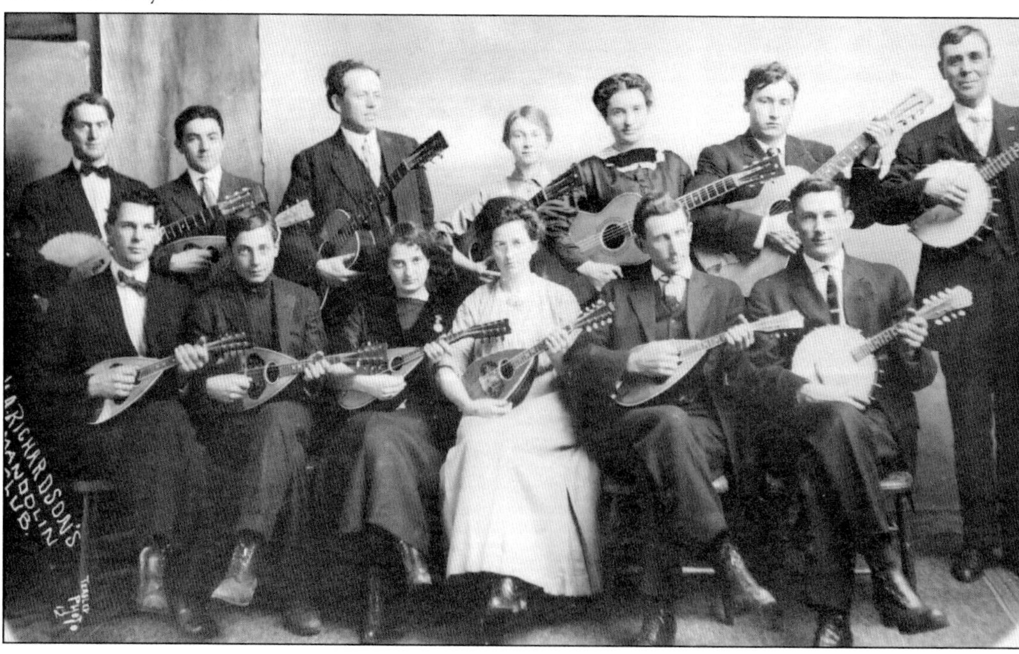

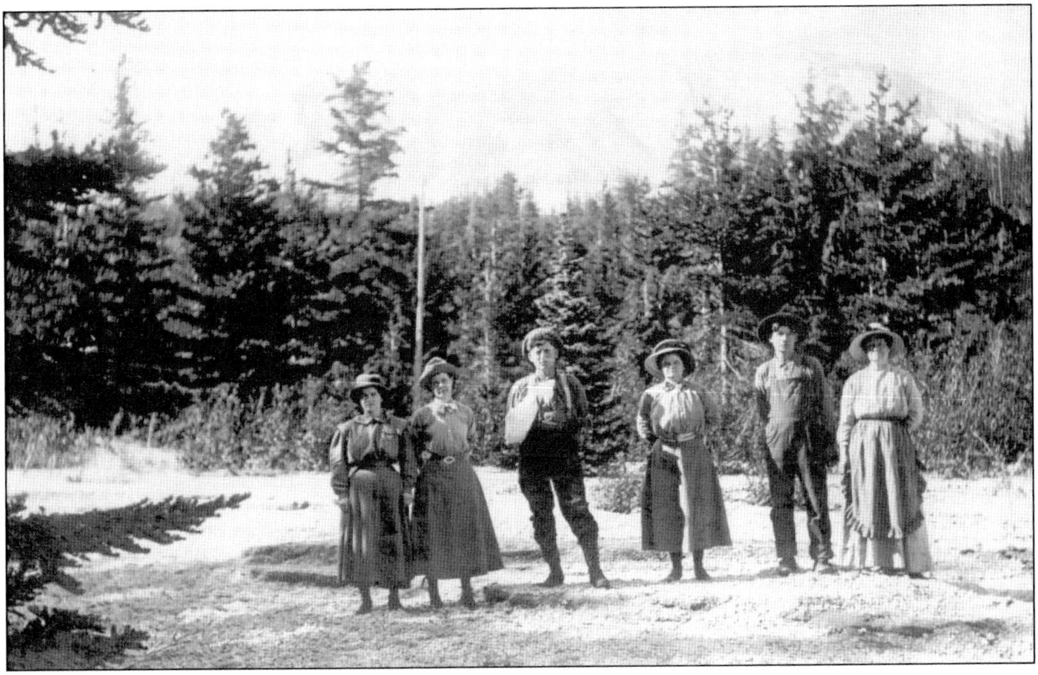

Even though people worked hard physically, they still enjoyed hiking or picnicking in some of the beautiful, scenic places nearby. Above, this group is on an outing at Spirit Lake. The beauty of Spirit Lake has drawn admirers since it was first seen. Its position at the foot of Mount St. Helens made it all the more attractive to all types of visitors. The girl on the left is Bertha Whittle Booth. The rest are unidentified. Being centers of community life, churches hosted activities other than worship, such as the St. Paul Lutheran Church Band in 1910 (shown below).

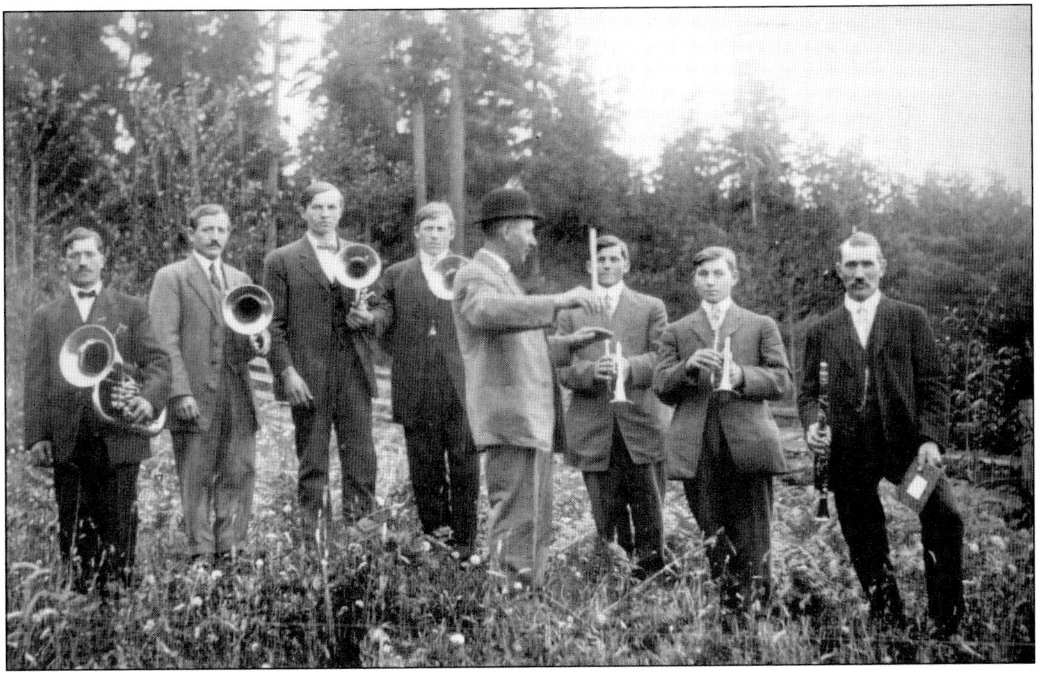

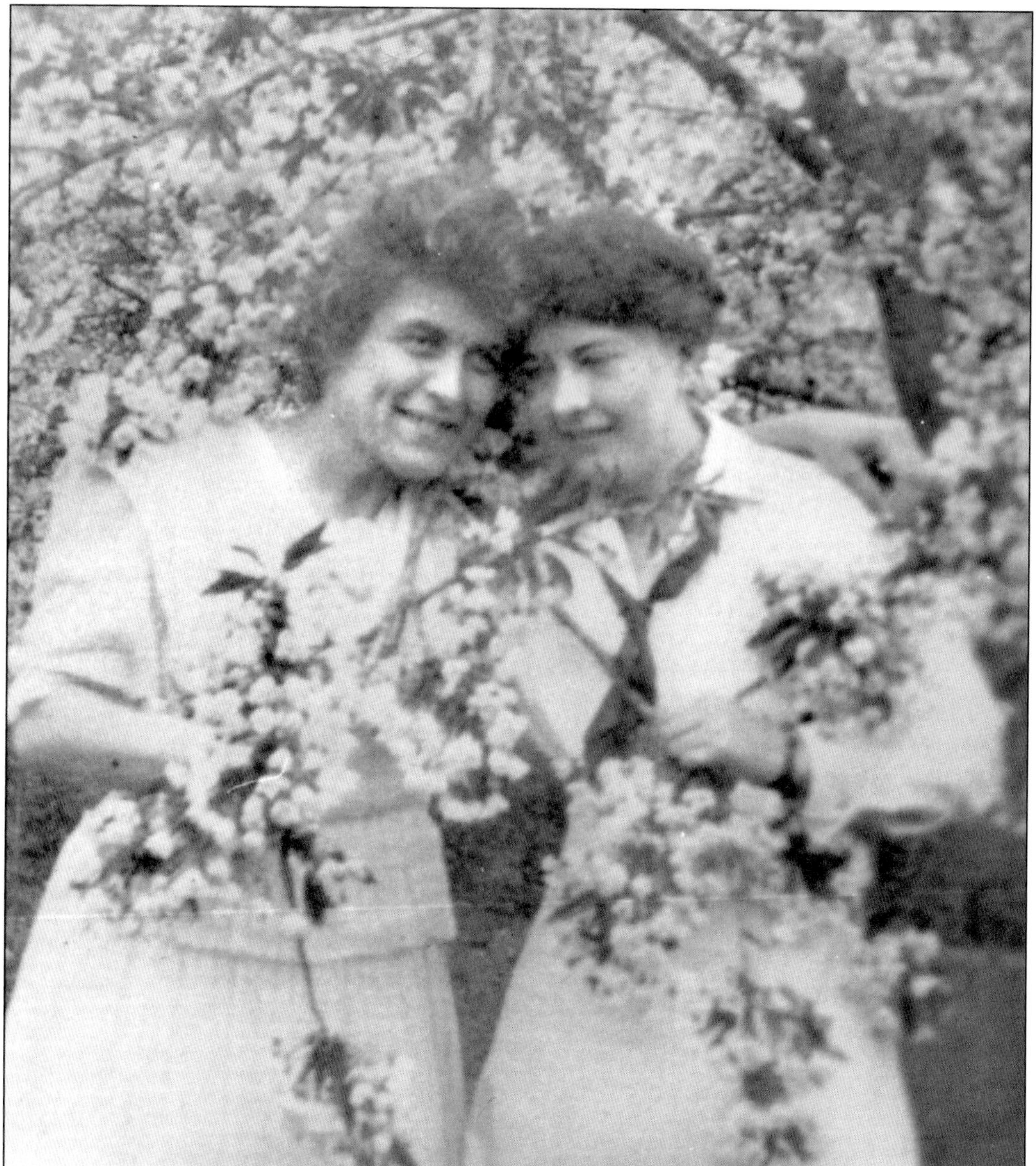

Rose Burnette (left) was a second grade teacher in 1915 when this photograph was taken. Alice Weidenheimer was a first grade teacher. They show off their spring finery among fruit blossoms in this unusually informal photograph.

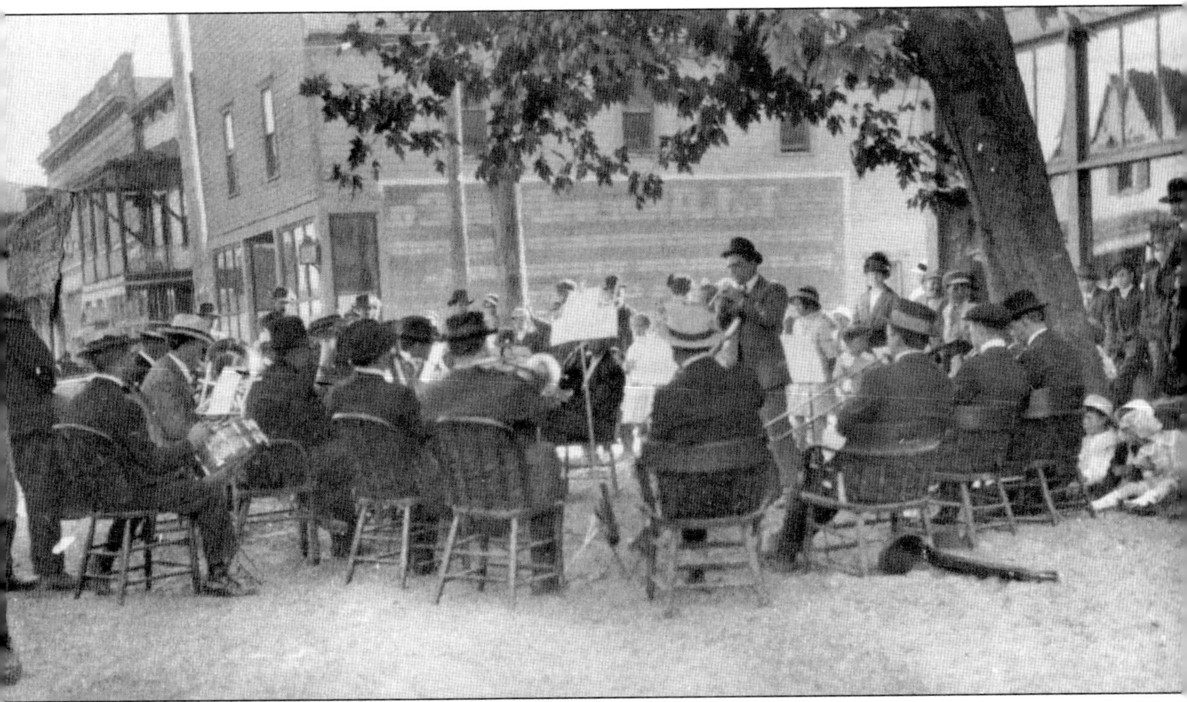

The Castle Rock Band is performing under a tree on Front Avenue and in front of the Castle Rock Hotel (formerly the Spencer House) at Jackson Street. A community band is another example of how people of that time made their own entertainment and shared it with each other. The phonograph was invented in the 1880s; however, recorded music and machines to play it on were not available to the average family until after World War I.

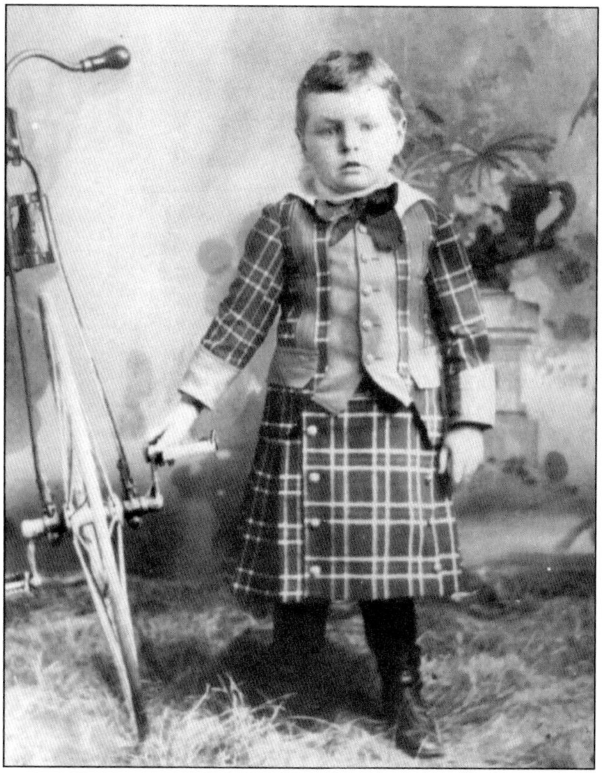

A grandson of William Whittle, son of Emma Whittle Mackinster, wears dress clothes for a young boy in the 1890s. His hair is cut short in a masculine way, but he is wearing a skirt. This was the accepted method of dress for very young boys, though his may have also been influenced by his father's Scottish heritage. The little girls are also Whittle grandchildren, though not identified either by names or by parent's name. They are also wearing dress clothes appropriate for young girls, though the dark color indicates that they may be dressed for a funeral.

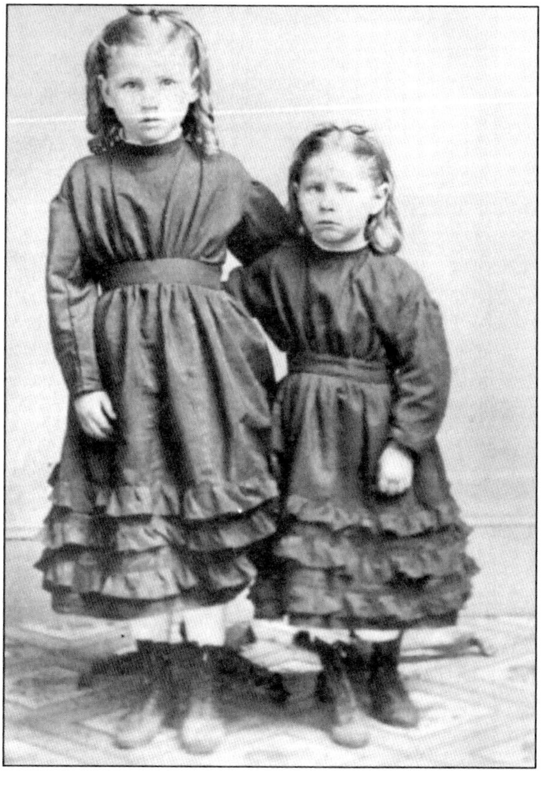

Bertha Whittle Booth (left) and Clydena Thurston Hyde (right) pose in their lovely coats and hats sometime between 1910 and 1920. They are also wearing dress shoes with high heels, so they are dressed for stepping out and not just going on everyday errands. They are standing on the west side of the river on the old ferry dock. The east pier of the high steel bridge that was built in 1910 is on the riverbank behind them. The photograph below, also taken about 1910, shows Frank Hubbard (left) and Clarence Dougherty (right) posed in their finery as young-men-about-town, both sporting hats. Dougherty wears the old, separate, hard and high starched collar with his tie, while Hubbard has gone with the newer, smaller collar. Hubbard also wears a waistcoat and watch chain.

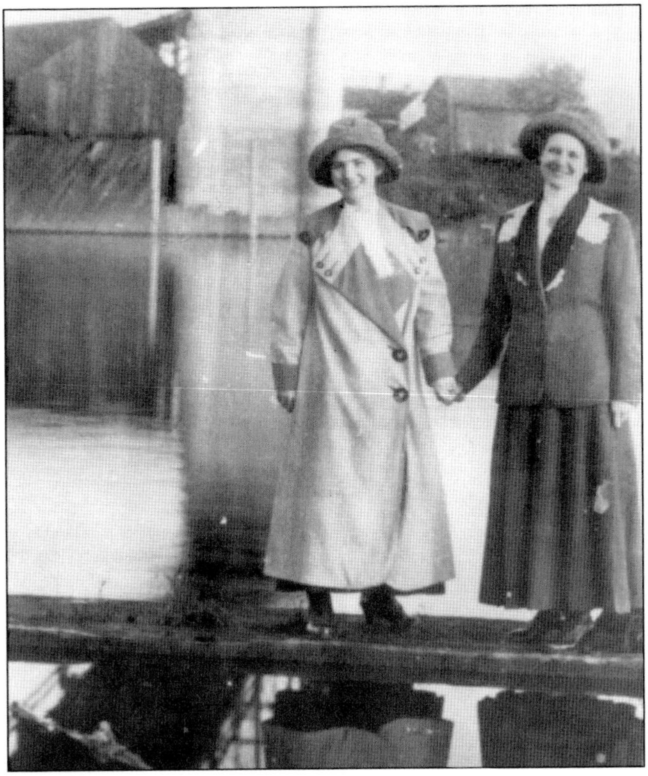

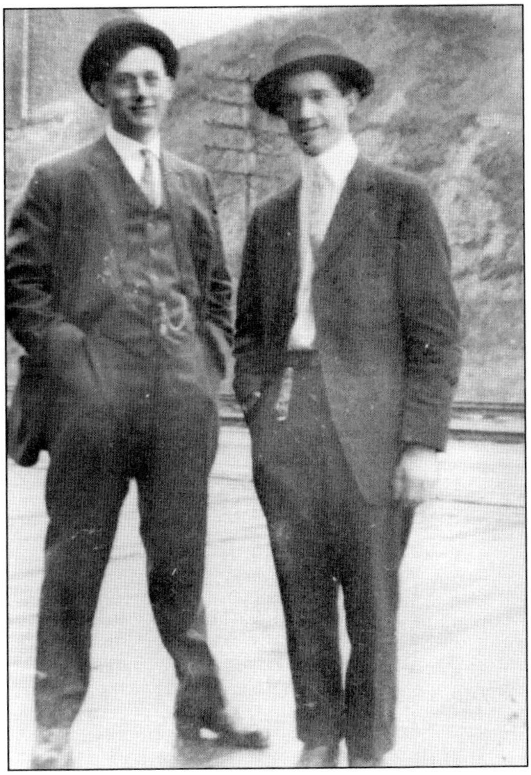

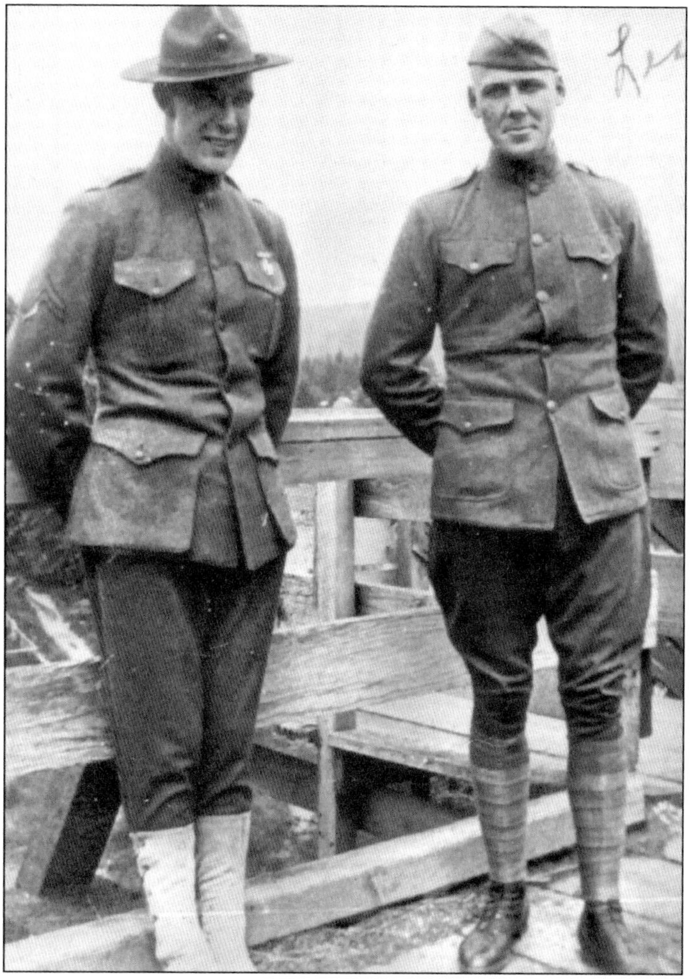

U.S. Marine C. F. "Fay" Breneman (left) and U.S. Army doughboy Lester Huntington (right) pose in their World War I uniforms. Huntington would later become a district judge. After the war was over, in 1921–1922, the citizens of Castle Rock erected a memorial in front of city hall to honor the sons of the town who did not survive the war. Below, the gentlemen to the left of the monument are unidentified. Kneeling directly in front of the monument is Richard Gaze. Then kneeling are, from left to right, George Gaze and Richard Johnston. Standing to the right of the monument are, from left to right, Sam C. Roake, Sam "Dad" Roake, unidentified, and Otto Stevens in the white shirt. The men in the third row are unidentified.

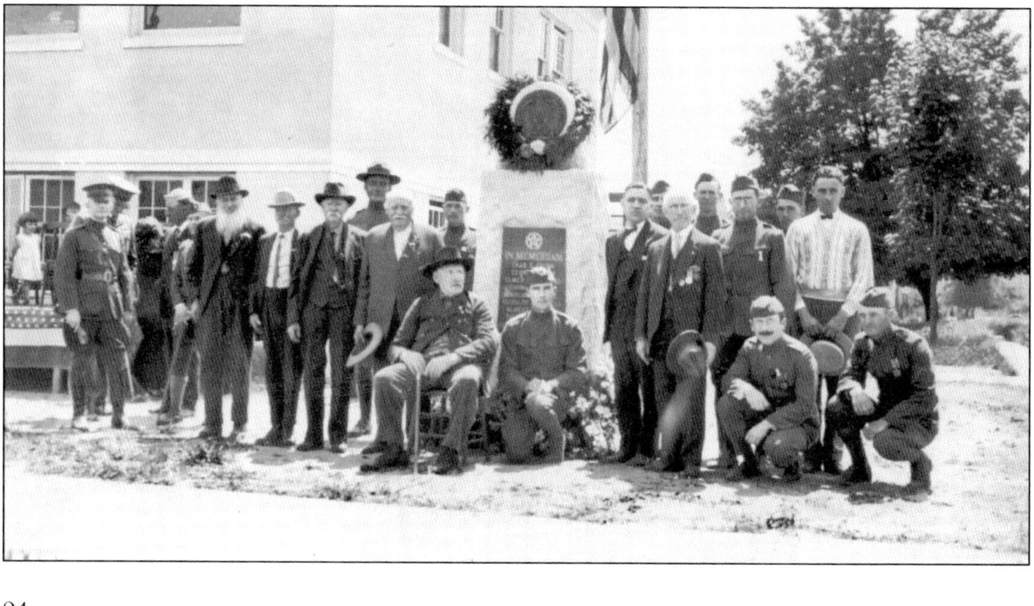

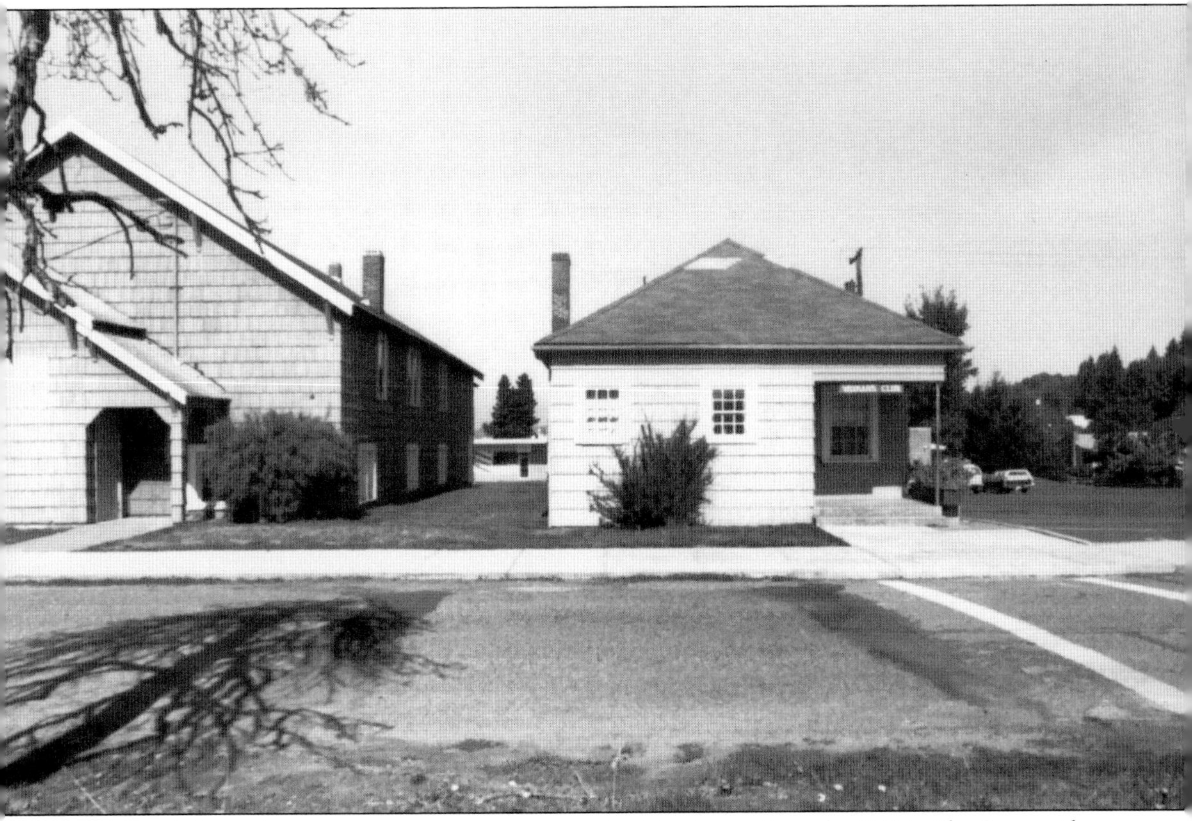

Buildings dedicated to community spirit are shown in this picture from the 1980s. The Sunnyside Grange hall (left) has a large room with a stage at one end upstairs and has been the site of many dances, parties, and other community events over the years, as well as Grange meetings and events. The Grange, or Patrons of Husbandry, was started as a social and political lodge for farm families in the early 1800s and is still active today. The Woman's Club building (right) has been the home of a group of women dedicated to the betterment of the community since 1912. Originally called the Castle Rock Woman's Commercial Club, it was founded by Ida Peabody and Beulah Dahlman to put garbage cans and street signs on the downtown streets. Within the first few months, they also inspired the city council to install a public drinking fountain on Cowlitz Street and petitioned to have the old boardwalks replaced by cement sidewalks. Over the years, the Woman's Club has also created (and for a time maintained) the town's library, established a garden club, supported the community fair, and supported and funded many other worthy projects.

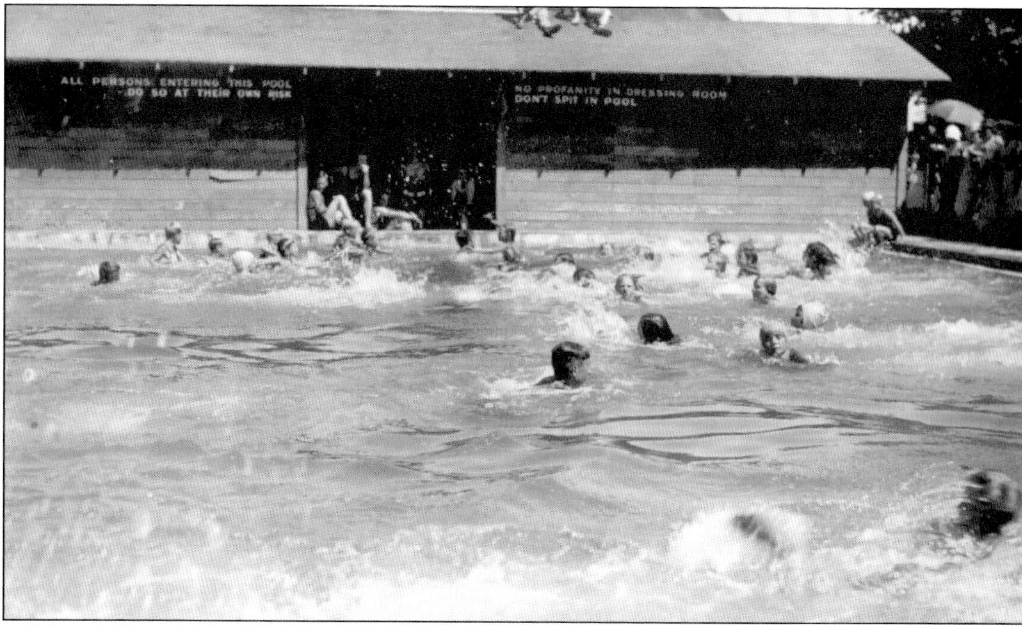

In the photograph above are unidentified children cavorting in the Castle Rock community swimming pool in the 1920s. Shown below is the Castle Rock public swimming pool in the late 1930s.

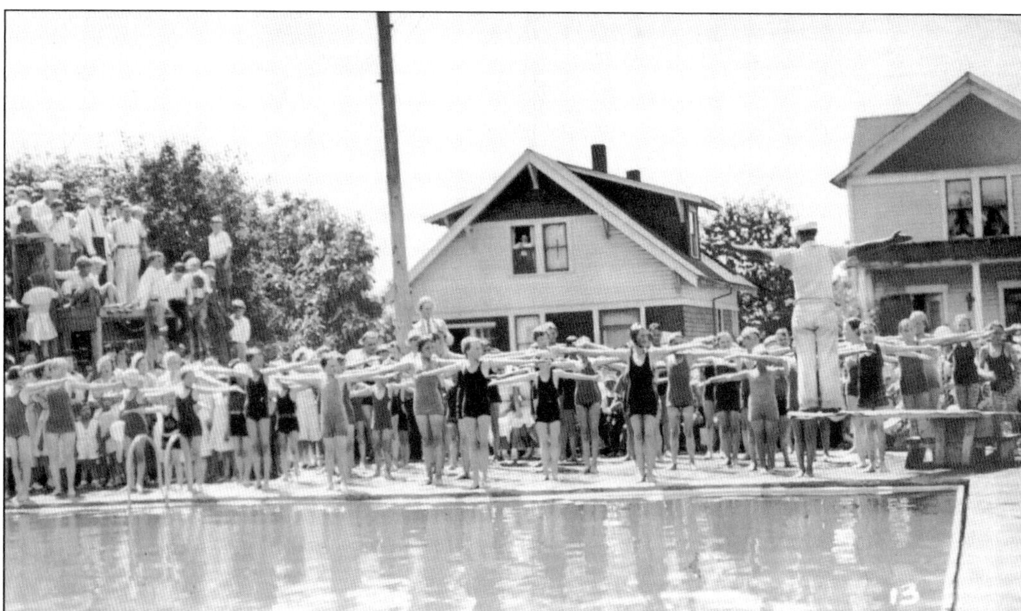

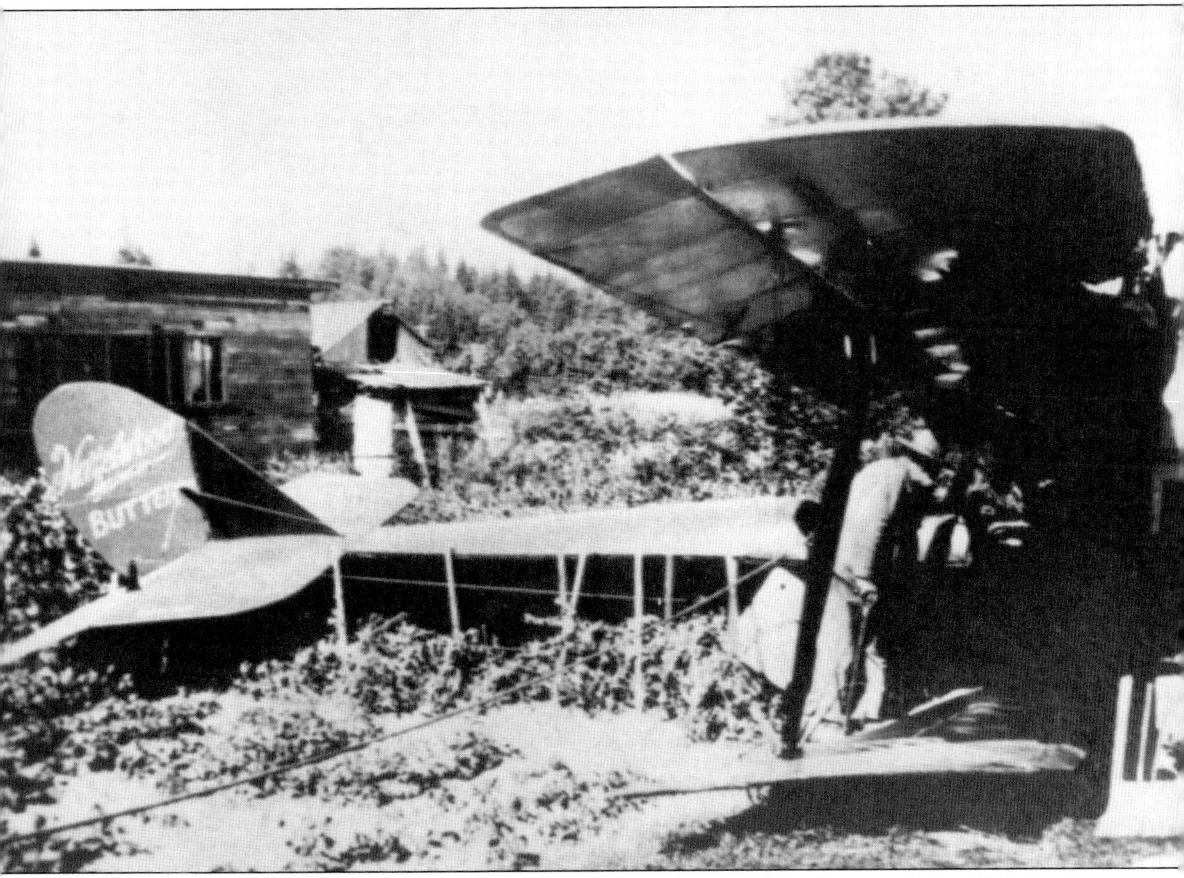

A biplane crashed in downtown Castle Rock on the north side of the home of John Kalmbach (pronounce Kum-bow) on the northeast corner of Front Avenue and B Street. In the first few years of the 1900s, after airplanes were invented, pilots started developing stunts with the airplanes to test the machine's abilities. This led to a type of daredevil pilot who traveled around the country from town to town doing shows for a small fee. This was called barnstorming. The flyers were usually young. They often slept in fields under the wings of their airplanes and did their own mechanic work. They performed more and more dangerous feats of flying to feed the voracious demand of the public for thrills. Some even traveled with an ambulance, which would go through the town with sirens blaring to lead people out to the airfield. This practice of extreme flying often led to wrecking the airplanes, and many of the pilots survived multiple crashes in their careers.

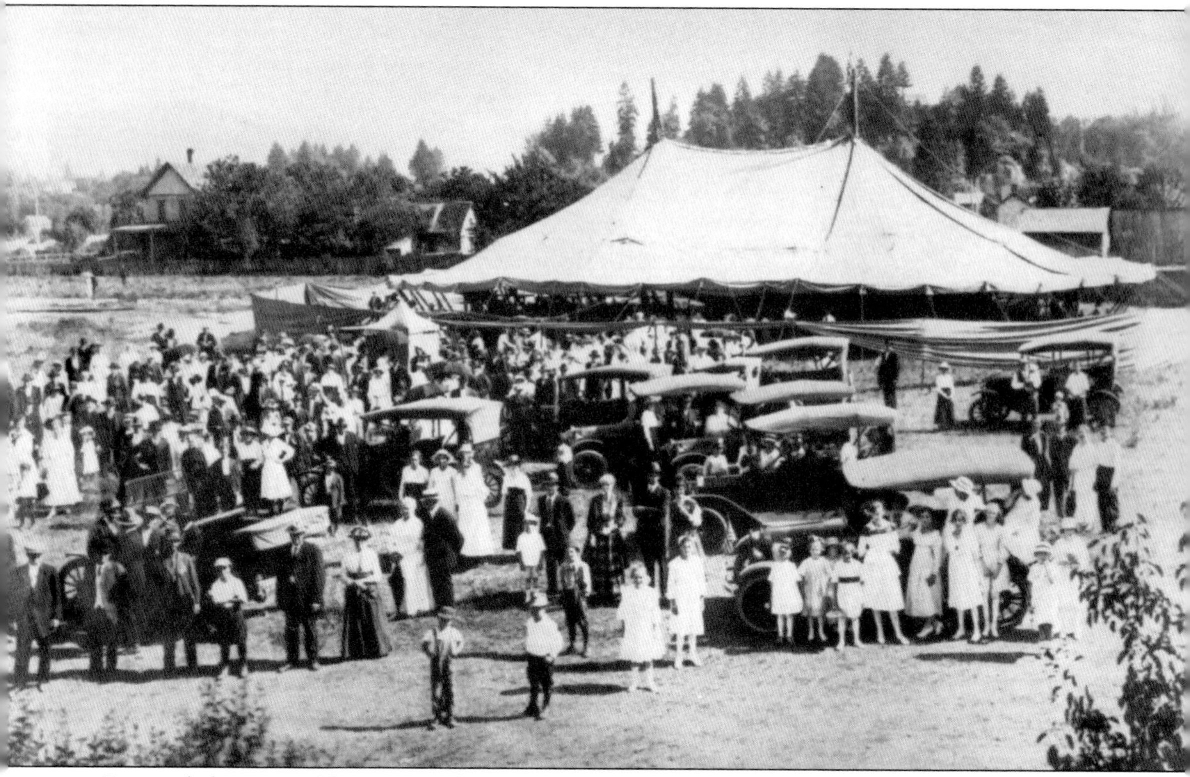

Pictured above is a Chautauqua show drawing a crowd in the 1920s. They set up their tent and performed in an empty field on the east side of Huntington Avenue, where the school bus barn is now. The first Chautauqua, the New York Chautauqua Assembly, was developed in 1874 by Methodist minister John Heyl Vincent and his partner businessman Lewis Miller at Chautauqua Lake in New York state. It was a religiously based, educational summer camp. These performances became so popular with families that a movement was spawned. Beginning in 1904, itinerant Chautauqua shows, formally dubbed Circuit Chautauquas and commonly known as tent Chautauquas, brought education and entertainment to towns all across the country. Educational, political, and religious lectures were the mainstay of these performances, but music and other entertainment were all a part of the Chautauqua presentation. After the Chautauqua tent was erected, it would stay for several days. Each performer appeared on a particular day of the program. So-called "first day" talent would move on to other Chautauquas, followed by "second day" performers and so on throughout the touring season. By the 1920s, Chautauquas were at their peak and had performed in 10,000 towns to crowds of more than 45 million. By the 1940s, they had run their course.

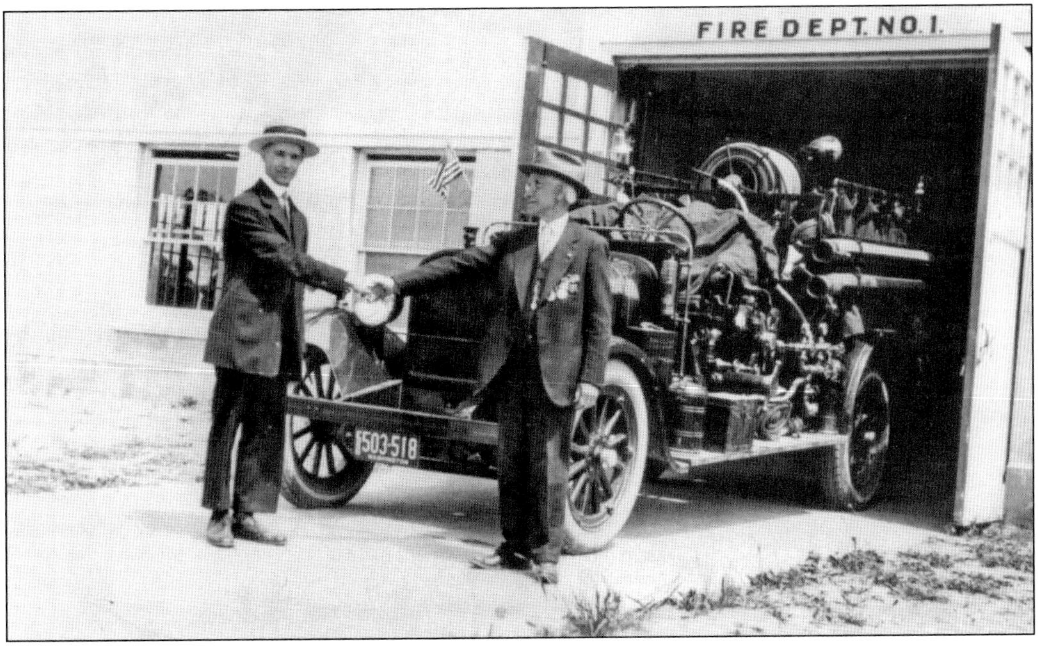

In the photograph above, fire chief Frank Hubbard (left) and Mayor Samuel "Dad" Roake (right) stand in front of the new, fully equipped fire truck and newly dedicated combined city hall and fire department building. Shown at right is fire chief Frank Hubbard modeling new protective gear for volunteer fire fighters. Hard hats with an elongated brim in the back were the newest design to protect firemen from burning embers or water falling down their collars. The waterproof coat was designed to provide some protection for fire fighters to keep them from getting soaking wet while operating or being in the way of the hoses.

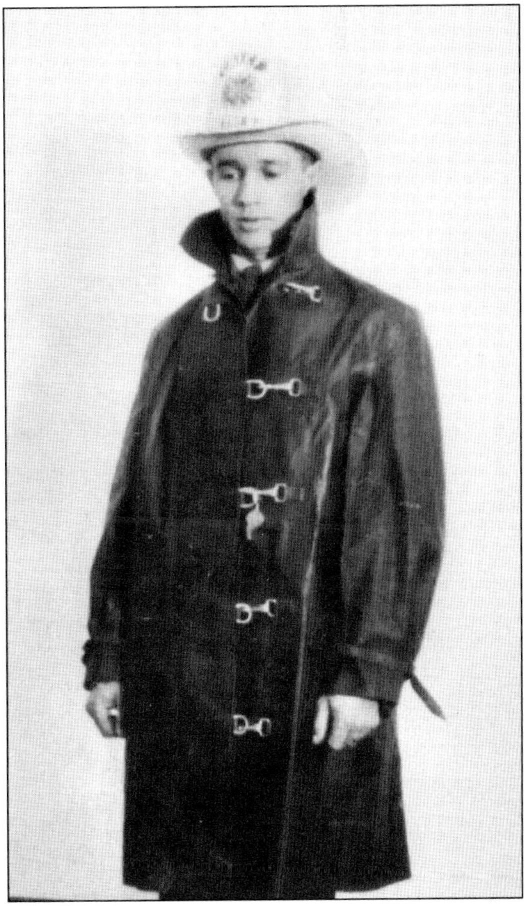

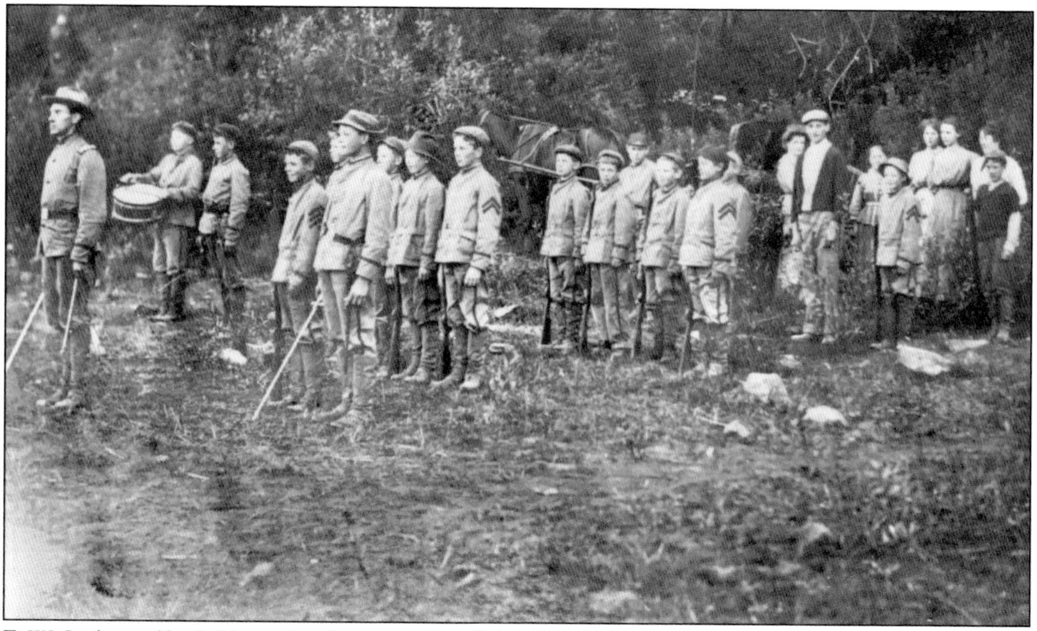

F. W. Jackson (far left), under the auspices of the Castle Rock Christian Church, was the leader of a Boy Scout troop in 1911. The Boys Scouts of America had just been incorporated in 1910, following the template of the Boys Scouts started in England about 1900 by Robert Baden-Powell. The idea had originally been to teach basic outdoor survival and first aid skills to boys as preparation for serving in the army because many soldiers of the time did not have these skills.

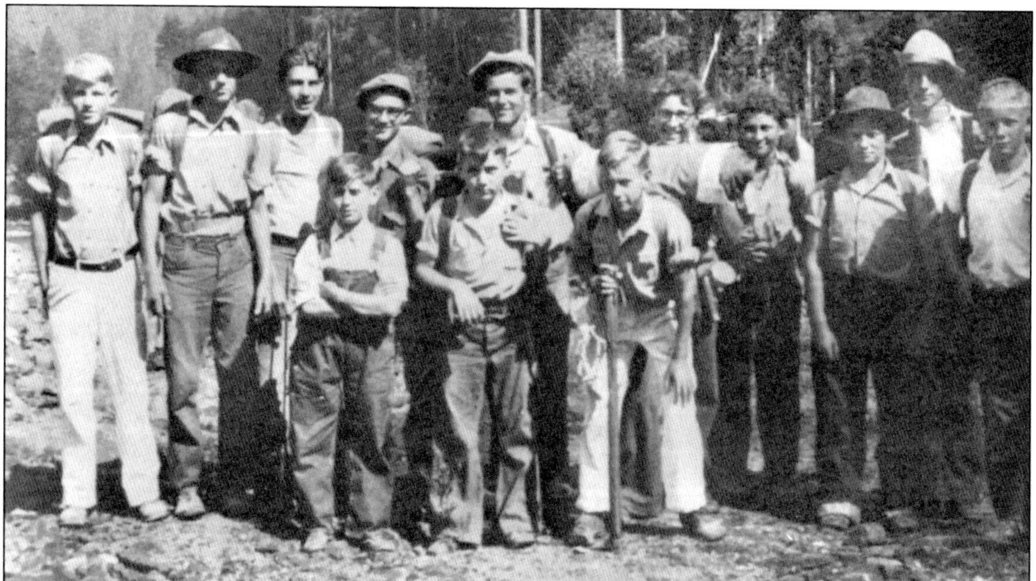

The Castle Rock Boy Scout troop in the 1930s posed before starting a hike. They are, from left to right, (first row) ? Chitester, ? Chitester, and unidentified; (second row) two unidentified, Wendell Dougherty, Jack Hubbard, Frank Hallet, four unidentified, and Glenn Hoyer. Frank Hallett went on to become a lawyer and FBI agent. He retired from the FBI to a private practice in Castle Rock, where he raised a family and contributed greatly to the community. Glenn Hoyer was a flyer in World War II and was killed in battle.

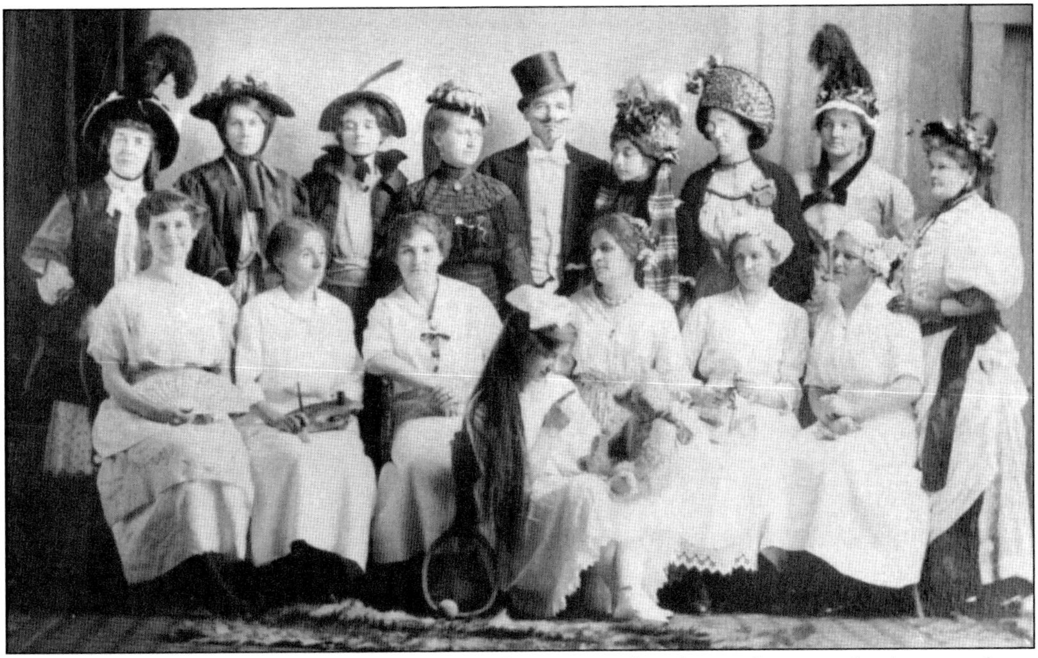

Local amateur actors put on a dramatic production in the above photograph. Among those pictured are, from left to right, (first row) unidentified; (second row) unidentified, Mrs. Willis Dykeman, Bertha Booth, and three unidentified; (third row) four unidentified, George Gaze, two unidentified, Maggie Dougherty, and unidentified.

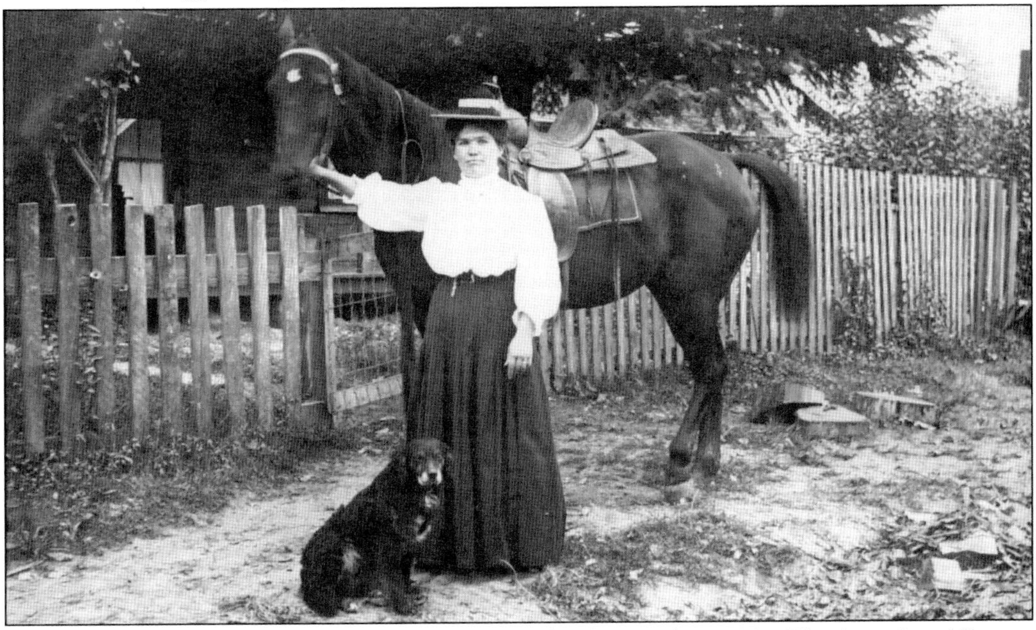

Bess Chism Price poses with a saddled horse and a dog in the 1900s. The horse's saddle is a high-cantled western style used by cowboys. If she is going to mount and ride the horse, she is not going to use the proper lady's style, sidesaddle. Young pioneer women often learned to ride astride out of necessity even before the acceptance of women's wearing trousers or bloomers. (Courtesy CCHM.)

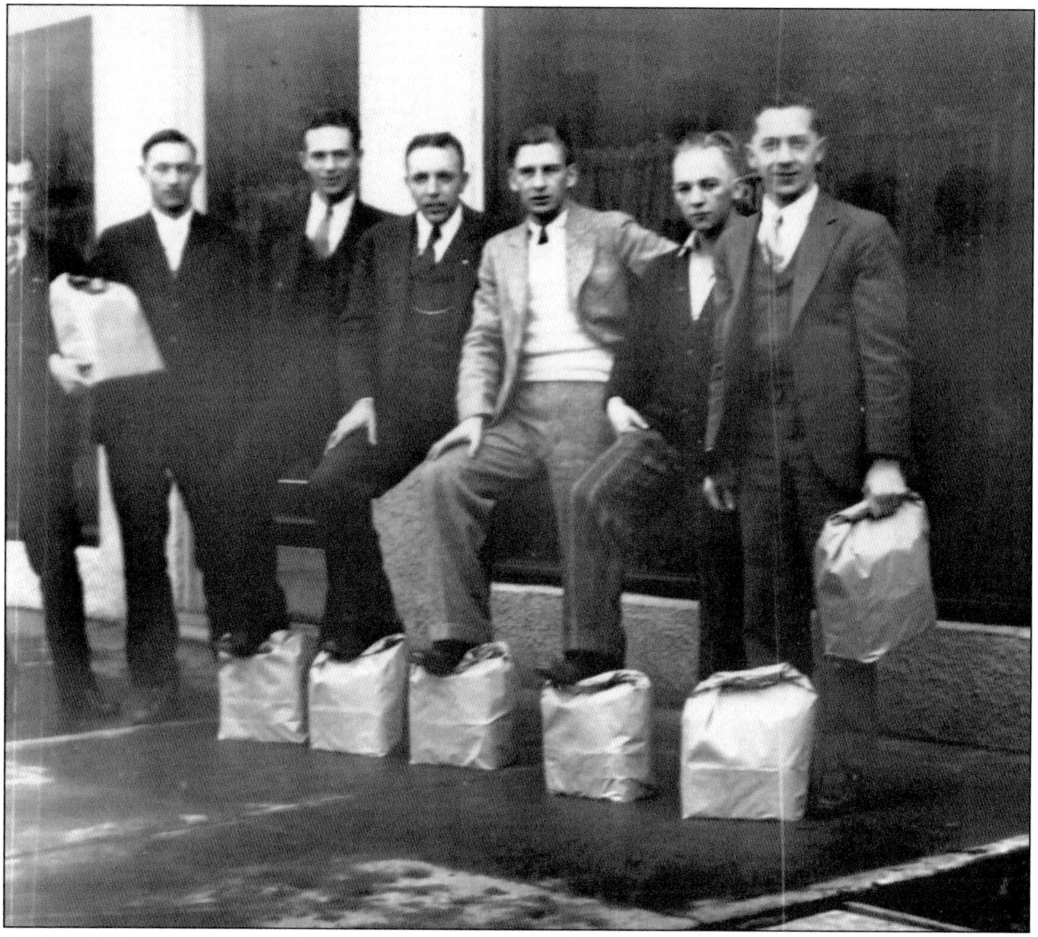

In the 1930s, members of the Castle Rock town basketball team are on their way to the state tournament. Team members are, from left to right, Keith Carnine, George Hall, Ted Perry, Ray Harris, Howard Hobson, L. Daggy, and Albert Ivie. The practice of the period was for each player to be sponsored by a local business. There is no record of which businesses sponsored these players. However, since they all have their things in paper grocery bags, it can be theorized that one or more of them was sponsored by the local Safeway store, as chain supermarkets were the first to put paper bags into widespread use.

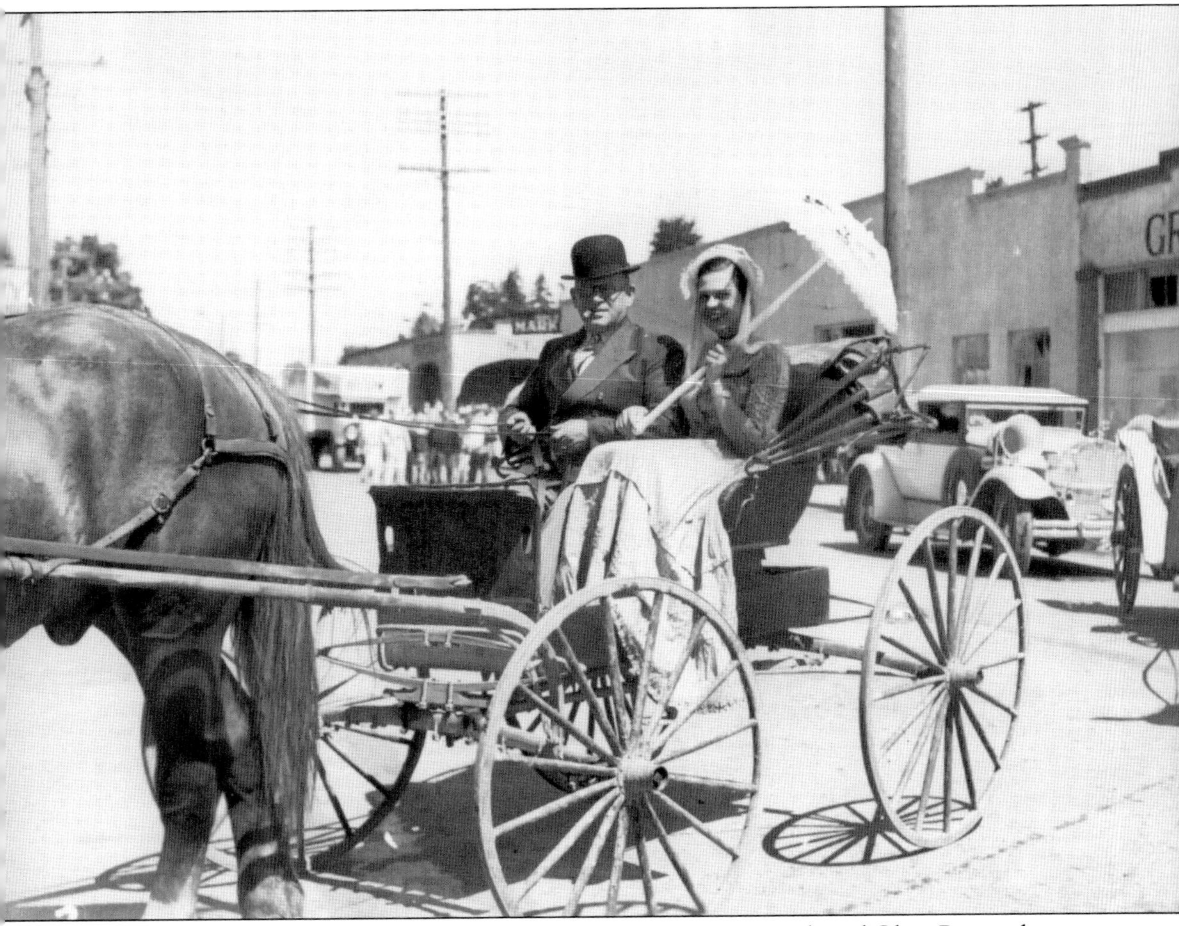

Participating in the 1936 community fair parade are Frank McCormick and Olive Pratt, who are shown in a horse-drawn buggy turning the corner from Front Avenue onto A Street. They are wearing old-fashioned costumes.

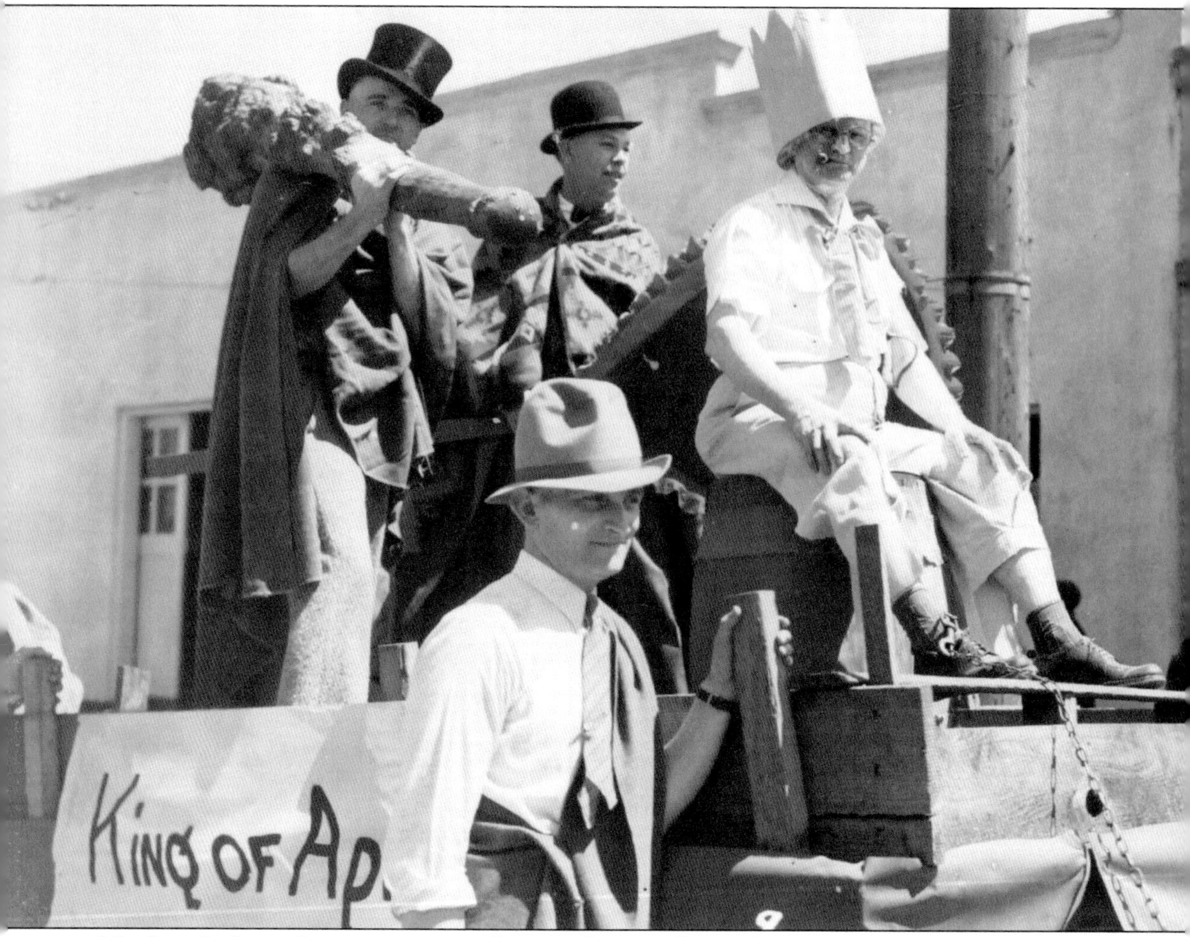

Unidentified parade participants in the 1936 fair parade are shown portraying the capture of the "King of the Apes." Locally, the legendary Bigfoot has long been called the Mount St. Helens Ape. Even before the advent of the white settlers, there were Native American legends telling of an ape-like creature in the mountains and forests of the Pacific Northwest. This legend was particularly strong around Mount St. Helens and Spirit Lake. In 1924, six miners reported that they were sleeping in a cabin on the lower slopes of Mount St. Helens when they were attacked by a group of huge, hairy creatures. They said the creatures came out of the night and hurled huge rocks and boulders down on the cabin. They managed to get out and hide until daylight, when they returned. Finding their rifles, they went after their attackers. They claimed to have shot one of the creatures, which rolled down into a steep canyon on the northeast side of the mountain. This place is still called Ape Canyon. The search party that went back from Longview and Kelso found no sign of the creature, but the cabin had been destroyed by boulders.

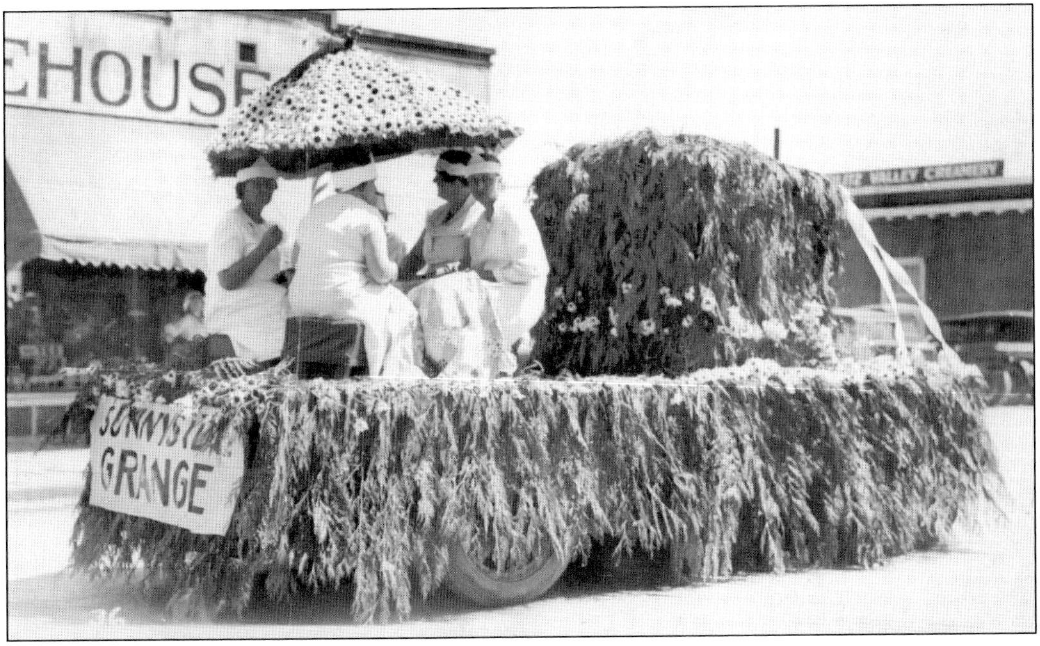

Shown above is the Sunnyside Grange float in the 1936 fair parade. The float is apparently a flatbed truck in disguise and holds five lovely ladies thoughtfully protected from the sun. The parade (shown below) began on Front Avenue with children in fanciful costumes. The marquis coming out over the sidewalk (center left) is the Castle Rock movie theater, an important business in town in 1936. Tents (far right) hold the exhibits and other parts of the fair, which was held on the vacant lots on the east side of Front Avenue until the fairgrounds were built in the 1950s.

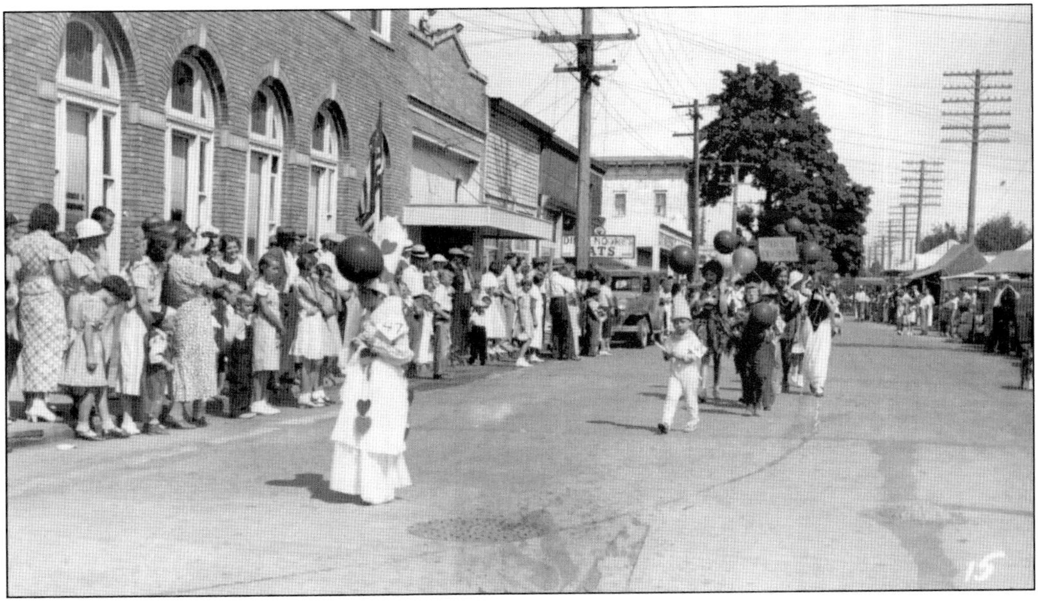

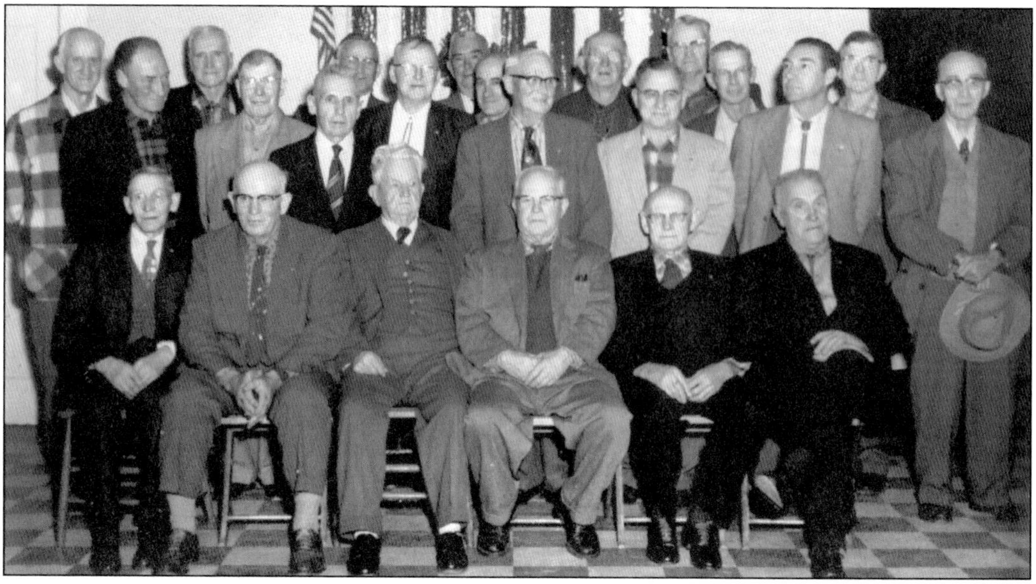

Lodges and other community service organizations have been active in Castle Rock since right after its founding. Shown above is a group of the Castle Rock chapter of the Fraternal Order of Eagles in the 1950s. Shown below is a group from the Masonic lodge in their regalia, also in the 1950s. From left to right, they are (first row) Herman Alexander, Albert Anderson, and "Cap" Anderson; (second row) Art Larson, Rev. Martin Skarbo, Alden Jones, and two unidentified; (third row) E. T. Cooney, ? Downey, and four unidentified. Both of these organizations have buildings in the downtown area and are still strong forces for good in the community today.

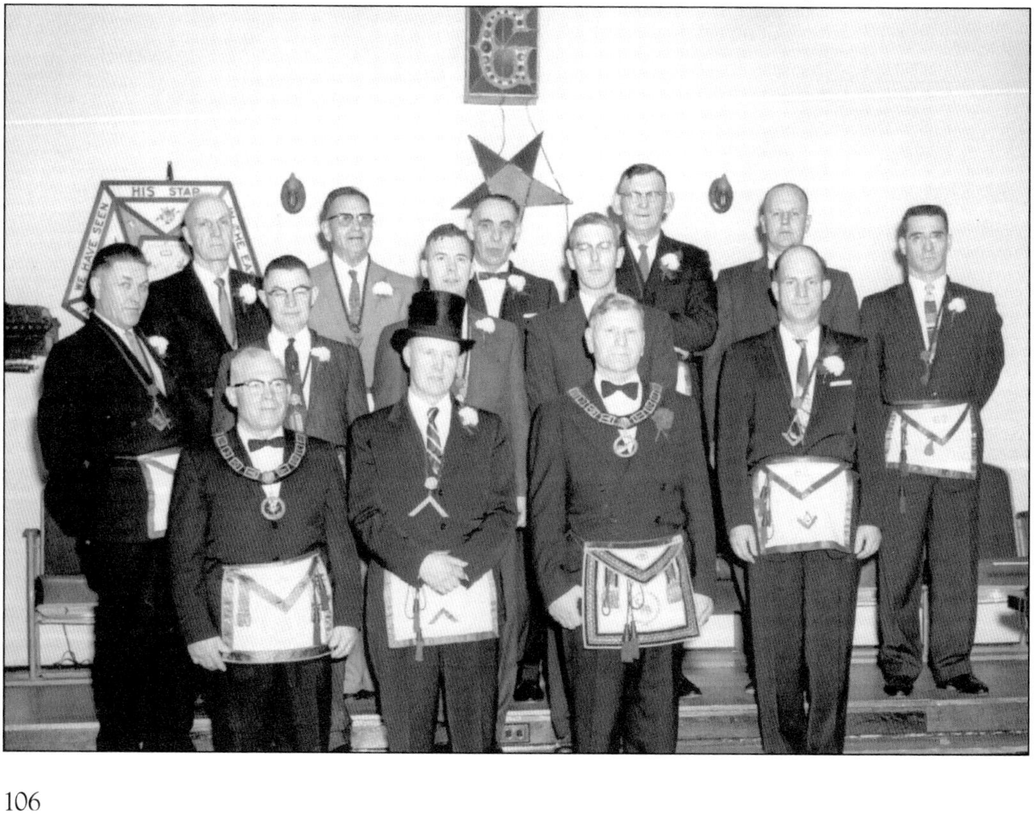

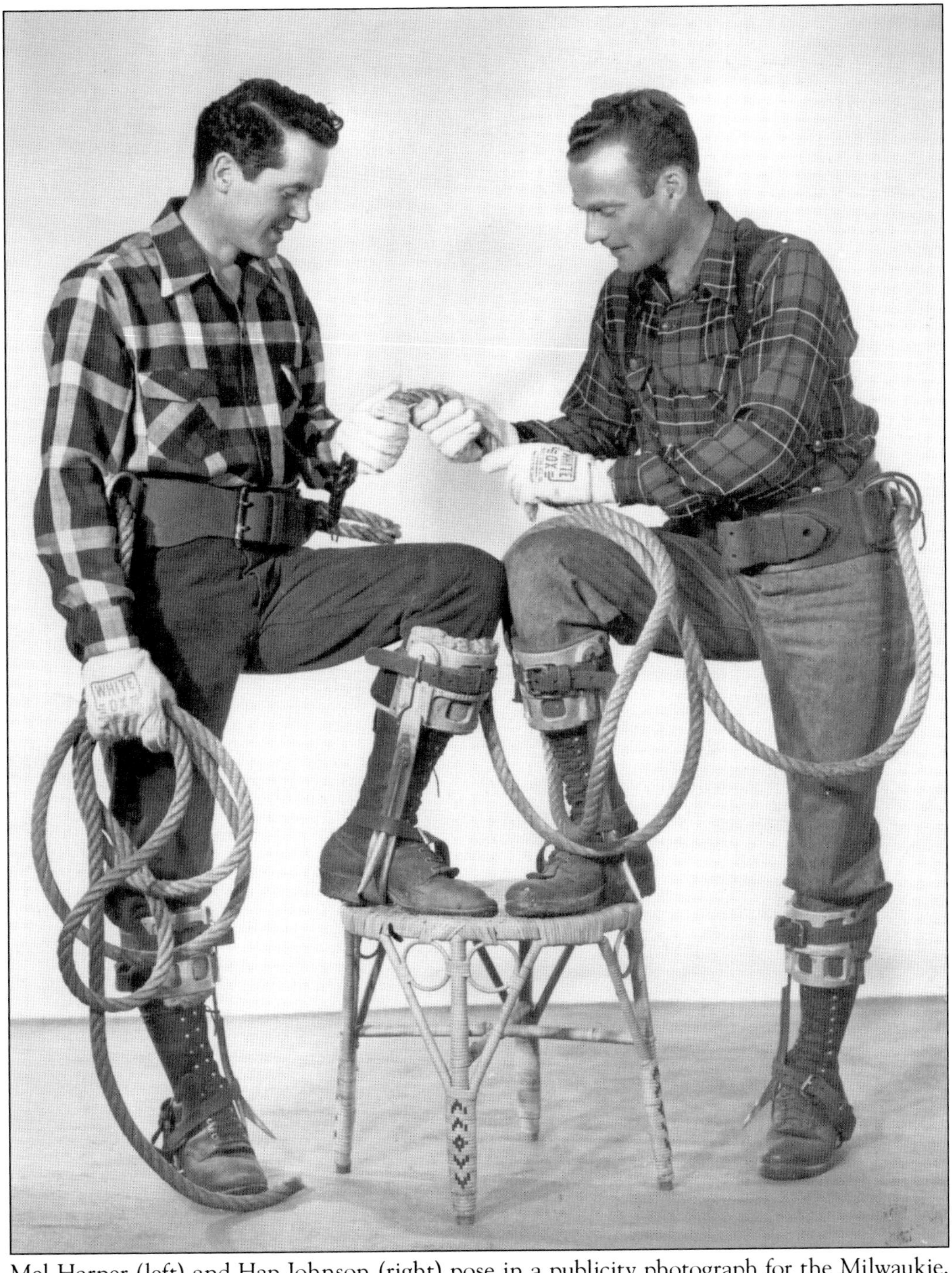

Mel Harper (left) and Hap Johnson (right) pose in a publicity photograph for the Milwaukie, Wisconsin, Central Sport Show in the 1950s. They are modeling the climbing gear worn in the speed climbing competitions in which they competed. Both men lived in Castle Rock. Hap Johnson was the World Champion Speed Climber multiple times.

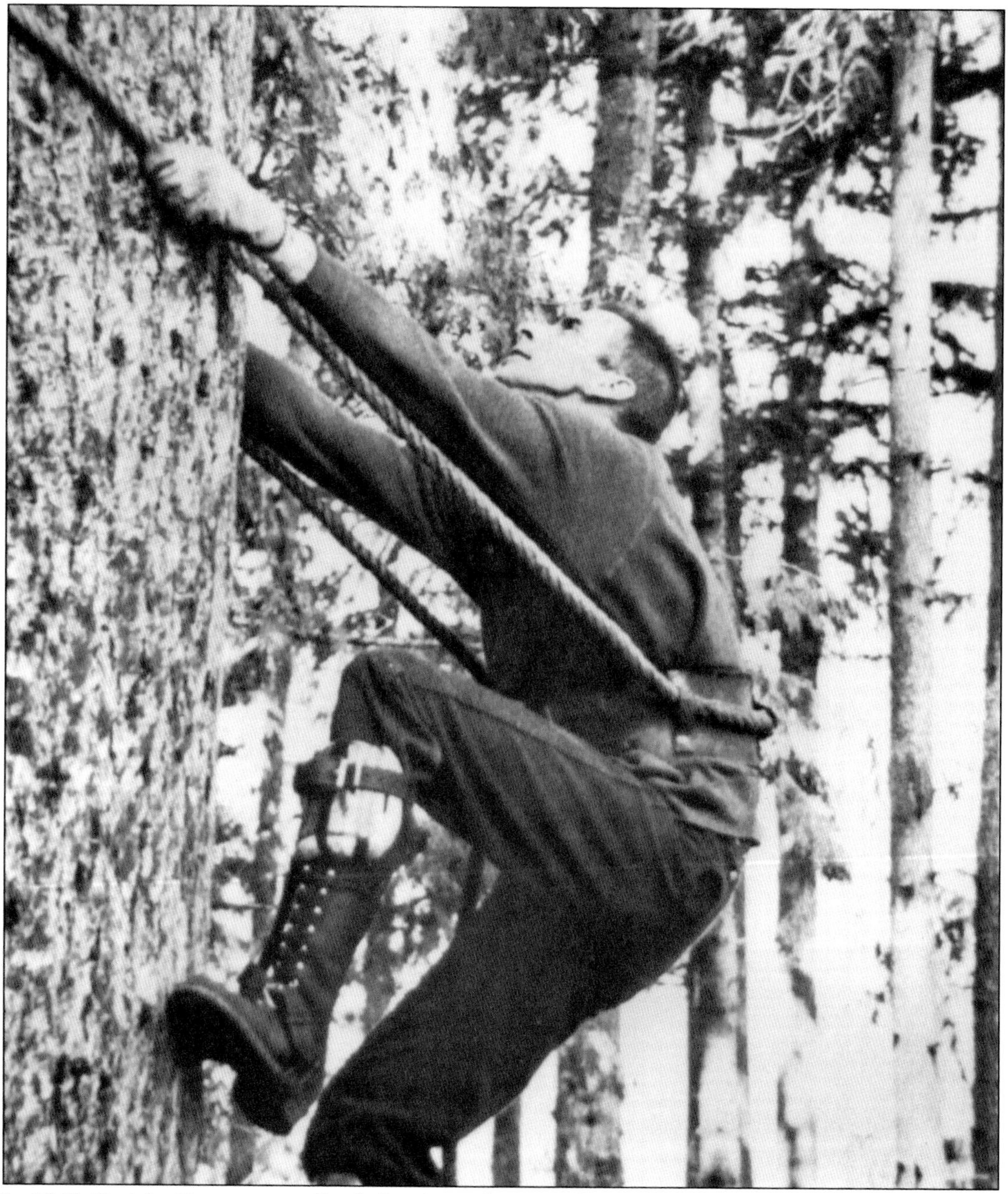

In 1967, Dwight Carpenter, a Castle Rock resident, readies to start a speed climb competition at the Longview Timber Carnival in Longview, Washington, 10 miles from Castle Rock. Carpenter was the defending first place speed climber and "All Around Logger" from 1966 at the Longview Timber Carnival. There is a story told that Carpenter was given a ticket for running a red light in Longview. He contested the ticket in court, saying that the light had turned yellow as he entered the intersection and he should have had five seconds before the light turned red. He contended that, being a speed climber, he could count seconds in his head and that the light did not stay yellow long enough. The judge, impressed by his statement, had a reconstruction of the event done at the light. It was discovered that Carpenter was right. The light did not stay yellow long enough for a driver to decided whether to stop or go on. His ticket was dropped.

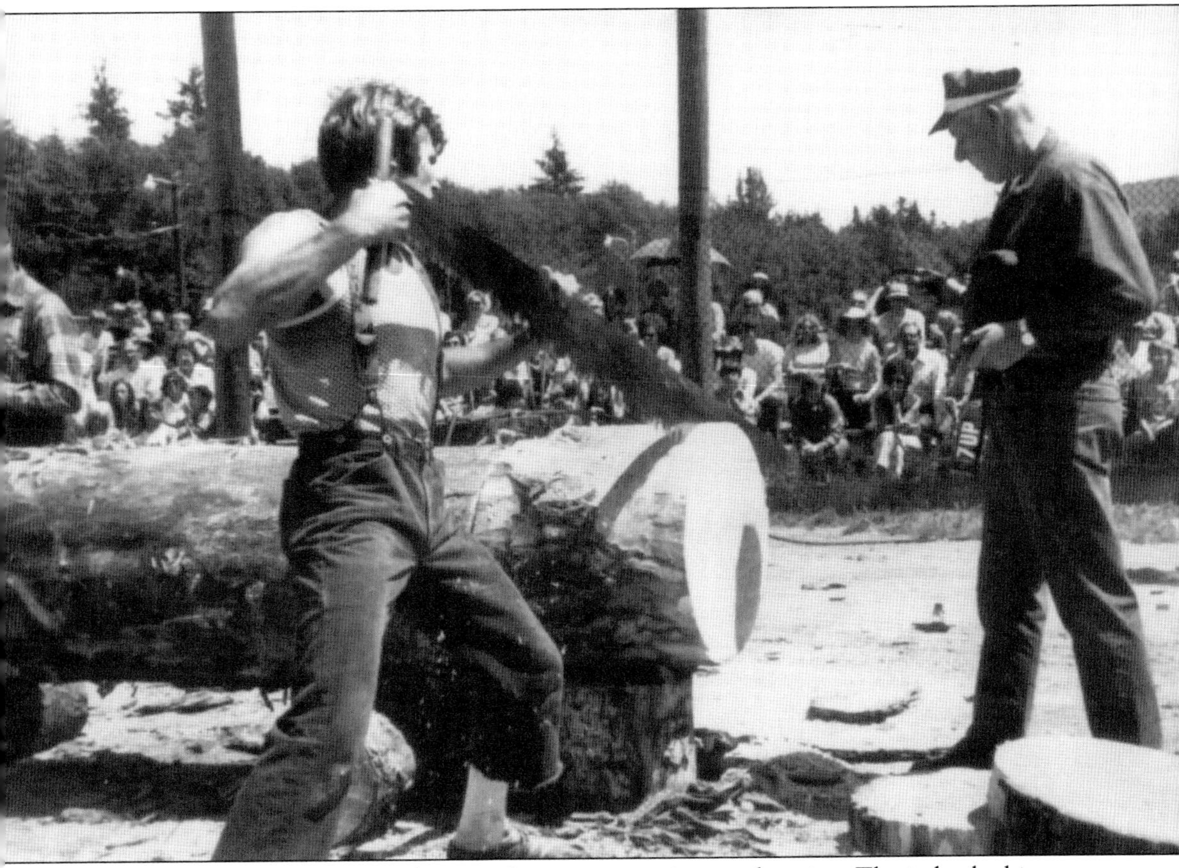

An unidentified competitor at a logging show competes in speed sawing. The judge looking on is also unidentified.

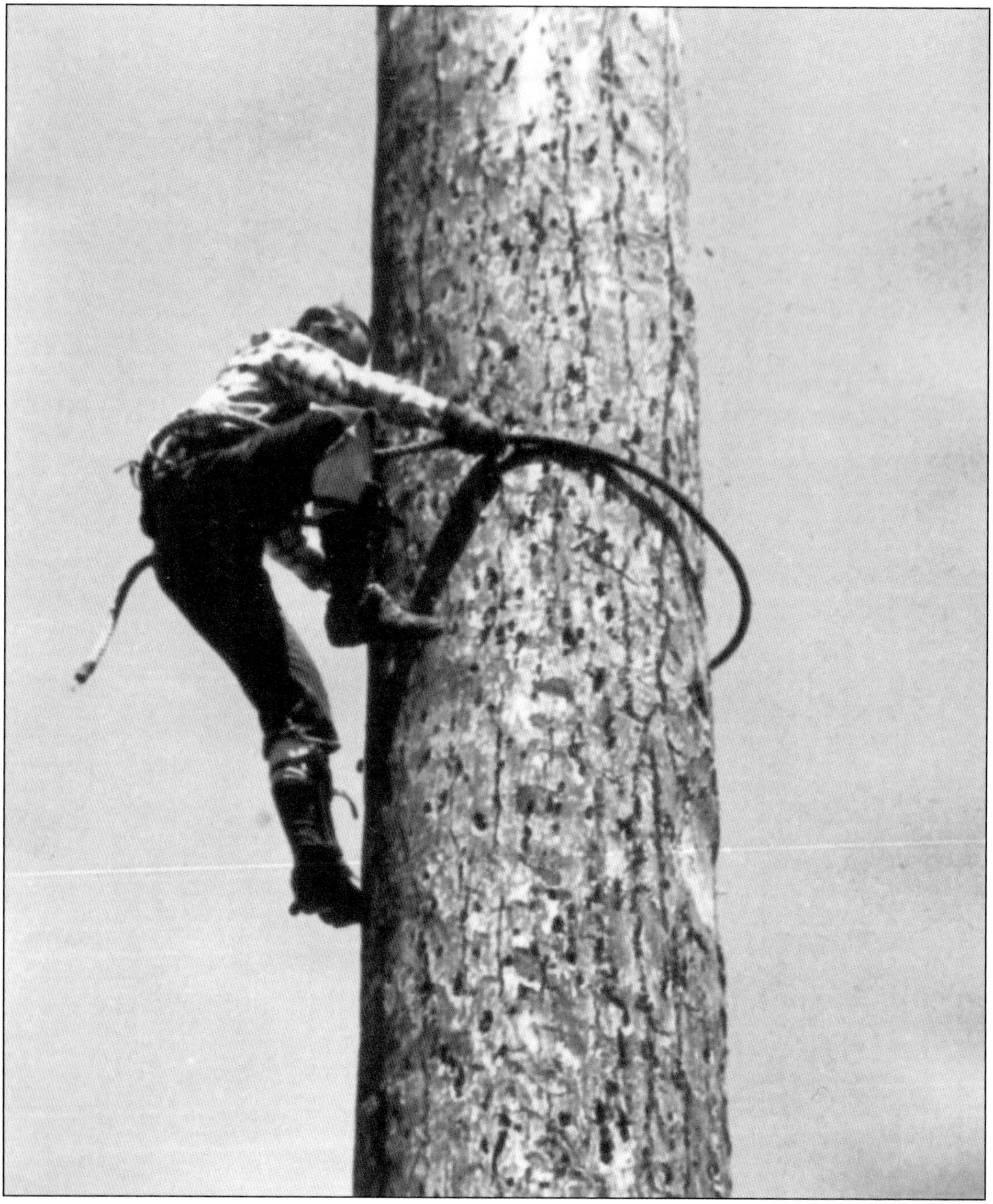

Ron Downing is speed climbing in a competition in the 1960s. Downing was also a champion speed climber for several years.

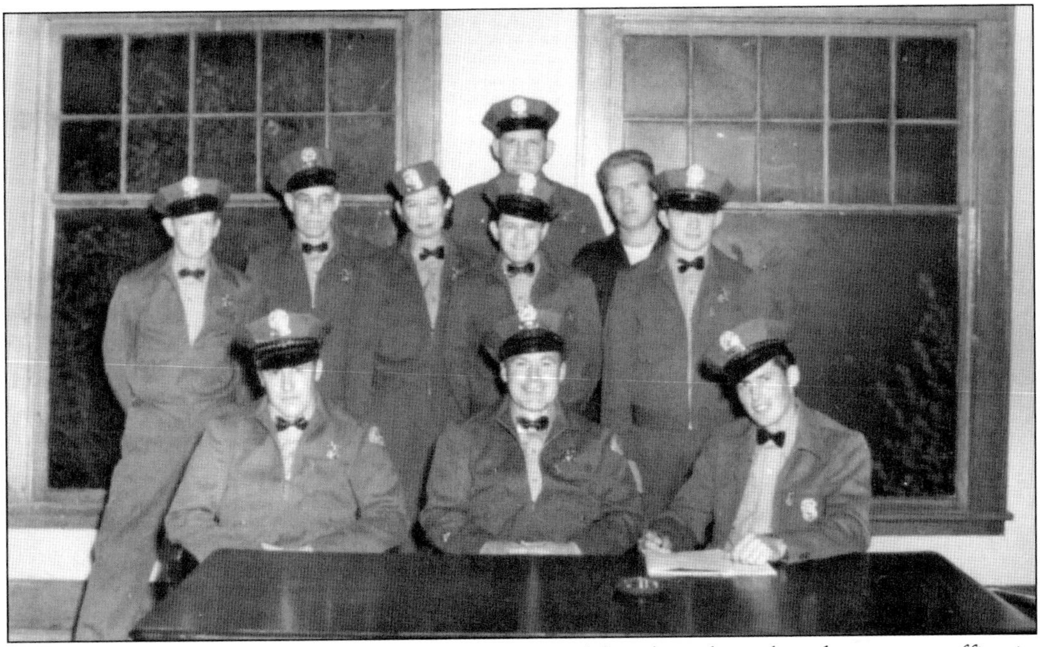

The Castle Rock Auxiliary Police in the 1950s pose (above) in the police department office in city hall. They are, from left to right, (first row) unidentified, Jay Van Tassel, and unidentified; (second row) unidentified, Denver Nazelrod, Roberta Lurene, and two unidentified; (third row) police chief George Eaton and an unidentified man. Lurene later became the city's justice of the peace. The city jail (below) still exists on Jackson Street NW. The jail was built by Albert Rosin and was constructed of concrete. The building is 12 feet by 24 feet. The walls, floor, and even the roof are made of concrete. There are four barred windows near the roof about 9 inches high and 12 inches wide. The door is a solid slab of steel. No one ever escaped from this jail in its many years of use. It is now a historical exhibit for visitors.

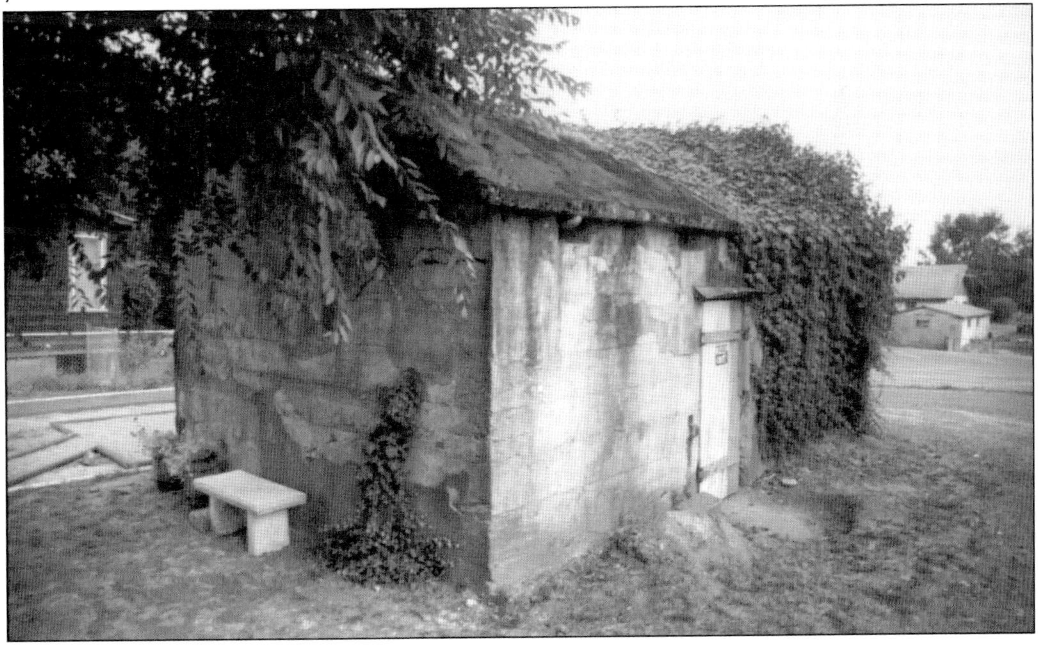

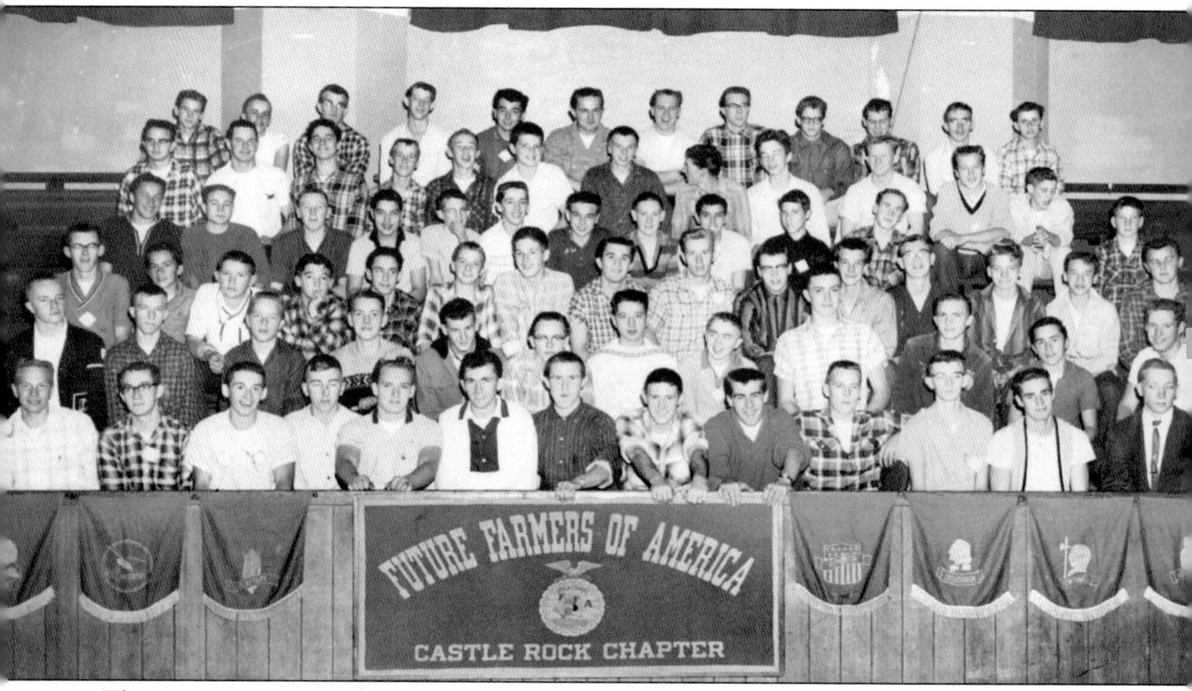

These young men are the 1959–1960 school year members of the Future Farmers of America club at Castle Rock High School. A vital part of the community in the middle decades of the 20th century, the Future Farmers of America did many projects outside of class time. They used a tractor and plow purchased with money they had raised to hire out to plow fields and gardens for residents of the community. They charged a reasonable fee for this service, raising money to maintain their equipment and fund other agriculture-related educational projects.

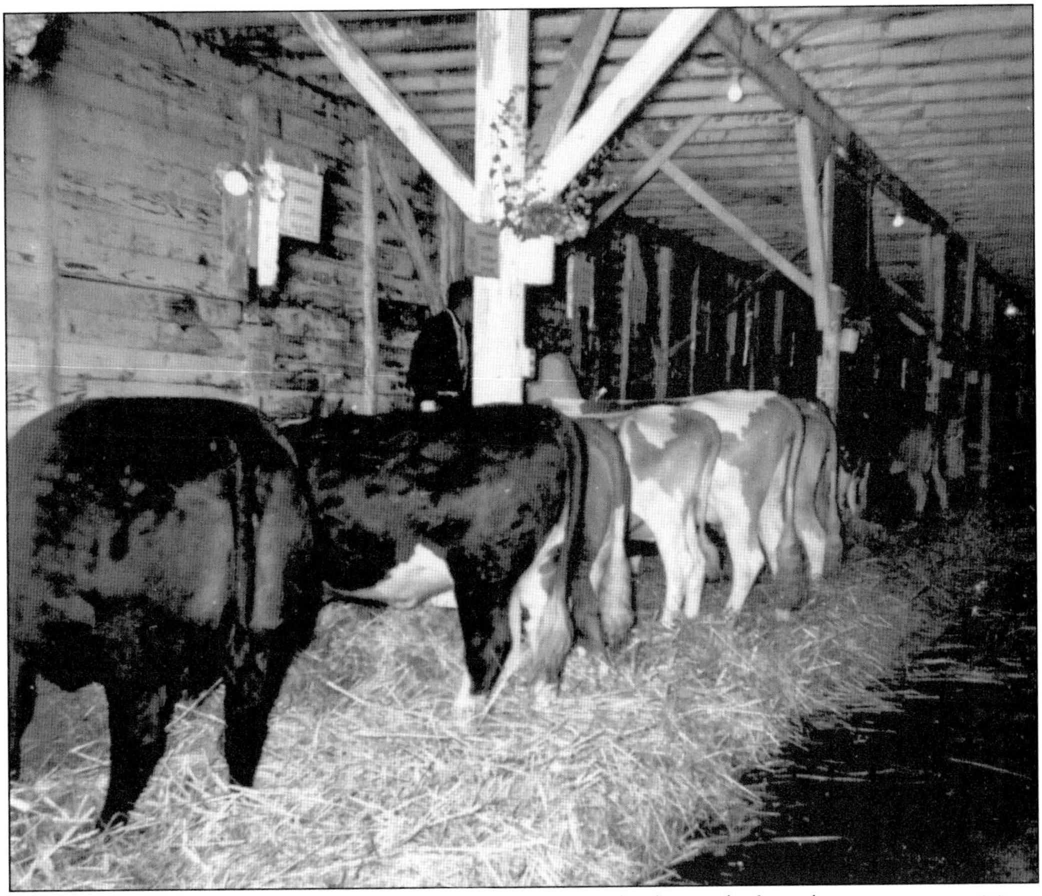

Future Farmers of America members' cattle are resting on display in the barn between competitions at the Columbia Empire Fair (Cowlitz County) in August 1960. Future Farmers of America participants from Castle Rock earned many ribbons for their livestock that year and in other years. The club members raised and showed purebred livestock while learning about breeding and caring for their animals. This increased their skills as possible future farmers and helped improve the quality of blood lines of the animals they raised and bred.

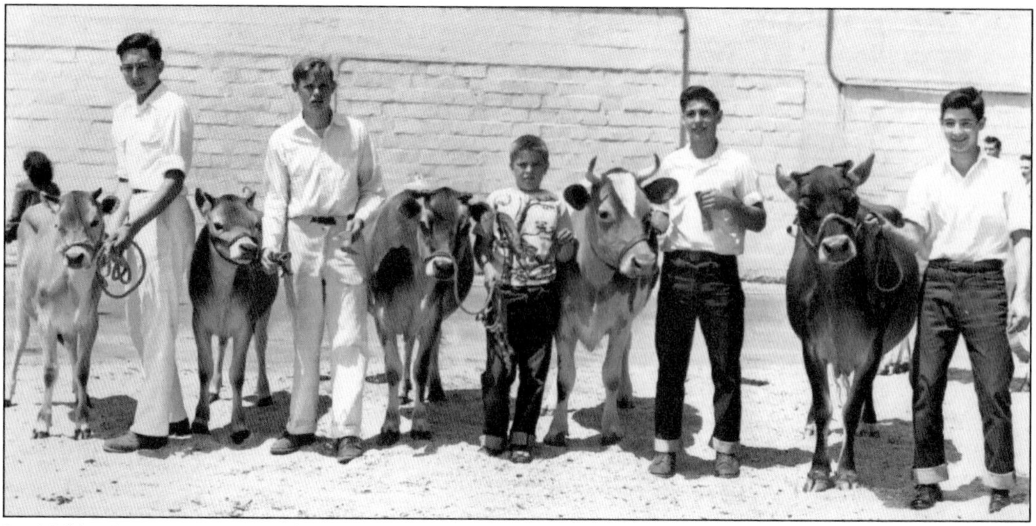

In 1950, the winners are shown in the Future Farmers of America Foundation project show (above) in Longview, Washington. They are, from left to right, Roger Gardner with his heifer, for which he won first place in Judging and fifth place in Fitting and Showing; Floyd Hadderly with his Jersey heifer, for which he won first place for breed and sixth place in Fitting and Showing; Keith Titus is holding Melvin Kayser's Jersey heifer, a third place winner; Butch Rebelin with his Guernsey cow, who won her breed class and came fifth in Fitting and Showing; and Melvin Kayser Jr., with his Jersey cow, for which he won first place in the breed category, first place in Jersey Judging, and third place in Fitting and Showing. Forty head of cattle were in the award show, which was sponsored by the Sears Foundation. Shown below is Dick Moore in March 1960 with his Holstein heifer dairy project for Future Farmers of America.

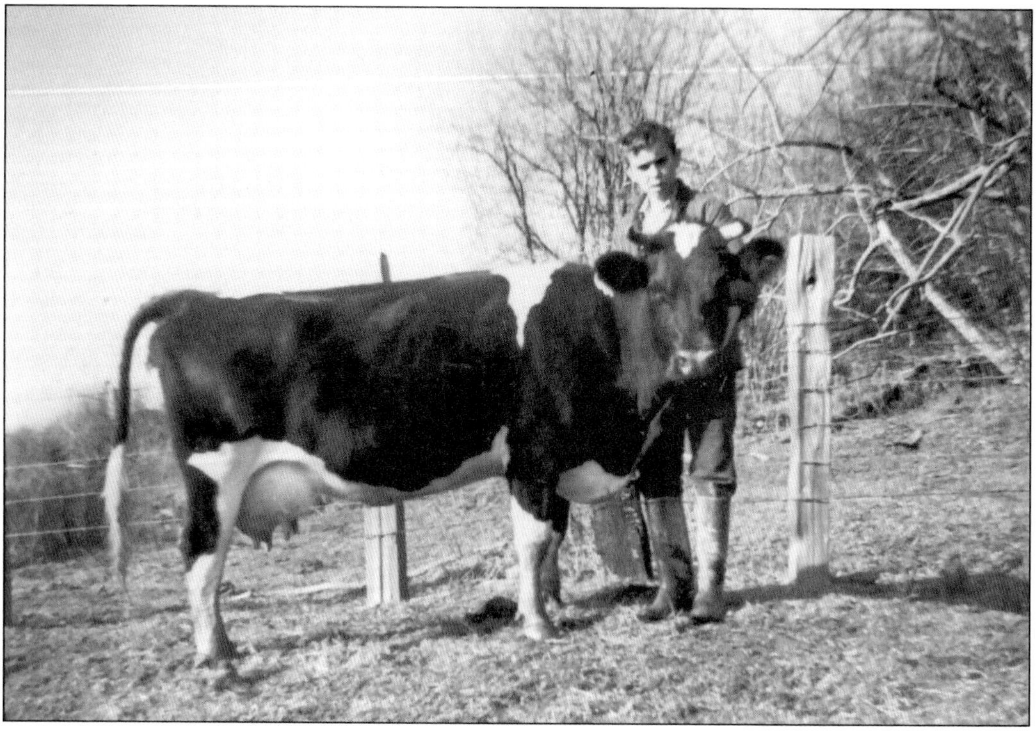

Five

Surviving Disaster

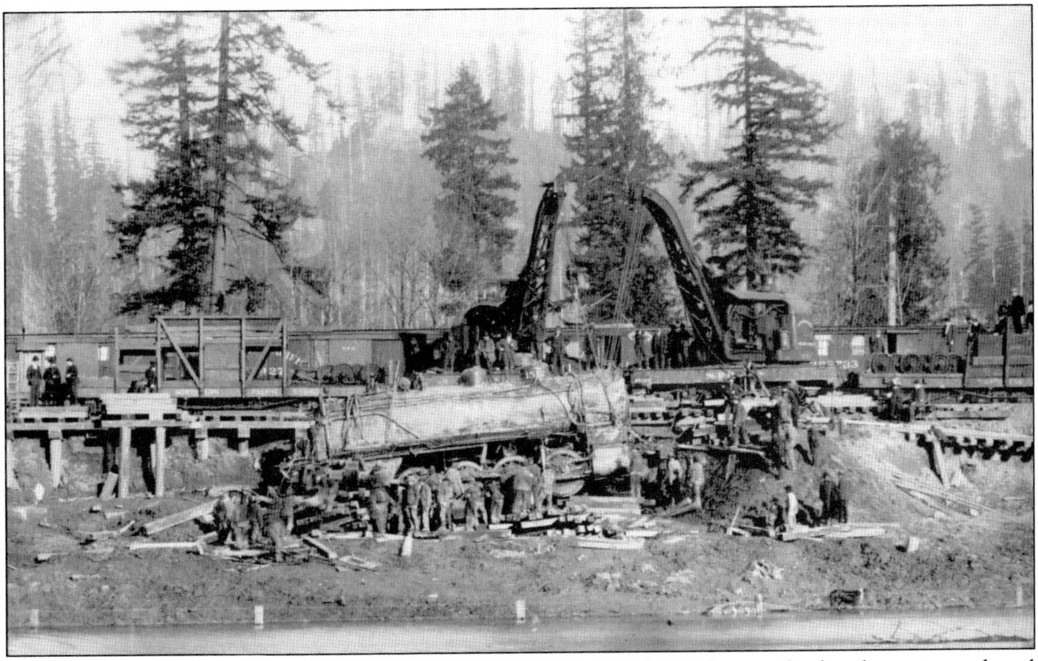

In 1910, the newly built railway roadbed sank under the tracks and caused a freight train to derail near town. The fireman on the train was killed in the wreck. Many men died in construction and train accidents in the early days of the railroads. When the tracks ran next to the downtown business area, a woman was killed by being hit by a train.

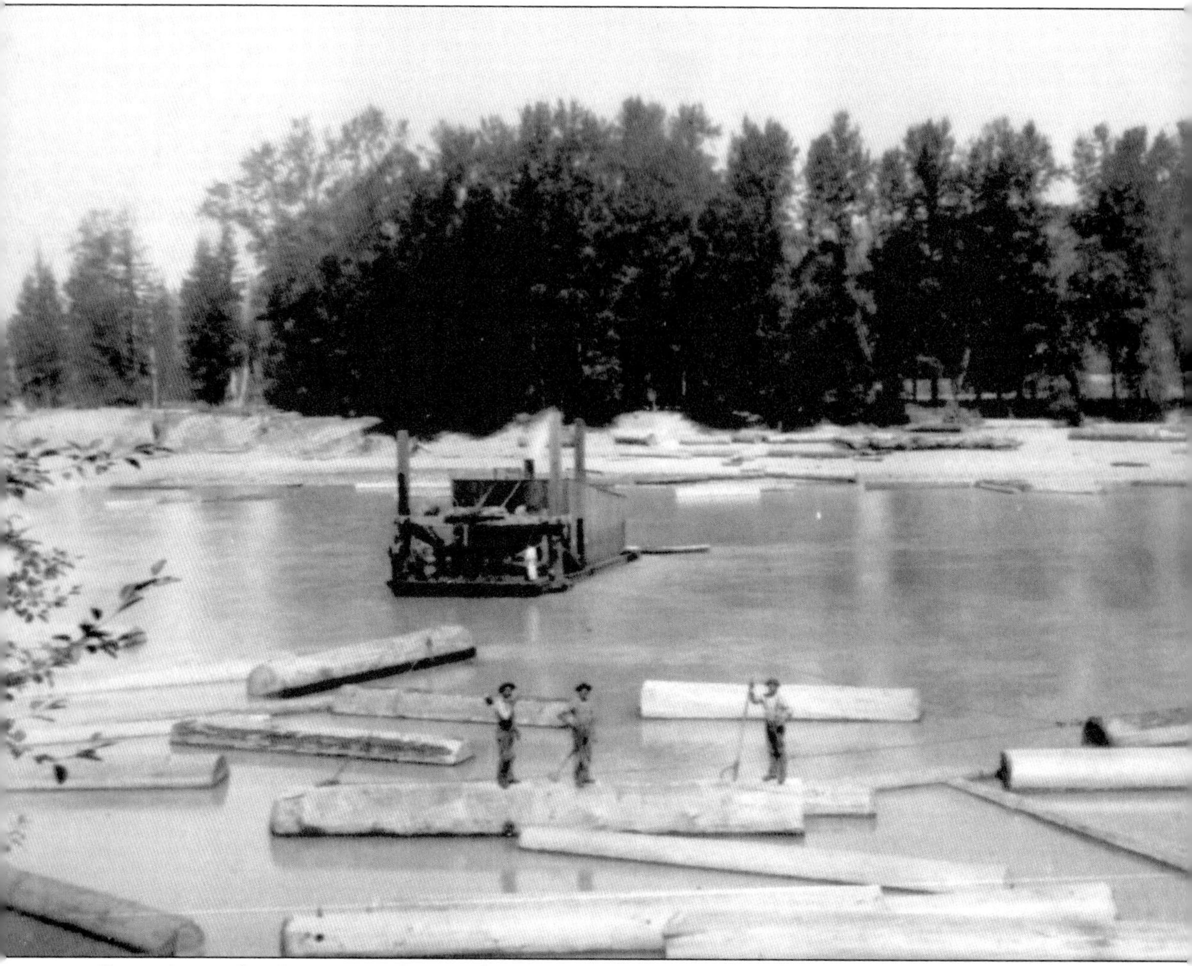

Being located right next to the Cowlitz River, Castle Rock was plagued by a series of floods. The first mentioned in historical writings was in 1894, but no photographs have been found of that flood. These men are salvaging logs and timber that were washed into the river or that have escaped from log rafts in the flood of 1906. The logging companies would either float logs down the creeks and into the river or bring them in by horse and wagon. They would collect the logs in floating groups called rafts, which were contained by chains. In time, ways of holding the log rafts together were developed so they could be towed down the river, into the Columbia River, out into the ocean, and down the coast to the booming cities of California in need of building materials. In the case of a flood, the chains could not hold against the force of the water. In the background, logs can be seen on the riverbank. These would have to be pushed back into the water and recollected in the rafts.

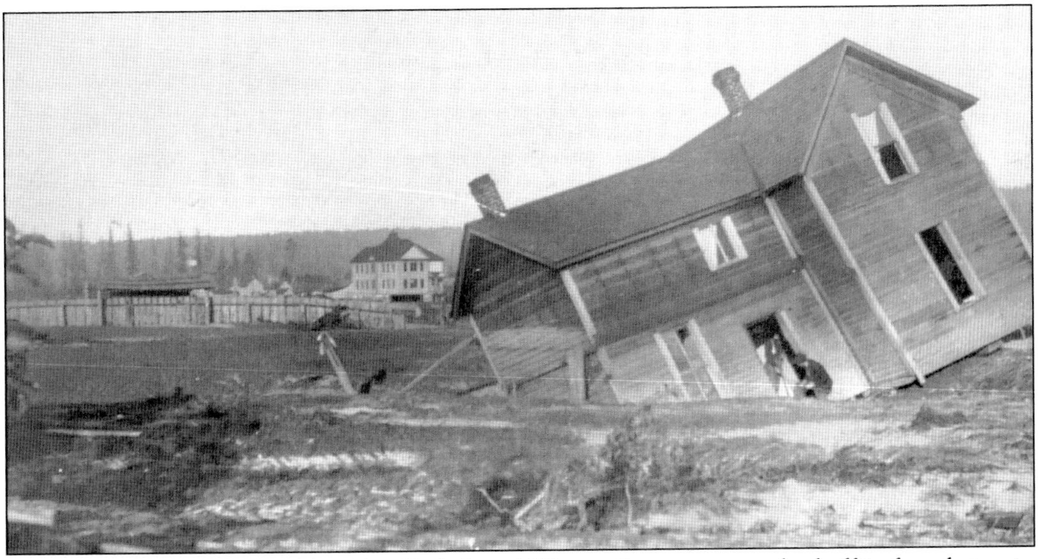

The Henry Johnson home (above) at Eighth and Warren Streets was washed off its foundation in the 1906 flood. Left tipped up in mud after the water receded, some of the contents were able to be salvaged. Many houses were washed away completely, and the river actually changed its course permanently. Some areas where houses had been were now under water and new land, which had been in the river, was now part of the town. The water reached halfway up the first story on the school buildings (below) in the 1933 flood. Again, the river changed its course slightly, and many people moved to land on one of the hills inside of or surrounding the town, such as the Heights, Jim Town, and the Buland neighborhood. These areas became the most valuable building sites until the dike was constructed.

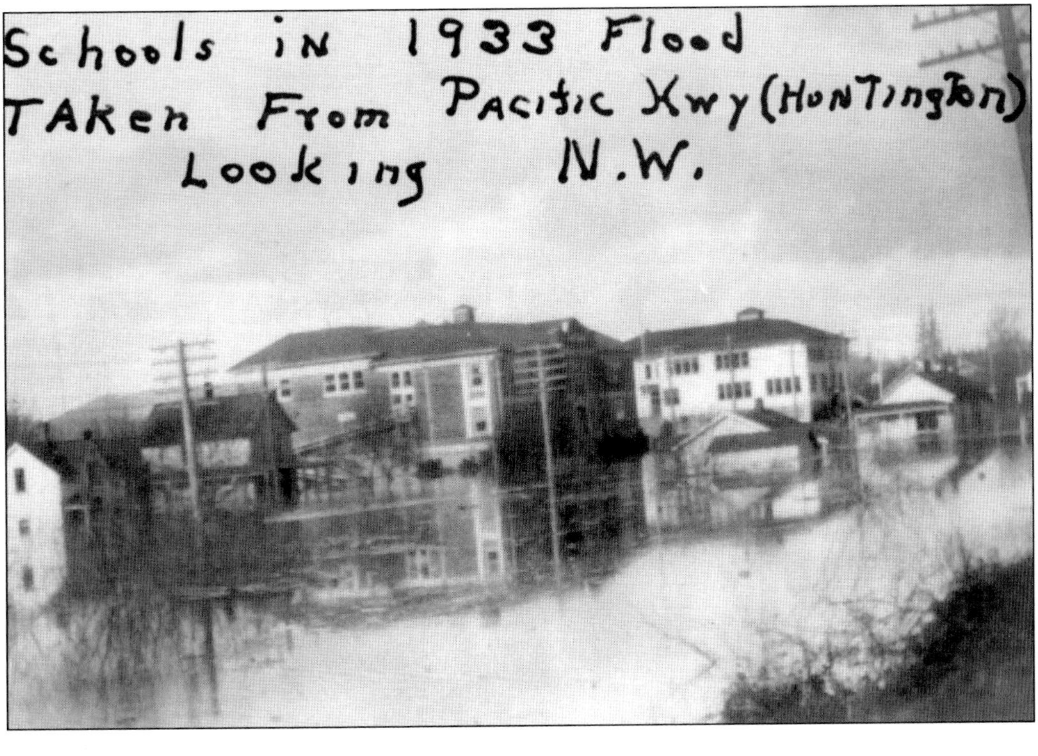

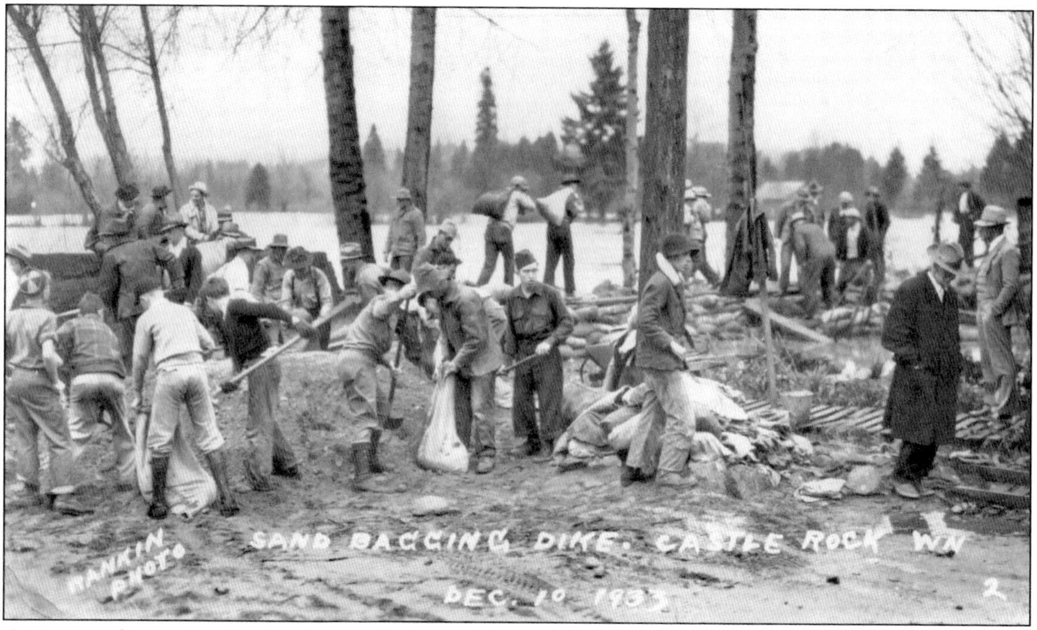

On December 10, 1933, the Cowlitz River was rising, and the people of the town banded together to fight the water. They filled sandbags and tried to construct an emergency barrier against the rising river. In the end, they were defeated. Many of the residential areas in the bend of the river were inundated, and many homes were lost. (Courtesy CCHM.)

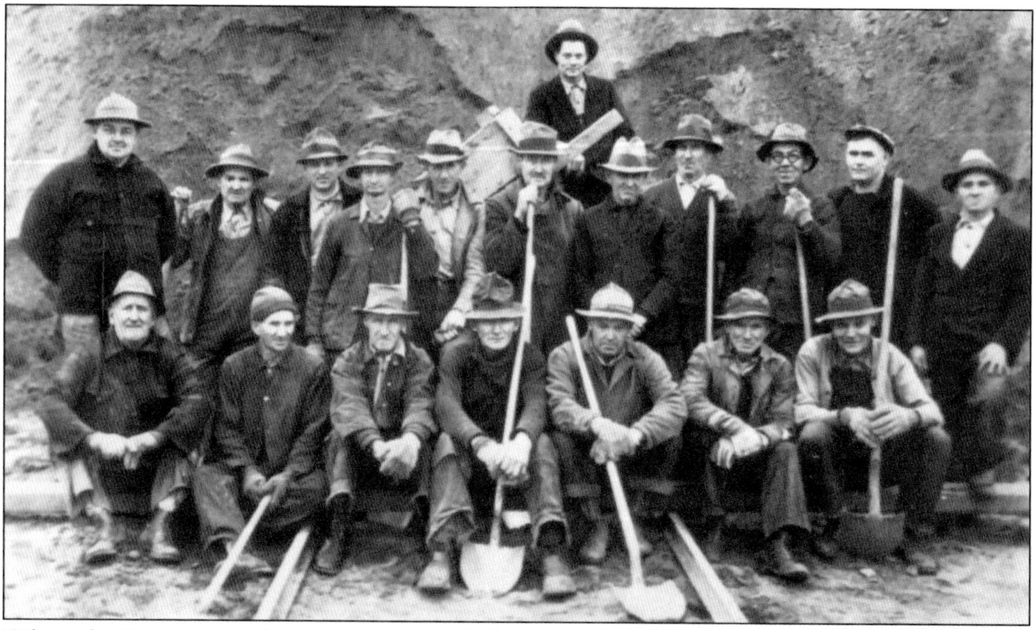

When the Roosevelt Administration decided that one of the ways to combat unemployment was to inject money into the economy during the Great Depression of the 1930s, it formed the Works Project Administration. One of the many projects funded by that department of the federal government was the construction of a dike on the Cowlitz River to protect the low-lying main part of town from future high-water events. This crew is building the dike on the Cowlitz River in 1936.

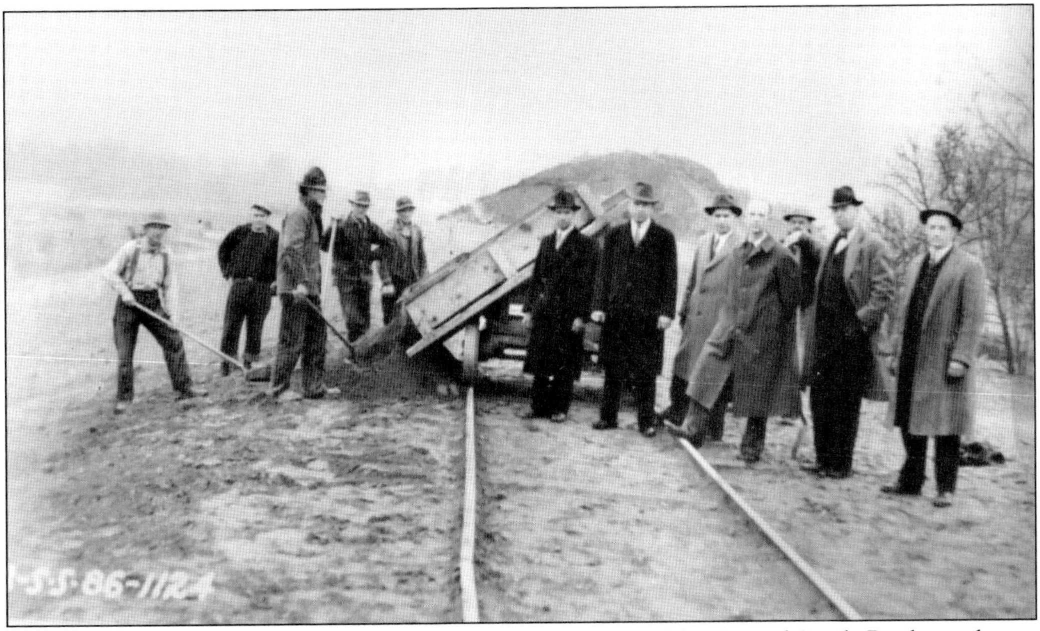

On March 10, 1936, members of the sponsoring committee of the City of Castle Rock are shown with part of the construction crew working on the Castle Rock dike under the auspices of the U.S. government Works Progress Administration. The committee members are the gentlemen in overcoats, suits, and ties. They are, from left to right, Frank Hubbard, William Graham, Dr. ? Windham, Everett Powellson, A. V. Peterson, and Clarence Dougherty.

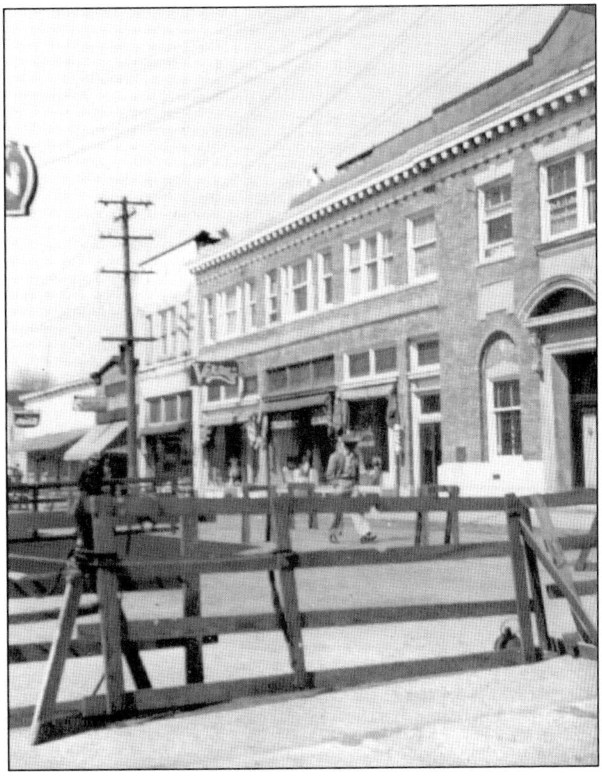

On April 18, 1949, barriers kept the unwary motorist from hitting open cracks in the pavement on Cowlitz Street after the huge earthquake. At noon on April 13, 1949, the earth all over southwest Washington heaved and bucked. The earthquake measured 7.1 on the Richter scale, and the epicenter was between Olympia and Centralia, but the only death that day occurred at Castle Rock. As the frightened students were rushing out of the old Castle Rock High School, a brick was dislodged from above the door. It hit Jack Roller, a senior and the student body president, who was killed instantly.

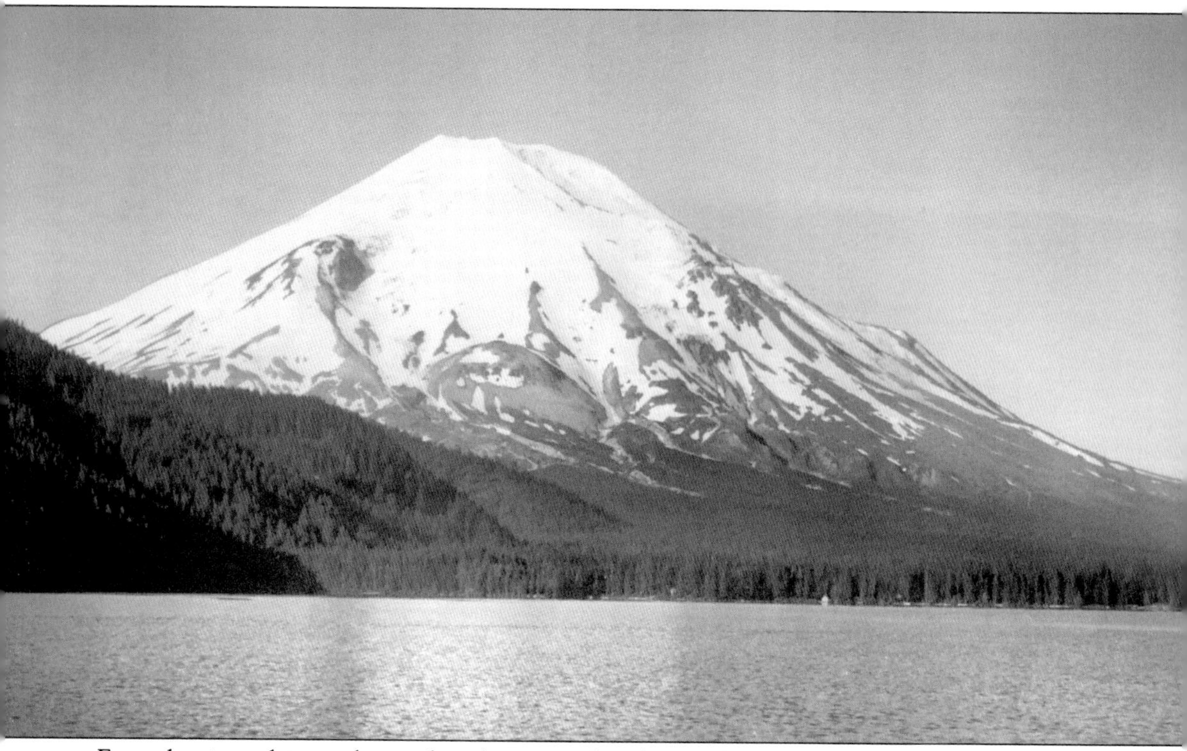

From the time white traders and settlers arrived in the Pacific Northwest, it appeared that Mount St. Helens was a beautiful, serene mountain. There were stories told by the Native Americans of the mountain spewing fire, but the people who chose to settle here assumed these were stories of long ago, possibly embellished over time. Scientists who came to study Mount St. Helens realized there was a possibility the volcano could awaken. By the 1970s, even though there were still glaciers on the peak, the timberline was moving higher up the mountain's sides. This indicated to volcanologists that the mountain was warming and allowing trees to survive at higher elevations. It appeared likely that magma was moving in the no-longer-dormant lava tubes inside the mountain itself. Some volcanologists felt that the volcano would erupt before the year 2000.

Before 1980, Spirit Lake lay in splendor at the foot of Mount St. Helens. Many legends surrounded the lake among both the Native Americans and the whites. Though it was the source of one part of the Toutle River, no one knew where the water to fill the lake came from. Early settlers told a story of a team of horses harnessed to a wagon that were swept away in either the Lewis River or the Kalama River, depending on the version of the story, and found floating in Spirit Lake. No one knew how deep the lake was. Scientists even used sonar to try to locate the bottom, but no instruments gave satisfactory results. Some of these mysteries would probably have been solved if it had not been for the awakening of the volcano sleeping next to the lake.

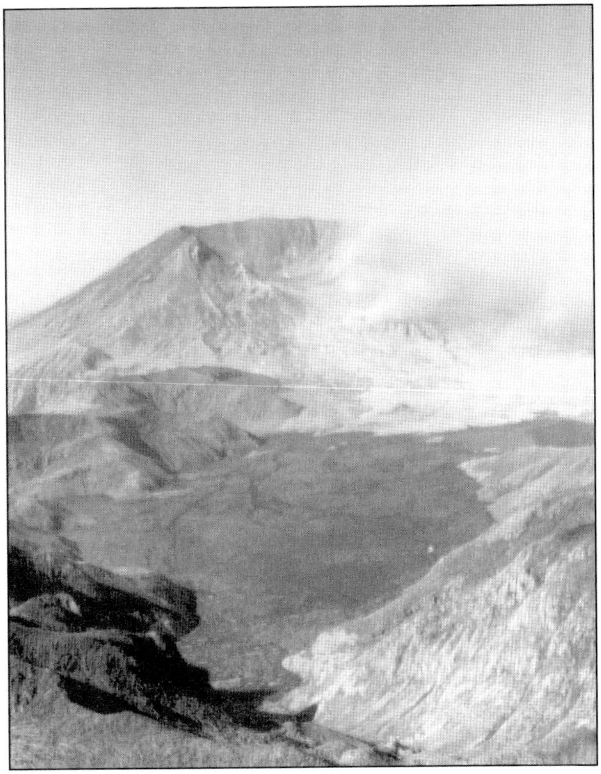

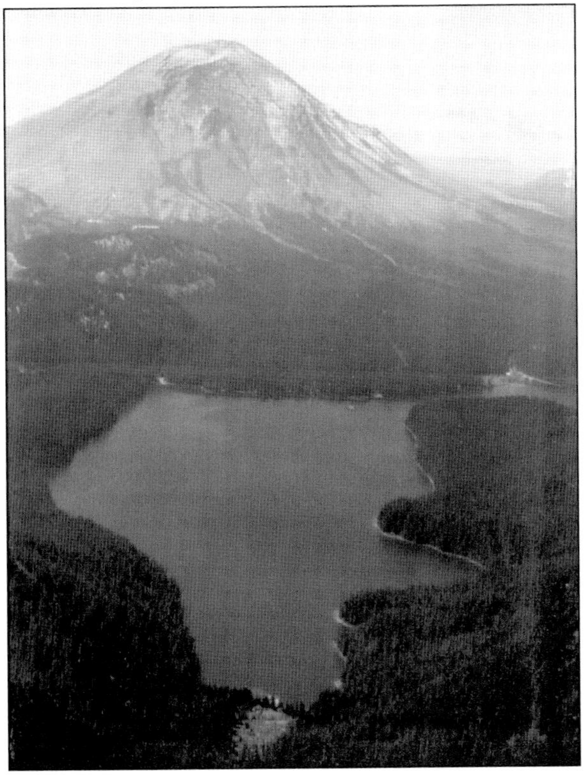

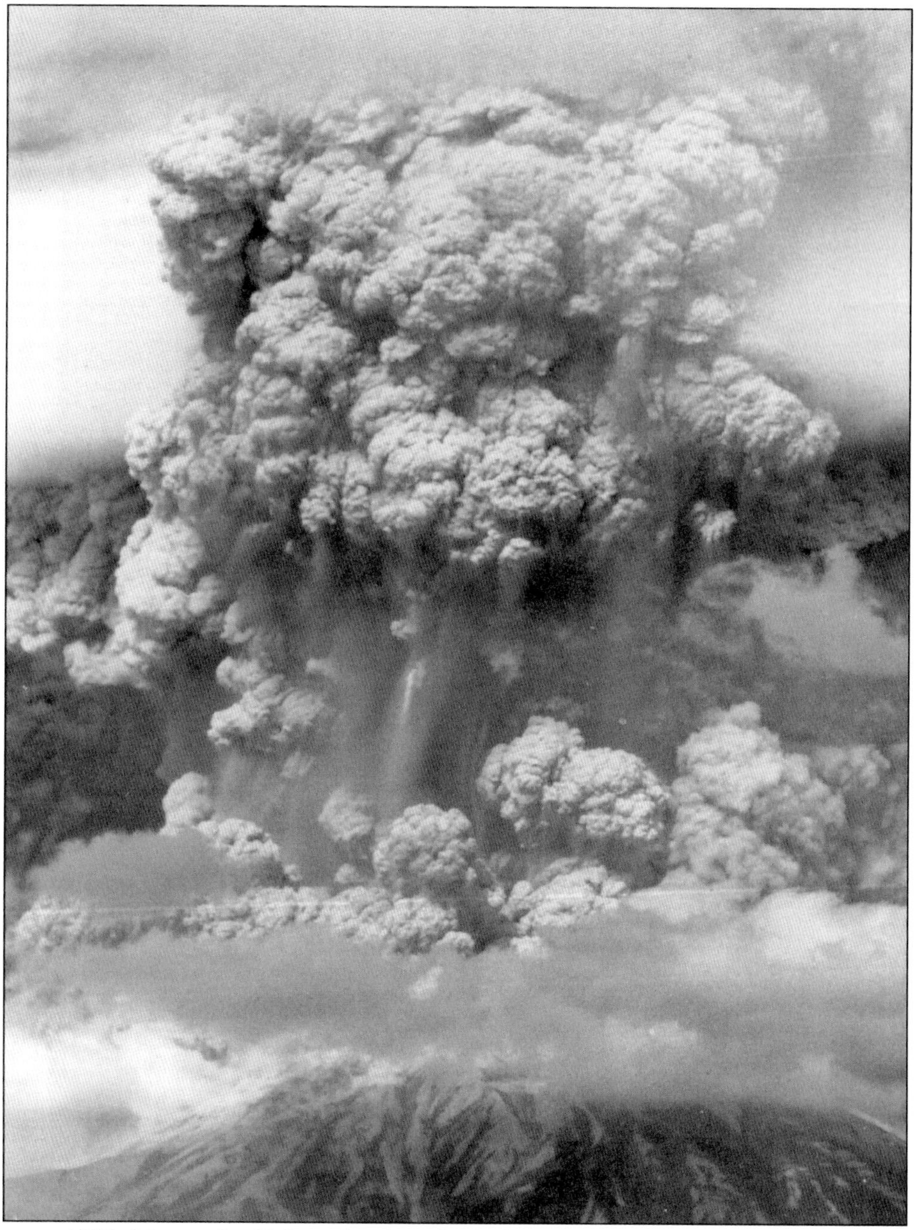

In January 1980, Mount St. Helens developed a bulge on the northwest side of the peak. On March 20, the first seismic activity was detected under the mountain. By March 27, plumes of steam and ash were venting out of fissures in the crust of the volcano. The sequence of the eruption had begun. Highways leading to the area were shut down. Residents and logging crews working within 10 miles of the mountain were evacuated and barred from returning. However, as weeks went by, people got used to the small bursts of steam and ragged holes appearing on the surface of the volcano. Residents wanted to go back inside the blockaded area. On May 18, 1980, the pressure that had been building inside the mountain was finally released by a small earth tremor. The mountain exploded. The side of the mountain that had been bulging collapsed and released a cloud of superheated gas and ash that rolled down the mountainside and into the Toutle River valley.

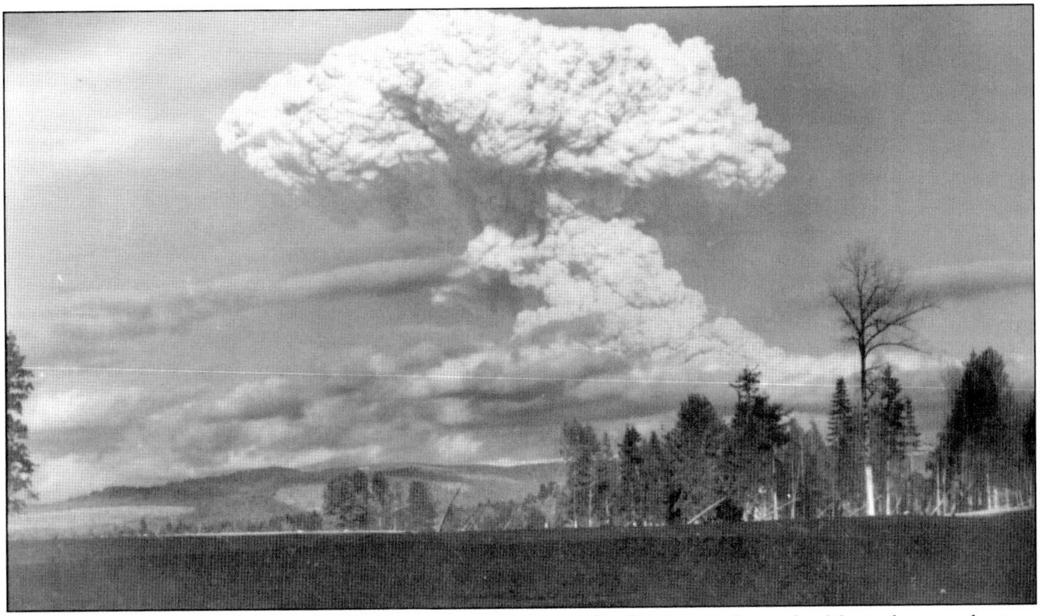

At 8:32 a.m. on May 18, 1980, the eruption of Mount St. Helens released a blast that geologists estimated was at the magnitude equal to 2,500 times the power of the atom bomb that destroyed Hiroshima. It buried North Fork Toutle River to an average depth of 150 feet (maximum depth 600 feet) and moved at a velocity of 70 to 150 miles per hour. The power of the blast followed the line of least resistance, which was sideways and to the north. The shock wave blew down 4 billion board feet of timber (enough to build about 300,000 two-bedroom homes) like matchsticks. Though a safety zone had been set up and maintained around the mountain, 57 people lost their lives in the blast. Harry Truman, the owner of Spirit Lake Lodge, was the only one who refused to leave the danger zone. He is now buried beneath several hundred feet of volcanic debris. All the rest were in areas that had been thought to be safe. Some campers, hunters, and volcano watchers did live to tell the tale.

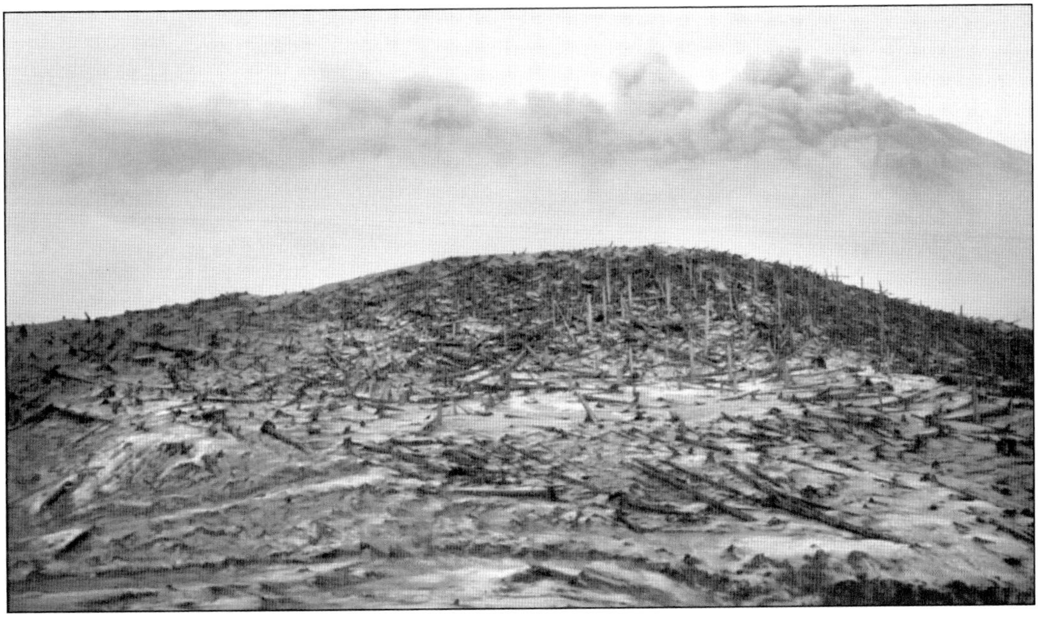

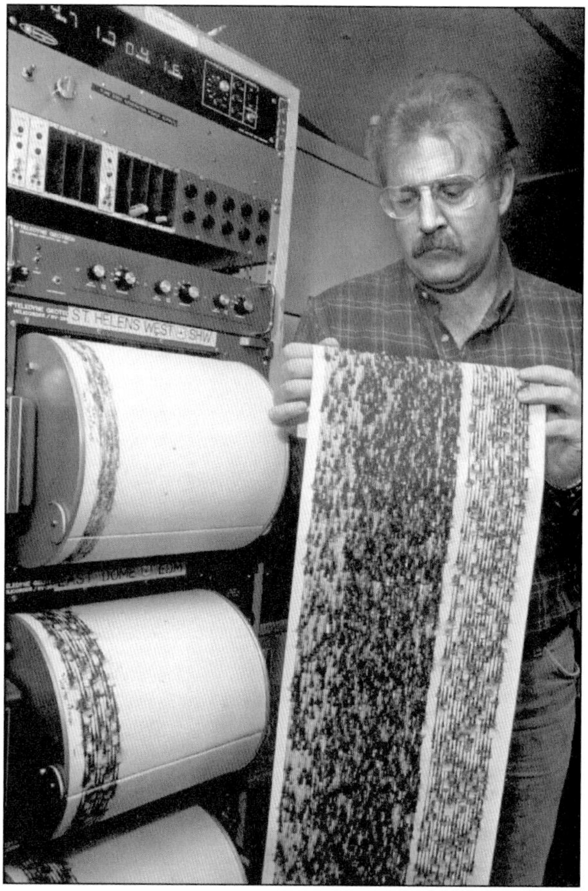

Geologists at nearby universities monitored the seismic activity at Mount St. Helens before March 1980. Now there is a Cascades Volcano Observatory with a permanent center in Vancouver, Washington. There is also a volcanic observatory at Johnston Ridge near Mount St. Helens itself that is only open in the summer. After the first burst of released power from the volcano, a plume of gas and ash rose 80,000 feet in less than 15 minutes. It carried 1.4 billion cubic yards of material across the United States in three days and circled the earth in 15 days. The Washington State Department of Game estimated nearly 7,000 big game animals (deer, elk, and bear) perished, as well as all birds and most small mammals. Many burrowing rodents, frogs, salamanders, and crawfish managed to survive because they were below ground level or the water surface when the disaster struck.

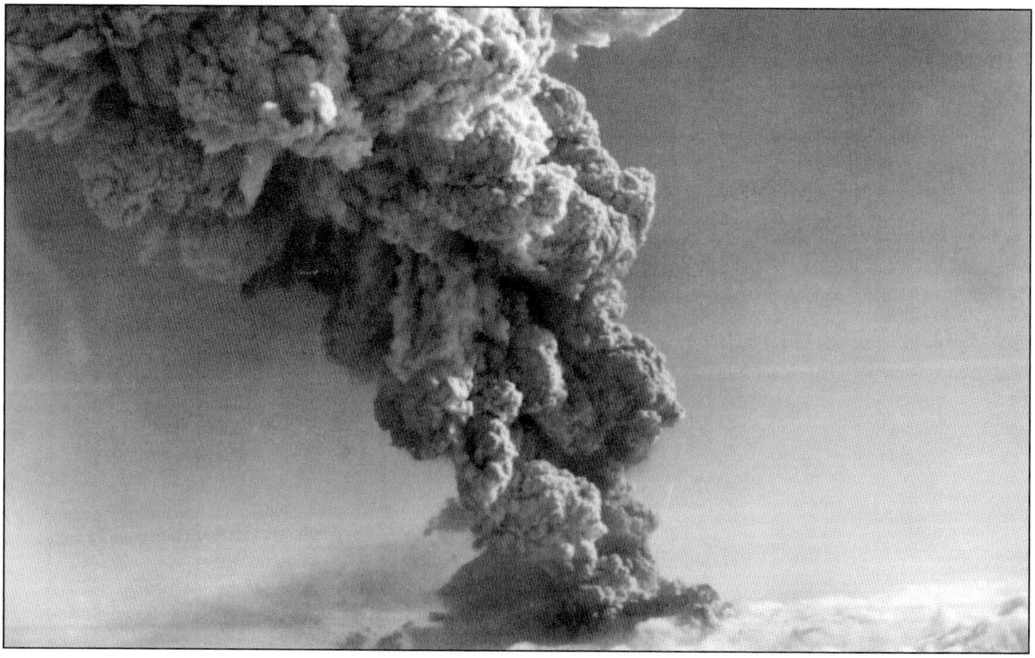

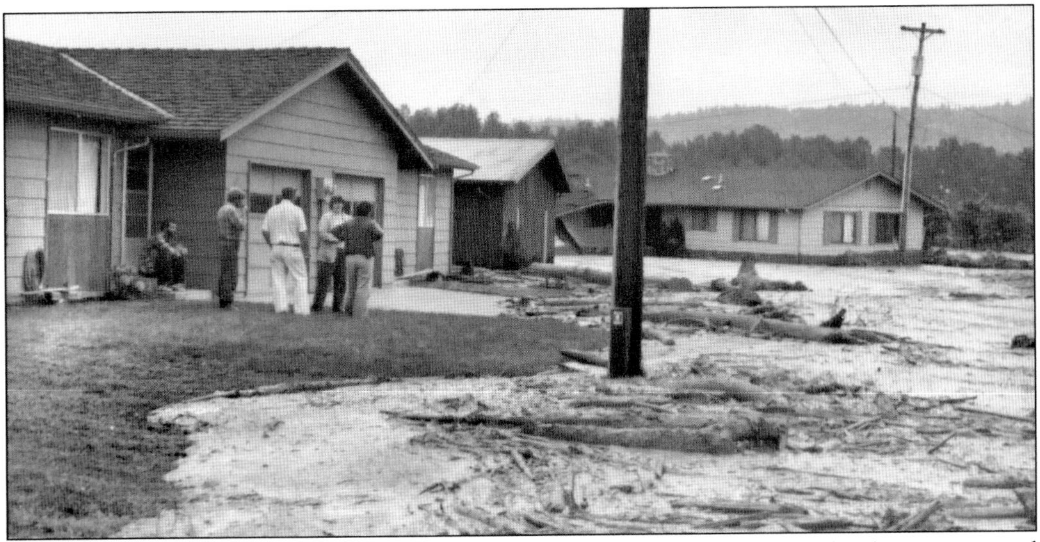

Houses at the Green Acres subdivision just north of the Castle Rock High School were impacted from the mudflow down the Toutle River and into the Cowlitz River. The melted glaciers from the mountain created a wave of mud and debris, including trees, smashed houses, and broken bridges, that damaged or ruined many buildings near the banks of the Cowlitz River at Castle Rock. The actual town of Castle Rock was protected by the dike built in 1936 to prevent flooding. The water from Mount St. Helens was so hot that the mud steamed in the riverbed and was said to look like hot chocolate pudding. The two bridges in the photograph below are at the mouth of the Toutle River where it enters the Cowlitz River 3 miles north of Castle Rock. One is the Interstate 5 freeway bridge, and the other is the Burlington Northern Railroad bridge. They were both closed for hours after the eruption but, though battered, survived the mudflow.

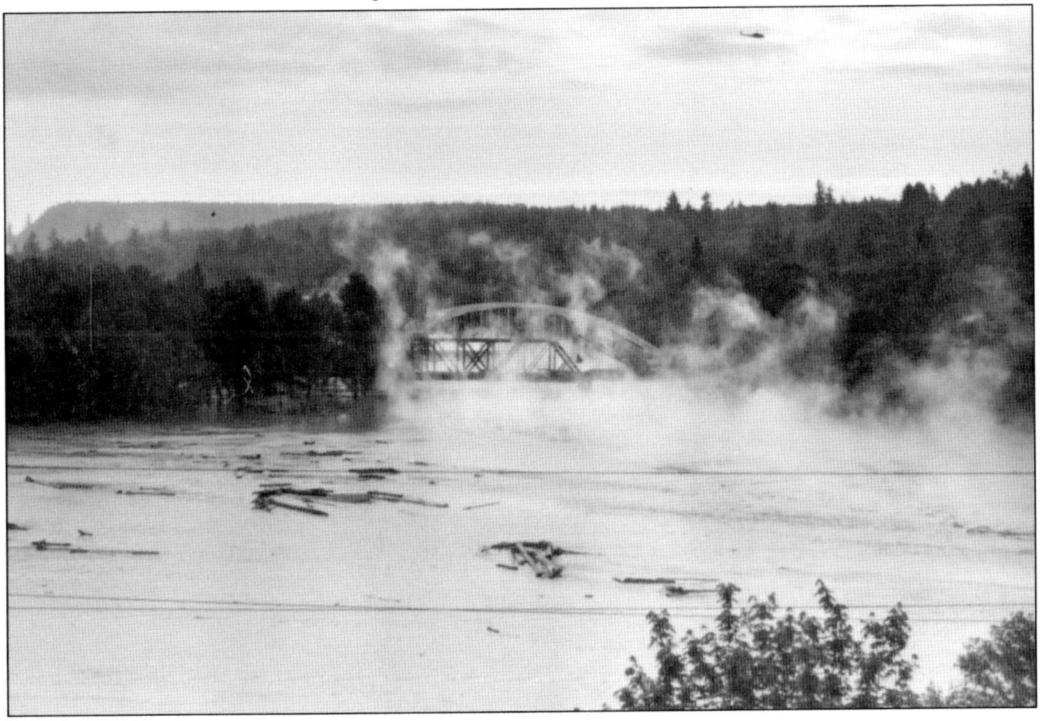

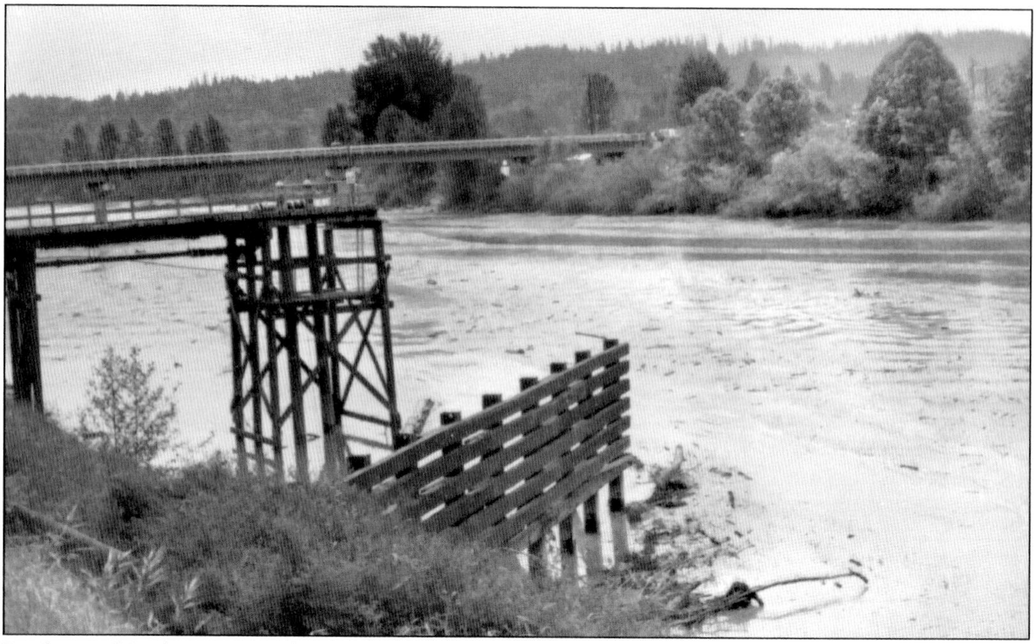

In the mid-20th century, the Castle Rock City Council deemed the old well-and-pump water system inadequate. It was replaced by a new water treatment plant that drew water from the Cowlitz River. On the morning of May 18, 1980, the pumping dock of the water intake (above) sits on the river with the bridge in the background. The next day after the mudflow from the eruption of Mount St. Helens came down the river, the dock (below) is gone as if it had never existed. The bridge supports are under much more water because the river is filled with tons of sand-like volcanic ash, which would require years of dredging.

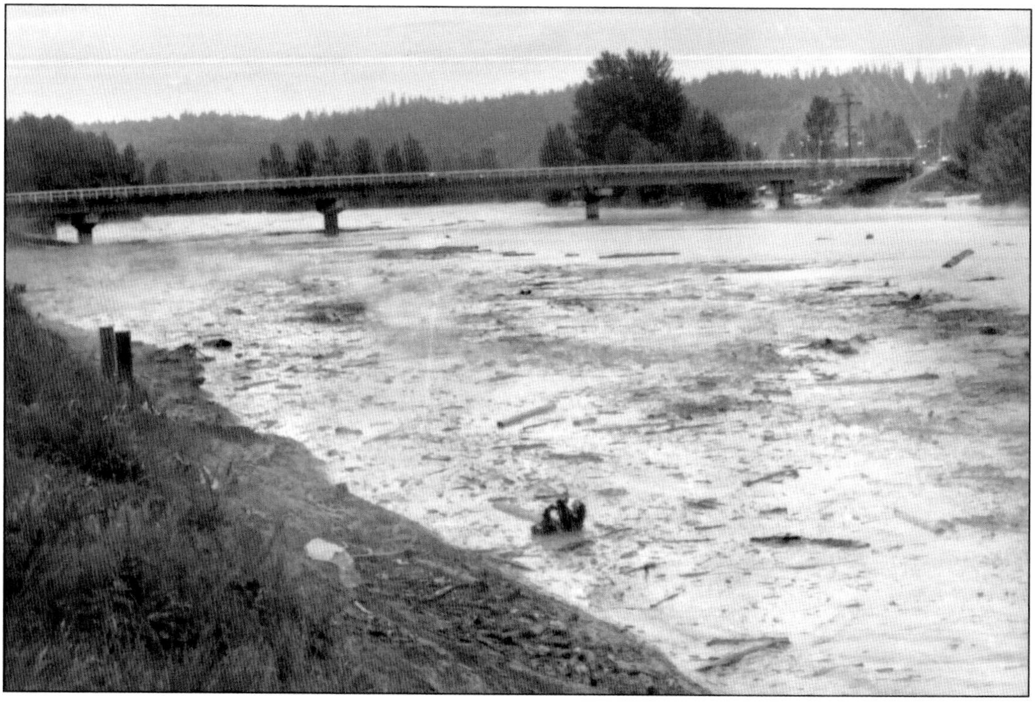

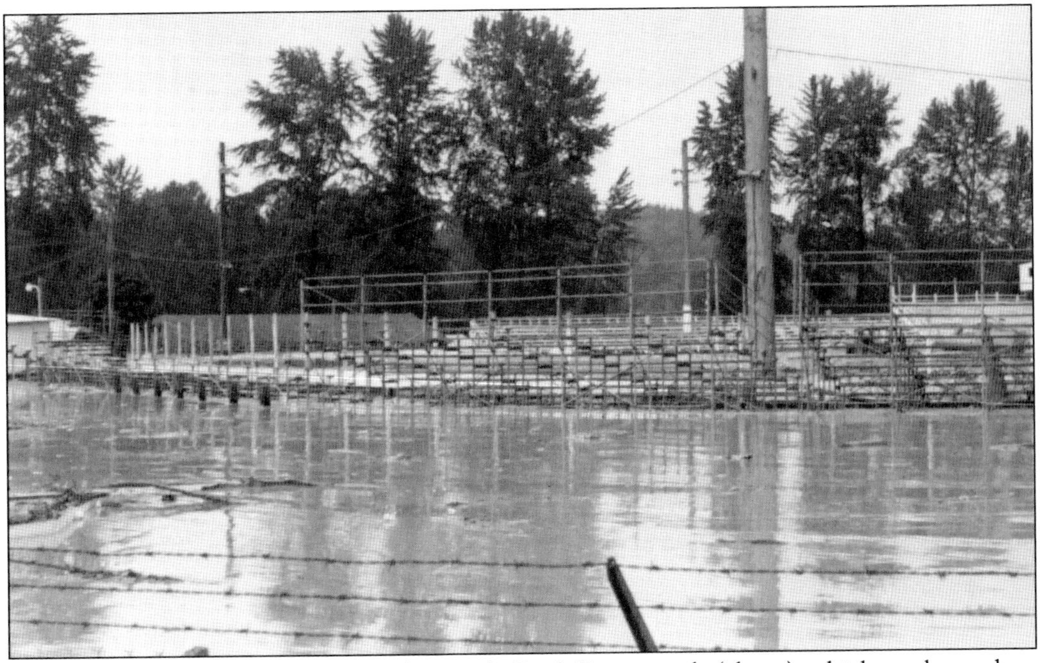

On May 19, 1980, the bleachers at the Castle Rock Fairgrounds (above), which are located on the west side of the Cowlitz River across from the town, were inundated with mud. The exhibit buildings and barns were filled with about 4 feet of volcanic mud. The historic log-built Toutle Post Office, which had been moved the fairgrounds as an exhibit, barely escaped destruction. Below, what looks like a mudflat is actually the Toutle River near where it empties into the Cowlitz River after the mudflow from the mountain filled in the riverbed with mud and debris. Pieces of dead trees can be seen sticking out of the mud. Along the banks of both rivers, trees were smothered by the volcanic ash that was left behind and died in the following months.

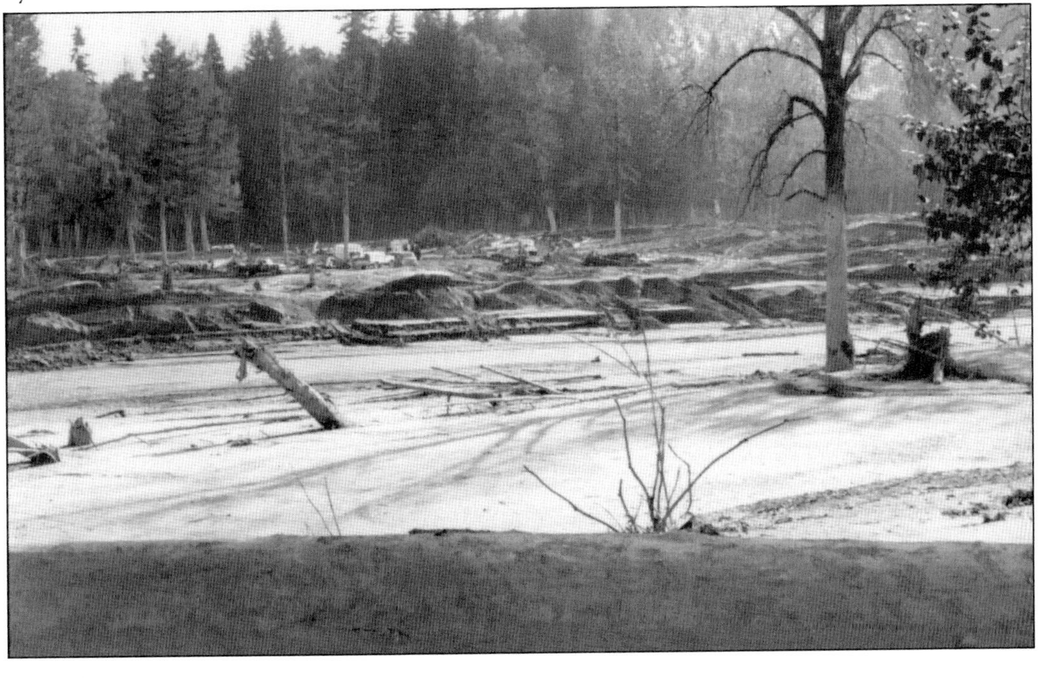

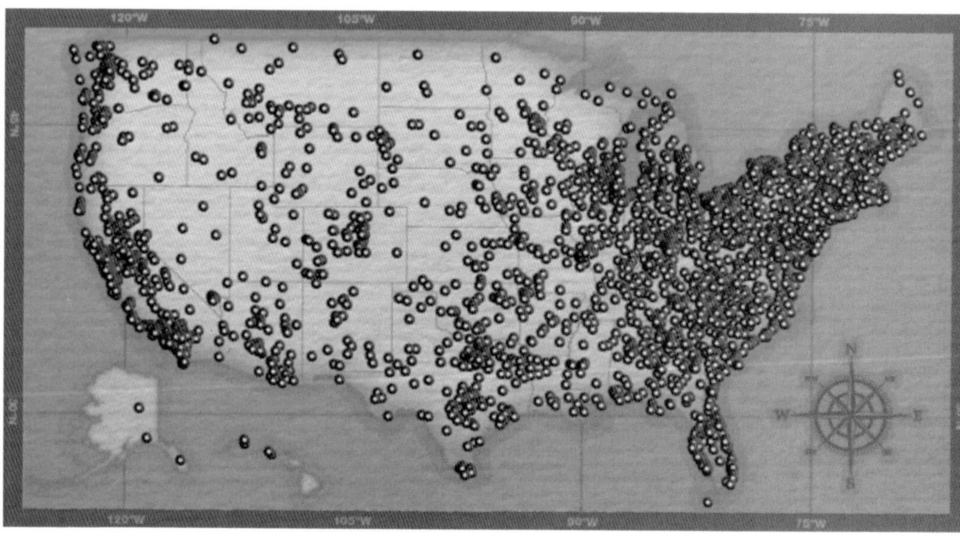